Third Workshop on Understanding Implicit and Underspecified Language (UnImplicit 2024)

St. Julian's, Malta
21 March 2024

ISBN: 978-1-7138-9464-3

Printed from e-media with permission by:

Curran Associates, Inc.
57 Morehouse Lane
Red Hook, NY 12571

Some format issues inherent in the e-media version may also appear in this print version.

Printed with permission by Curran Associates, Inc. (2025)

For permission requests, please contact the Association for Computational Linguistics at the address below.

Association for Computational Linguistics
209 N. Eighth Street
Stroudsburg, Pennsylvania 18360

Phone: 1-570-476-8006
Fax: 1-570-476-0860

acl@aclweb.org

Additional copies of this publication are available from:

Curran Associates, Inc.
57 Morehouse Lane
Red Hook, NY 12571 USA
Phone: 845-758-0400
Fax: 845-758-2633
Email: curran@proceedings.com
Web: www.proceedings.com

UnImplicit 2024

The Third Workshop on Understanding Implicit and Underspecified Language

Proceedings of the Workshop

March 21, 2024

Association for Computational Linguistics (ACL)
209 N. Eighth Street
Stroudsburg, PA 18360
USA
Tel: +1-570-476-8006
Fax: +1-570-476-0860
acl@aclweb.org

Introduction

Welcome to UnImplicit: The Third Workshop on Understanding Implicit and Underspecified Language. The focus of this workshop is on implicit and underspecified phenomena in language, which pose serious challenges to standard natural language processing models as they often require incorporating greater context, using symbolic inference and common-sense reasoning, or more generally, going beyond strictly lexical and compositional meaning constructs. This challenge spans all phases of the NLP model's life cycle: from collecting and annotating relevant data, through devising computational methods for modeling such phenomena, to evaluating and designing proper evaluation metrics.

In this workshop, our goal is to bring together theoreticians and practitioners from the entire NLP cycle, from annotation and benchmarking to modeling and applications, and to provide an umbrella for the development, discussion and standardization of the study of understanding implicit and underspecified language.

In total, we received 15 submissions (4 of which non-archival), out of which 12 were accepted. All accepted submissions are presented as posters. The workshop also includes three invited talks on topics related to implicit language. The program committee consisted of 21 researchers, who we'd like to thank for providing helpful and constructive reviews on the papers. We'd also like to thank all authors for their submissions and interest in our workshop.

Valentina, Daniel, Elias, Alisa and Sandro

Organizing Committee

Organizers

Valentina Pyatkin, Allen Institute for AI and University of Washington
Daniel Fried, CMU
Elias Stengel-Eskin, UNC Chapel Hill
Alisa Liu, University of Washington
Sandro Pezzelle, University of Amsterdam

Advisory Committee

Michael Roth, Stuttgart University
Reut Tsarfaty, Bar-Ilan University and AI2
Yoav Goldberg, Bar-Ilan University and AI2

Program Committee

Program Committee

Vera Demberg, Saarland University
Yanai Elazar, AI2 & University of Washington
Daniel Hershcovich, University of Copenhagen
Jennifer Hu, Harvard University
Lucy Li, UC Berkeley
Aida Nematzadeh, DeepMind
Sebastian Pado, University of Stuttgart
Roma Patel, Brown University
Chris Potts, Stanford University
Elior Sulem, Ben Gurion University
Tiago Torrent, Federal University of Juiz de Fora
Sara Tonelli, Fondazione Bruno Kessler
Nathan Schneider, Georgetown University
Michael Elhadad, Ben Gurion University
Zhaofeng Wu, MIT
Michael Elhadad, Ben Gurion University
Sofia Serrano, University of Washington
Dmitry Nikolaev, University of Stuttgart
Nan-Jiang Jiang, Google
Julian Michael, NYU
Ece Takmaz, University of Amsterdam
Sahithya Ravi, University of British Columbia

Invited Speakers

Alex Warstadt, ETH
Malihe Alikhani, Northeastern University
Benjamin Bergen, UCSD

Table of Contents

Program

Thursday, March 21, 2024

09:30 - 09:45	*Welcome and Opening Remarks*
09:45 - 10:45	*Invited Talk 1 - Alex Warstadt*
10:45 - 11:15	*Coffee Break*
11:15 - 12:30	*In-Person Poster Session*
12:30 - 13:45	*Lunch*
13:45 - 14:30	*In-Person Oral Presentations*
14:30 - 15:30	*Invited Talk 2 - Malihe Alikhani*
15:30 - 16:00	*Coffee Break*
16:00 - 17:00	*Invited Talk 3 - Benjamin Bergen*
17:00 - 17:10	*Closing Remarks*

Taking Action Towards Graceful Interaction: The Effects of Performing Actions on Modelling Policies for Instruction Clarification Requests

Brielen Madureira[1] **David Schlangen**[1,2]
[1]Computational Linguistics, Department of Linguistics
University of Potsdam, Germany
[2]German Research Center for Artificial Intelligence (DFKI), Berlin, Germany
{madureiralasota,david.schlangen}@uni-potsdam.de

Abstract

Clarification requests are a mechanism to help solve communication problems, *e.g.* due to ambiguity or underspecification, in instruction-following interactions. Despite their importance, even skilful models struggle with producing or interpreting such repair acts. In this work, we test three hypotheses concerning the effects of action taking as an auxiliary task in modelling iCR policies. Contrary to initial expectations, we conclude that its contribution to learning an iCR policy is limited, but some information can still be extracted from prediction uncertainty. We present further evidence that even well-motivated, Transformer-based models fail to learn good policies for *when to ask* Instruction CRs (iCRs), while the task of determining *what to ask about* can be more successfully modelled. Considering the implications of these findings, we further discuss the shortcomings of the data-driven paradigm for learning meta-communication acts.

Figure 1: Clarification requests posed by an instruction follower, demonstrating uncertainty on deciding what actions to take due to ambiguity or underspecification. From: CoDraw dialogue game 8198, CC BY-NC 4.0, cliparts from Zitnick and Parikh (2013).

1 Introduction

The concept of *graceful interaction* (Hayes and Reddy, 1979, 1983) was proposed as a set of skills that machines should exhibit to properly engage in cooperative dialogue with humans, among which are being able to ask for, understand and offer clarification. More than forty years later, the ineptitude of large language models and voice assistants to handle underspecifications and to properly process or produce clarification requests (CR) is still being documented (Larsson, 2017; Kuhn et al., 2022; Li et al., 2023; Deng et al., 2023; Shaikh et al., 2023). It is also one of the acknowledged limitations of the currently prevailing commercial chat-optimised LLM.[1]

Given that they are modulated for instructions, this seems to be a peculiar fault: CRs are a crucial mechanism used to repair misunderstandings in instruction following interactions (Benotti, 2009), as we see in Figure 1. On second thought, it comes as no surprise. Clarification exchanges are meta-communication acts that do not normally appear in non-interactive data (Kuhn et al., 2022) and are also relatively rare in dialogue data. As a specific dialogue phenomenon, CRs have an empirical frequency of 4% of turns in spontaneous conversations to 11% of turns in strictly instruction-following interactions (Purver et al., 2001; Benotti and Blackburn, 2021; Madureira and Schlangen, 2023b). Therefore, it is still unclear to what extent CR strategies can be learnt with data-driven approaches (Benotti and Blackburn, 2021).

Many existing CR datasets, despite their utility for applications like conversational search (Keyvan and Huang, 2022; Rahmani et al., 2023), either have not been collected via real interactions or are synthetic, so that learnt CR policies may not correspond to genuine human behaviour. Moreover, current best-performing data-driven models are still

[1]In the blogpost releasing chatGPT, the limitations section says: *"Ideally, the model would ask clarifying questions when the user provided an ambiguous query. Instead, our current models usually guess what the user intended."*. Source: `https://openai.com/blog/chatgpt`.

Proceedings of the Third Workshop on Understanding Implicit and Underspecified Language, pages 1–21
March 21, 2024 ©2024 Association for Computational Linguistics

not doing very well in deciding when to request clarification (see §2), and we must understand why.

CRs can occur in all four levels of communication (Clark, 1996): Attention (due to problems in the channel), identification (due to acoustic impediments), recognition (when the signal is understood but a lexical, parsing or reference problem manifests) and consideration (when the intention is unclear) (Rodríguez and Schlangen, 2004). Instruction CRs (iCR) emerge mostly at Clark's 4th level of communication (Clark, 1996), *i.e.* at the level of uptake (Schlöder and Fernández, 2014), to solve ambiguities and underspecifications.

Recently, Madureira and Schlangen (2023b,a) have argued that the multimodal CoDraw game (Kim et al., 2019) is a rich resource for iCRs, naturally produced as a by-product of game playing via actions, as in the example in Figure 1. This dataset offers a balance between size (in comparison to well-curated but small corpora) and retaining ecological validity (as opposed to massive datasets collected or crafted artificially). Supposing underlying iCR strategies can emerge from data, we can reasonably assume that action-taking is a key component in modelling policies for deciding when and what to repair in this type of game.

However, one major drawback of the proposed baseline models is the *overhearer* paradigm: Models are not trained to act as authentic dialogue participants. Instead, they process other people's interactions, and at some points have to predict when to ask iCRs, a decision detached from the actual actions required by the game. Understanding is different for overhearers and addressees, and the latter have advantages in building common ground (Schober and Clark, 1989). Clark (1992) argues that subjects in psycholinguistics are actually usually treated as overhearers; we add to that that many NLP approaches are also modelling overhearers.

Contributions Given that background, this work aims to expand the boundaries of the open question of learning meta-communication acts from human data. We do that by (i) implementing a more well-motivated model for learning *when to ask* iCRs in CoDraw; (ii) taking another step towards a more realistic agent by defining and modelling the task of *what to ask* about; and, most importantly, (iii) testing three hypotheses to study the effect of action-taking in learning iCR policies, verifying whether a measure of certainty can be used to probe for iCR abilities and inform predictions.

2 Related Work

Learning *when to ask* questions The problem of knowing when to ask questions in an interaction appears in various contexts. Relevant work has been done in language-aided visual navigation (Nguyen and Daumé III, 2019; Thomason et al., 2020; Chi et al., 2020; Nguyen et al., 2022), in which the agent must take actions in an environment and decide when to ask for help, where RL is a suitable method. Similar policies are necessary in interactive settings like visual dialogue games that require deciding when to stop asking (Shekhar et al., 2018) or incremental predictions on when to answer a question (Boyd-Graber et al., 2012).

Modelling clarification requests A vast literature exists on describing and modelling clarification strategies (Purver et al., 2003; Gabsdil, 2003; Schlangen, 2004; Rodríguez and Schlangen, 2004; Rieser and Lemon, 2006; Stoyanchev et al., 2013, *inter alia*). In the age of neural network-based NLP, the problem has commonly been broken down into various tasks that are learnt from data: *When to ask* (Narayan-Chen et al., 2019; Aliannejadi et al., 2021; Shi et al., 2022; Kiseleva et al., 2022), *what to ask* about (Braslavski et al., 2017; Aliannejadi et al., 2021; Hu et al., 2020), and how to generate (Kumar and Black, 2020; Gervits et al., 2021; Majumder et al., 2021) or select/rank appropriate CRs (Rao and Daumé III, 2018; Aliannejadi et al., 2019; Mohanty et al., 2023). Ideally, these tasks should be tied into a single agent, but several works are still approaching the problem in a "task-framed" fashion without integration of all capabilities (Schlangen, 2021).

Modelling policies for *when to ask* for clarification in instruction following is far from being a solved problem, as models perform well below the ceiling. The performance in the Minecraft Dialogue dataset is 0.63 accuracy for the CR class (Shi et al., 2022). In the recent IGLU challenge (Kiseleva et al., 2022), the best model in the leaderboard[2] reaches 0.75 weighted average F1 Score. In predicting underspecification for code generation, the highest performance is 0.78 binary F1Score (Li et al., 2023). In Codraw-iCR, the baseline achieves a similarly suboptimal 0.34 average precision (Madureira and Schlangen, 2023b). These policies are failing to fully capture the human behaviour from data, but the reasons as still obscure.

[2]Reported in the NeurIPS 2022 IGLU challenge platform.

Another open issue is how to collect high-quality CR data in enough amounts for machine learning purposes. In the annotated Minecraft Dialogue Corpus (Narayan-Chen et al., 2019; Shi et al., 2022), TEACh dataset (Padmakumar et al., 2022; Gella et al., 2022) and CoDraw (Kim et al., 2019; Madureira and Schlangen, 2023b,a), CRs occur by own initiative of the players in real, multi-turn interaction, ranging from hundreds to less than ten thousand identified CR utterances. Still in the same size range, the IGLU dataset (Kiseleva et al., 2022; Mohanty et al., 2022) has been collected in a setting that avoids pairing up players, with a one-shot opportunity to ask for clarification (and without a partner to answer it and allow further actions).

Other procedures have been used to collect CR data in larger amounts. Massive datasets are DialFRED (Gao et al., 2022), created via crowdsourcing with workers who are explicitly asked to generate a question, and answer it, for a situation they are not actually involved with. In neighbour domains like virtual assistance, conversational search and code generation, large-scale datasets containing CRs have been constructed with data augmentation methods (Aliannejadi et al., 2021), user simulation (Kottur et al., 2021), templates (Li et al., 2023) and crawling QA online forums (Rao and Daumé III, 2018; Kumar and Black, 2020). These strategies can reflect CR form and facilitate data collection but abstract away the fundamental triggers of Instruction CRs (joint effort, real-time interaction and action-taking), being arguably not suitable for learning CR policies for instruction following.

Evaluating CR mechanisms in dialogue models We need more evaluation campaigns and methods to shed light on what a model has actually learnt with respect to CR strategies and why it fails. Some initiatives towards more detailed assessment are in progress. Chiyah-Garcia et al. (2023) evaluate the abilities of multimodal models to process CRs in coreference resolution by interpreting the difference in the object-F1 score at turns before and after a CR as the improvement provided by incorporating the clarification; they also analyse results by considering various CR properties. In the realm of LLMs, recent studies have employed evaluation techniques via prompts to test the models abilities, concluding that they can detect ambiguity to some extent but even so do not generally attempt to repair it and when they do request clarification there is little alignment with human strategies (Kuhn et al., 2022; Shaikh et al., 2023). When Deng et al. (2023) first induce the LLM to predict whether the appropriate dialogue act is to ask for clarification the best LLM achieves only 0.28 F1 Score.

3 Definitions

CoDraw (Kim et al., 2019) is a multimodal dialogue game where an instruction follower (IF) uses a gallery of 28 (out of 58) cliparts to reconstruct a scene (from the Abstract Scenes dataset (Zitnick and Parikh, 2013)) they cannot see. They exchange text messages in a turn-based fashion with an instruction giver (IG), who sees the original scene but has no access to the state of the reconstructed scene, except for one chance to peek at it during the game. The available actions are adding or deleting, moving, flipping and resizing cliparts in a canvas. Game success is measured by a scene similarity score based on its symbolic representation. The authors collected 9.9k such dialogues in English, containing around 8k iCRs (11.3% of the game turns), annotated by Madureira and Schlangen (2023b,a) both under the license CC BY-NC 4.0.

Note that not all iCRs are *questions*. In terms of mood, most CoDraw-iCRs are polar questions, followed by wh- and alternative questions, but there are also declarative and imperative forms. Almost 60% of instances refer to only one object and around 33% refer to two objects. The attributes being clarified are, in order of frequency, relations between objects, positions in the scene, disambiguation of persons, direction, size and disambiguation ob objects (Madureira and Schlangen, 2023a).

We can split the space of possible IF models for this game regarding their CR capabilities:

1. Overhearer: *A model that observes the current game state (dialogue context and scene) to predict when to ask iCRs, without any additional game-play actions or linguistic decisions.*
2. Action-Taker: *A model that plays the game by only taking clipart actions, without iCR decisions.*
3. iCR-Action-Taker: *An Action-Taker with the extra decision of when to ask iCRs.*
4. Full agent: *A model that makes all game-play decisions, including natural language generation.*

The Overhearer is a common paradigm in NLP in which models resemble an observer of the actual player, deciding what to do *as if it were in their shoes*. It is, however, a rather rough simplification of a full-fledged agent, which is an idealised target not yet reached. (iCR-)Action-Takers are an intermediate step examined in this work.

Task 1 We follow the formalisation of the task of *when to ask* for iCRs in CoDraw by Madureira and Schlangen (2023b). In short, given the game state up to the last IG utterance, the IF has to decide whether to ask for clarification. This policy is modelled as a function $f_{when} : s \mapsto [0, 1]$ that maps the game state s_t at the current turn t to the probability of asking an iCR at this point, performing a binary decision task at each turn in the game. Here, the state s comprises the dialogue history, the gallery and the situation of the scene.

Task 2 Additionally, once the decision to ask has been made, a player should also know what objects are subject to clarification at that point. We thus define the subsequent task of *what to ask* about: at an iCR turn t, a function $f_{what} : (o_i, s) \mapsto [0, 1]$ outputs, for each of the 28 objects o_i in the gallery, the probability of asking an iCR about it, given the state s_t. These are binary decisions over each available object in the gallery. Both of these tasks are steps happening before the actual generation, which we do not address in this work.[3]

4 Hypotheses

In this section, we motivate and state the three hypotheses we test as our main contribution. We refer to related findings in the Minecraft game, but note that CoDraw has a more challenging asymmetry regarding the players' common ground: the IG does not observe the IF's actions throughout the game.

Chiyah-Garcia et al. (2023) argue that auxiliary learning objectives of detecting objects' attributes in a scene (Lee et al., 2022) are useful for referential CRs at Clark's 3rd level, elicited during reference resolution.[4] Our expectation is that action prediction should be equivalently relevant for 4th level iCRs, which emerge when deciding how to act. More concretely, iCR-Action-Takers should have a more genuine motivation to decide to request clarification in comparison to Overhearers.[5] To investigate it, our first hypothesis is:

Hypothesis 1: *iCR-Action-Takers can learn a more accurate policy for predicting* ***when to ask*** *an iCR than Overhearers.*

Here, we can also test whether action *detection* has a similar effect, by letting the model learn to detect actions given the scene before and after, as in Rojowiec et al. (2020). It is a framing even more equivalent to Lee et al. (2022), since, in their model, the attributes are already available in the images. The access to post-action scene can be examined in this dialogue game because it is turn-based: The IF would have done all actions they want (thus seeing the newly edited scene) at the point they press the button to send the next message or iCR.

Next, we aim to investigate if Action-Takers, which are trained without any explicit iCR signal, still build representations that encode the need for repair. The study done by Xiao and Wang (2019) on quantifying uncertainty in NLP tasks shows that the examined models output higher data uncertainties for more difficult predictions. Besides, Yao et al. (2019) propose the assumption that if a model is uncertain about a prediction, it is more likely to be an error, and use uncertainty as a score to decide whether the prediction requires user clarification in semantic parsing. Based on that, we conjecture that the need for repair should manifest as less certainty in the Action-Taker's decisions. Therefore, the second hypothesis we test is:

Hypothesis 2: *At iCR turns, Action-Takers predict actions with less certainty than at other turns. Similarly, less certainty is expected for actions upon objects subject to iCRs than for other objects.*

For this step, we set the linking hypothesis that certainty is expressed in the probability the model assigns to taking action, or not, at a given turn. It is a reasonable assumption, because the objective function is expected to push the predictions to be either 0 or 1, so predictions close to 0.5 can be seen as indecisive.[6]

Finally, iCR policies for *when to ask* should be grounded in a fine-grained representation of what exactly is unclear. Thus our last hypothesis is:

Hypothesis 3: *Pre-trained iCR-Action-Takers can learn a more accurate policy for predicting* ***what to ask about*** *in iCR turns than Overhearers.*

[3]We leave the additional decisions of what *attributes* to mention and which *form* to realise for ongoing parallel work dealing specifically with iCR generation.

[4]CoDraw-iCR also contains referential CRs, but directly related to uptake of instructions.

[5]Experiments in the Minecraft dataset point to the opposite direction: Generating action sequences slightly harmed the accuracy on *when to ask* (Shi et al., 2022). We seek to dive deeper into understanding this issue.

[6]An investigation of the predictive uncertainty of the IF model in the Minecraft data has been done by Naszad et al. (2022) using length-normalized log-likelihood and entropy of generated action *sequences*. Negative results are reported in an unpublished short manuscript concluding that uncertainty is not a direct signal for when to ask CRs in their setting.

5 Models

In this section, we present the models we analyse in our experiments. We do not intend to propose a novel architecture, since our aim is to understand why current SotA models are failing and the effect that learning to take actions has on them. We implement a model that addresses the limitations of the baseline model (iCR-baseline) from Madureira and Schlangen (2023b) by incorporating techniques from top-flight models in recent multimodal dialogue challenges, namely IGLU (Kiseleva et al., 2022) and SIMMC 2.0 (Kottur et al., 2021). The basic architecture of the Overhearer and (iCR-)Action-Taker is illustrated in Figure 2. We provide here an overview of its informationv flow; see Appendix for detailed specifications.

The CoDraw IF has access to a gallery of 28 objects, which is an informative source in the game (*e.g.* if it contains just one of the three tree cliparts, it is less likely that disambiguation is needed) but was absent in iCR-baseline. We follow a symbolic approach to represent the objects' attributes (presence in the scene, orientation, position, size, pose, facial expression) based on the original drawer in Kim et al. (2019) (which, however, had unrealistic access to all possible objects in the database).

Previous works did not employ Transformers (Vaswani et al., 2017) to model iCR policies in CoDraw. Given its leading performance in several scenarios, we bring them to the scene, in an approach inspired by DETR (Carion et al., 2020). We use a Transformer decoder[7] module to create contextual embeddings of each object in the current game state, *i.e.* by building a representation that considers the dialogue so far and the actual scene.

This is done by passing each object to the Transformer decoder ("target"), to allow self-attention to the state of the gallery, and subsequent cross-attention with the game state representation ("memory"). The state has two components: The dialogue so far, represented via token-level contextual embeddings constructed by BERT (Devlin et al., 2019), and the current scene, represented as image features constructed by a ResNet (He et al., 2015) backbone, followed by a trainable convolutional layer to reduce the number of channels, as in the DETR model (Carion et al., 2020). We make text

[7]The full Transformer encoder-decoder was detrimental in almost all cases, so we report results using only the decoder component. This is probably due to the fact that the scene and dialogue had already been encoded by the pretrained components.

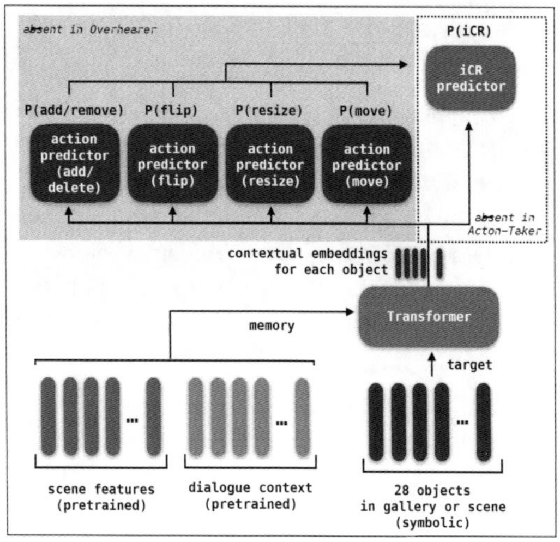

Figure 2: The basic structure of our iCR policy models. The full structure represents the iCR-Action-Taker. The Overhearer contains no action predictor (area shaded in grey), whereas the Action-Taker contains no iCR predictor (area in the dotted box).

and scene available as one sequence like Lee et al. (2022). The variation of iCR-Action-Detecters access the scene before and after the actions.

The Transformer outputs a contextual representation of each object. The steps so far are represented in the lower portion of Figure 2. Now we proceed to the predictions in the upper part, which differs according to the type of model. To test our hypotheses, we implement models that predict the game actions (or detect them, if the updated image is used) and/or make iCR decisions via multi-task learning. We take inspiration from Shi et al. (2022) to train the contextual object embeddings as joint encodings for all the classifiers.

Action predictors and iCR predictors are implemented as 2-layer feed-forward networks with dropout, which take a representation as input and output a probability. In (iCR-)Action-Takers, we model each action prediction (add/delete, flip, resize, move) as a binary classification done upon each object embedding.[8] The iCR decision is also performed as a binary classification task. In Task 1 (when to ask), it predicts whether an iCR should be made at the current turn. In Task 2, (what to ask) it predicts, for each object, whether it is subject to and iCR. In iCR-Action-Takers, we let the action logits be part of the input to the iCR predictor.

[8]To facilitate evaluation, we add an additional meta-action prediction which is 1 whenever *any* action is made to a clipart.

6 Experiments

For our experiments, we implement variations of Overhearers and (iCR-)Action-Takers, all trained on the CoDraw dataset. Results are compared by varying the complexity of the input, which can be comprised of the gallery G, the dialogue context D with varying length, the scene before S_b and after S_a the current actions, and the actual actions A or their logits L_A.

To test H1, we compare Overhearers with iCR-Action-Takers and iCR-Action-Detecters in Task 1, predicting *when to ask* iCRs at turn level. For H2, we examine the predictions of the Action-Taker using the certainty measure we discuss next. Finally, H3 is tested by a similar analysis as H1, but in Task 2, *i.e. what to ask* about. Here, iCR predictions are done at clipart level and only the turns where iCRs actually occurred are used (*i.e.*, we assume the decision to ask for iCR has already been taken). For H3, Overhearers are compared with pretrained iCR-Action-Takers/Detecters whose action modules' parameters are initialised with the best Action-Taker/Detecter checkpoint.

	iCRs		actions				
	when	what	any	add/del	move	flip	resize
train	11.24	14.32	5.43	3.11	2.13	0.23	0.42
val	11.84	14.43	5.47	3.11	2.17	0.24	0.39
test	11.26	14.69	5.40	3.12	2.11	0.21	0.39

Table 1: % of the positive labels in the dataset.

Table 1 shows the proportion of each type of label in the dataset. Actions at each turn are sparse (mean=1.65, std=1.69) because only a small subset of the full action space is actually performed.

Implementation Our implementation uses PyTorch Lightning. We run hyperparameter search and other manual combinations, and then use the configuration that led to the best results in the validation set for the Overhearer G+D model. The training objective is to minimise a sum of binary cross-entropy losses for each task. Optimisation relies on the Adam algorithm (Kingma and Ba, 2015), with early stopping. Details of the model configuration, data processing and experiment setup are in the Appendix. Our code is available at `https://github.com/briemadu/icr-actions`.

Evaluation metrics We report test results for the best epoch in the validation set.[9] H1 and H3 are analysed based on the performance on iCR predictions. To facilitate comparison to existing works, we report Average Precision (AP) and binary and macro-average F1-Score (bF1 and mF1) for each model and task (*i.e.* one measure for iCR labels and one for all action labels). To inspect how much information can be extracted from clipart states alone (*e.g.* some cliparts are less often subject to iCRs), we report metrics for a model that only gets the gallery as input. For H2, we need an additional prediction certainty metric. We adapt the classification margin metric used for uncertainty sampling in active learning (Settles, 2012), which is the difference between the probability assigned to the first and the second class, like in Chi et al. (2020). In our binary task, we define it as $|P(iCR) - P(\neg iCR)|$, which is 0 when both are 0.5 (highest uncertainty) and 1 when one or the other is 1 (highest certainty). We analyse whether we can derive a signal for *when to ask* iCRs by finding a decision threshold upon this metric, as in similar works (Yao et al., 2019; Naszad et al., 2022; Khalid and Stone, 2023).

7 Results

Table 2 presents the main results for all experiments. We begin with overall observations, and then walk through the table to analyse the findings for each hypothesis. In the next section, we discuss the implications of these findings.

Firstly, for deciding *when to ask* an iCR, the base Overhearer achieves 0.38 AP and the highest performance comes from the iCR-Action-Detecter with 0.41. This is noticeably higher than the 0.34 Overhearer baseline in Madureira and Schlangen (2023b), but the gain is not as substantial as expected given the improvements in the architecture.[10] When the Overhearer is ablated to have no access to the dialogue, performance drops to close to random, as expected. The addition of scenes before and after the current actions and the inclusion of an explicit signal with the last actions, however, cause only marginal variation and do not really contribute to a better performance. The Action-Taker similarly does not profit from having access to the image. We have no precedent results for the

[9] We compared Overhearers using a context from 0 to 5 previous turns. 0 or 1 turns had worse results, but 2 to 5 were almost equivalent, so we report results using 3.

[10] Note that we use the second released version of the annotation, containing a marginally different proportion of iCRs.

		Task 1: When to Ask						**Task 2: What to Ask**					
	predictions:	iCR			actions			iCR			actions		
	inputs	AP	bF1	mF1	AP	bF1	mF1	AP	bF1	mF1	AP	bF1	mF1
Baseline	D, S_a	.347	-	.645	-	-	-	-	-	-	-	-	-
Overhearer	G	.138	.000	.470	-	-	-	.332	.289	.593	-	-	-
	G, D	.384	.349	.642	-	-	-	.697	.665	.801	-	-	-
	G, D, S_b	.372	.267	.604	-	-	-	.697	.666	.799	-	-	-
	G, D, S_b, S_a	.378	.304	.620	-	-	-	.694	.660	.799	-	-	-
	G, D, A	.372	.404	.662	-	-	-	.711	.683	.810	-	-	-
	G, D, S_b, A	.379	.377	.654	-	-	-	.712	.675	.808	-	-	-
	G, D, S_b, S_a, A	.388	.377	.655	-	-	-	.706	.674	.808	-	-	-
Action-Taker	G	-	-	-	.149	.005	.498	-	-	-	-	-	-
	G, D	-	-	-	.769	.710	.853	-	-	-	.571	.550	.770
	G, D, S_b	-	-	-	.762	.708	.851	-	-	-	.547	.530	.761
iCR-Action-Taker	G, D	.378	.393	.658	.755	.702	.848	**.753**	.688	**.815**	.652	.621	.807
	G, D, L_A	.393	.372	.652	.764	.708	.851	.751	.683	.811	.657	.619	.806
	G, D, S_b	.384	.380	.655	.760	.702	.848	.739	.681	.810	.612	.592	.792
	G, D, S_b, L_A	.378	.311	.625	.771	.709	.852	.743	.684	.812	.630	.600	.796
iCR-Action-Detecter	G, D, S_b, S_a	**.416**	**.418**	**.676**	.859	.763	.880	.733	.684	.811	.834	.730	.862
	G, D, S_b, S_a, L_A	.409	.366	.652	.864	.777	.886	.739	**.689**	.813	.838	.738	.867

Table 2: Main results of average precision, binary F1 Score and macro-average F1 Score for all models in the test set. The inputs are G: gallery, D: dialogue, S_b: scene before the actions, S_a: scene after the actions, A: last gold actions, L_A: predicted logits of the actions. Shaded cells means the models were pre-trained on actions.

task of *what to ask* about, but even the Overhearer achieves more than .70 AP. Given the imbalance of the labels, we consider it a favourable result, showing this task is easier to model. Introducing iCR decisions does not cause drastic changes to the performance on taking actions for *when to ask*, but fine-tuning on *what to ask* causes a drop, which is probably due to the fine-tuning occurring only on iCR turns. See Appendix for additional analysis.

Hypothesis 1 In H1, we study the effect of action-taking on the decision of *when to ask* iCRs. To analyse it, we compare the results of the Overhearer with the iCR-Action-Taker/-Detecter in the left block of Table 2. Integrating multi-task learning for taking actions is slightly helpful for iCR prediction only if the action decision logits are passed to the iCR classifier. If instead of *predicting* actions we let the model learn the auxiliary task of just *detecting* them from the scenes, the results are better.[11] Interestingly, the magnitude of the positive difference is comparable to the difference (in accuracy) found in the Minecraft dataset (Shi et al., 2022), which was, however, negative. These effects are not large enough to provide us with definite evidence that H1 holds.

[11]Again, this is still plausible: In CoDraw, we can assume that the actual player has taken actions before generating the iCR, as discussed by Madureira and Schlangen (2023b).

Hypothesis 2 For H2, we examine the certainty scores assigned by the Action-Taker to performing *any* action upon each clipart. For the task of *what to ask* about, we compare two distributions: Scores of cliparts subject to iCRs *versus* scores of cliparts not subject to iCRs. For *when to ask* iCRs, we inspect the distributions of the lowest score at turns where iCRs occur *versus* turns where no iCR is made. Using the two-sample Kolmogorov-Smirnov test (Hodges Jr, 1958), we compare the underlying empirical cumulative distributions of the two samples, shown in Figure 1, under the null hypothesis that they are equal, and a two-sided alternative.

	clipart (what to ask)		**turn (when to ask)**	
	iCR	**non-iCR**	**iCR**	**non-iCR**
mean (std)	.838 (.251)	.952 (.147)	.363 (.283)	.525 (.328)
KS test	.524*		.219*	
AP	.009		.080	

Table 3: Mean (std) of certainty scores for each sample, results of the two-sided Kolmogorov-Smirnov test and average precision. * means p-value < 0.001.

Table 3 shows the statistically significant test results. It means that, on the whole, Action-Takers behave differently regarding action certainty for cliparts or turns with iCRs. In Figure 3, we can see that the certainty for non-iCR cliparts is more concentrated around 1 than for cliparts subject to iCRs. Similarly, the distribution of the minimum certainty score at iCR turns is more concentrated at lower values. In that sense, we find support for H2. Still, using these scores directly as a signal for iCR prediction does not result in high AP, in line with the findings by Naszad et al. (2022). This seems to occur because, although the distributions are different, both samples have values in the whole range, with overlap in their standard deviation.

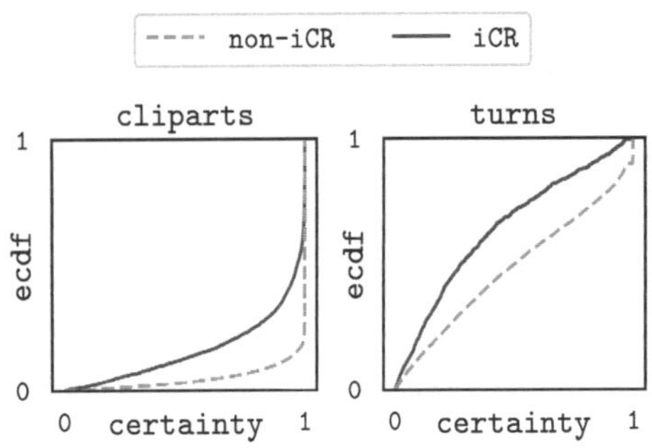

Figure 3: Empirical cumulative distribution function of the certainty of taking actions for each clipart (left) and the minimum by turn (right).

Hypothesis 3 Lastly, we assess the effect of taking actions in deciding *what to ask* about. Here, we focus on the right columns of Table 2, again comparing the Overhearer with the pretrained iCR-Action-Takers/Detecters. We observe a positive effect of learning to take actions on the iCR policy, with AP increasing from .69 to .75. Differently from the task of *when to ask*, here *predicting* actions leads to better results than merely *detecting* them. The difference is not negligible, which is stronger support in favour of H3 in this context.

8 Discussion

Our setting allowed us to differentiate between *understandability* and iCR *policy*. The first refers to learning a mapping from linguistic input to actions. The latter is an additional decision on top of action-taking that regards knowing when the information available to the agent at a given moment is not enough for the current purposes of wanting to commit to an outcome.

Learning to take actions does not seem to be a signal informative enough for deciding *when to ask* for iCRs, although it has a more prominent effect on deciding *what to ask* about in iCR turns. Besides, we investigated whether there is a signal in the purely understanding models that predicts what to clarify. Indeed, a model trained without any explicit iCR signal made predictions whose certainty distribution differ at iCR turns and cliparts. Even though the raw score cannot be directly used as a predictor of human iCR behaviour, further investigation can be done on extracting an agent's implicit iCR policies, *e.g.* with probing or attribution methods and in-depth analysis of the model's internal states.

The five sources of improvement (integration of the gallery, token-level representations of utterances, learnable scene features, attention mechanism to construct contextual object embeddings and action predictions) over the existing CoDraw baseline formed together a conceptually superior model design. We expected this more sophisticated architecture, aligned with the latest literature, to lead up to a clear-cut improvement in the task of when to ask iCRs. The fact that the gain is not more than 10% in our main metric over that baseline compel us to join the ranks of works that question whether the current NLP paradigm (employing imitation learning or behavioural cloning to learn with supervision from limited human data) is the right way to go when it comes to meta-discursive acts in interactions (Hayes, 1980; Nguyen et al., 2022; Min et al., 2022; Naszad et al., 2022; Bohg et al., 2023, *inter alia*). It is also possible that the actions signal is too weak; the action space is large (four actions on 28 objects) which makes the actually performed actions at a given turn be sparse.

In a static dataset of human play, the underlying CR policies of each player may differ by nature and also in visibility in the data. We cannot know with certainty if other humans would have behaved differently at each point than what is realised in the data; consequently, it is hardly possible to set a standard against which to judge the trained model's policy. We are, after all, trying to learn a "customary" policy from what is actually a mixture of policies with observations sampled from various players. It may be the case that we have reached the limits of the generalisable policies we can capture from this data with supervised training, even though the actual metrics are not close to the ceiling.[12] As Hayes (1980) discussed, graceful interaction requires developers to aim for non-literal aspects of communication that are effective for the

[12]Though, as pointed out by a reviewer, this may be a limitation of the class of models we tested, and results can possibly be improved with more powerful vision/language encoders.

human-agent interaction, instead of trying to imitate human patterns exactly. This connects to the over confidence problem in LLMs: In some situations, they should produce an *I don't know* or a CR, but their limited abilities in meta-semantic communication often cause failures.

Ambiguity arises under competing communicative pressures (Piantadosi et al., 2012). Thus CRs are not a problem: They are a solution emerging from joint effort (Clark, 2002). If many bits of information are to be conveyed, the IG may produce minimally sufficient messages and leave it to the addressee to identify gaps. The IF may also take actions that are only approximately good, since mistakes can normally be fixed later. Moreover, crowdworkers seem to lack incentive to try to build perfect reconstructions, and often seem to use implicit knowledge to make only satisfactory actions (see Appendix). Therefore, the iCR signal may not be "out there" in the data, but live in the internal state of the agents. Treating the task as *iid* predictions under supervised learning is also not ideal because game decisions are actually made sequentially. Like some works on learning when to ask questions, modelling iCR policies may call for reinforcement learning (see *e.g.* Khalid et al. (2020)), with evaluation methods that capture the effectiveness of the agent's policy for the game, beyond comparison with human behaviour.

9 Conclusion

We have examined the effects of performing actions on learning iCR policies in the CoDraw game. The assumption that learning to take actions would make the underlying *when to ask* policy emerge does not fully hold. Still, we find that prediction certainty of actions differs at iCR turns. Then, if we assume that a given policy has informed us on *when* iCRs have to be made, we show that it is possible to predict *what to ask* about more successfully, with action-taking having a stronger positive effect. Exploring larger datasets with CRs produced as a by-product of action-taking is desired. Still, the suboptimal performance of various SotA models in deciding *when to ask* for clarification speaks against approaches that seek to imitate human behaviour. We recommend more investigation with RL and evaluation methods that capture the effectiveness of iCR policies in dynamic contexts.

10 Limitations

We have only explored one dataset because there are very few genuine iCR datasets available yet. Minecraft, which is relatively comparable in terms of the underlying instruction following setting, is smaller and has a different form of common ground due to full visibility by the IG. It has been explored in related work, to which we refer in the related work section. SIMMC 2.0 is not suitable in this context for two reasons: Its CRs are not at Clark's level 4 (uptake), but mostly level 3 (reference resolution). Besides, it is a simulated dataset, and we are interested in exploring the limits of modelling human iCR behaviour.

The models are thus task-specifically fitted to CoDraw and cannot be applied out of the box to other domains. Still, we believe that CoDraw is representative of iCRs and that solving the task in one domain is a first step towards generalisation, which has not been achieved yet even with other datasets, as we discussed.

In this work, our models do not predict all fine-grained game actions, *i.e.* they are not full-fledged Action-Takers. In preliminary experiments, we first attempted to model an agent that predicts all features of each clipart at each turn. However, since the vast majority of the 28 available cliparts remain unchanged from one turn to the other, the model could simply learn to output a copy of the current state. We thus opted to turn all tasks into binary predictions for our analysis, as we observed results that are good enough for our purposes, given the imbalanced nature of the actions in the data. For each object in the gallery, it makes high level decisions on which actions are needed (add/delete, move, resize, flip). A full agent should include the subsequent tasks of deciding where to place cliparts and what exact (discrete) size to set (presence and orientation can be deduced in post-processing with the current version).

Further investigation can be done to improve the performance of the Action-Takers. Since the actions are very sparse, it may be the case that models just learn to detect mentioned cliparts in the utterances. A detailed error analysis should look closer at the predictions and also examine how good the scene similarity scores of the reconstructions are. Instead of predicting probabilities, the model could also output parameters of a distribution from which the actions would be sampled; we do not investigate that option here. Besides, we use a supervised learning approach that treats turns as *iid*. In reality, what the player does in one turn influences its next moves, so other methods like RL could be more appropriate, as we discussed.

Although our models take several epochs to overfit the training data, performance in the validation set saturates very early. The techniques we tried (for instance, dropout, variations of the architecture and filtering the training data) did not lead to better results. We performed a limited hyperparameter search that could be done more extensively in the future, also to investigate in more detail how the method scales with larger and smaller models.

For the task of *what to ask* about, we did not include the utterances for which the annotation does not provide the reference cliparts due to ambiguity. Still, that happens for very few cases and should not have a considerable impact on the results.

To conclude, we do not have human performance to use as an upper boundary for our results. It would be interesting to collect human data by letting humans decide *when to ask* for clarification and *what to ask* about, so that we can better understand to what extent the task itself is possible for humans acting as overhearers. Still, since our aim is to do an intrinsic analysis on whether taking actions improve a model's performance, human results are not strictly necessary, because comparison within models suffices for testing our hypotheses.

11 Ethical Considerations

Merely posing clarification requests can be a source of miscommunication regarding intentions, which has ethical implications and may also weaken the application of moral norms by the interlocutors, as discussed by Jackson and Williams (2018) and Jackson and Williams (2019). Besides, the risks regarding privacy and biases of learning actions from individual behaviour also apply, as well as the current topics being discussed in the field of responsible NLP.

Acknowledgements

We thank the anonymous reviewers for their valuable comments that helped improve the paper. We also thank Philipp Sadler and Javier Chiyah-Garcia for helpful discussions regarding this research project.

References

Mohammad Aliannejadi, Julia Kiseleva, Aleksandr Chuklin, Jeff Dalton, and Mikhail Burtsev. 2021. Building and evaluating open-domain dialogue corpora with clarifying questions. In *Proceedings of the 2021 Conference on Empirical Methods in Natural Language Processing*, pages 4473–4484, Online and Punta Cana, Dominican Republic. Association for Computational Linguistics.

Mohammad Aliannejadi, Hamed Zamani, Fabio Crestani, and W Bruce Croft. 2019. Asking clarifying questions in open-domain information-seeking conversations. In *Proceedings of the 42nd international acm sigir conference on research and development in information retrieval*, pages 475–484.

Luciana Benotti. 2009. Clarification potential of instructions. In *Proceedings of the SIGDIAL 2009 Conference*, pages 196–205, London, UK. Association for Computational Linguistics.

Luciana Benotti and Patrick Blackburn. 2021. A recipe for annotating grounded clarifications. In *Proceedings of the 2021 Conference of the North American Chapter of the Association for Computational Linguistics: Human Language Technologies*, pages 4065–4077, Online. Association for Computational Linguistics.

Jeannette Bohg, Marco Pavone, and Dorsa Sadigh. 2023. Principles of robot autonomy. http://web.stanford.edu/class/cs237b/. [Stanford lecture notes available online; session 12.].

Jordan Boyd-Graber, Brianna Satinoff, He He, and Hal Daumé III. 2012. Besting the quiz master: Crowdsourcing incremental classification games. In *Proceedings of the 2012 Joint Conference on Empirical Methods in Natural Language Processing and Computational Natural Language Learning*, pages 1290–1301, Jeju Island, Korea. Association for Computational Linguistics.

Pavel Braslavski, Denis Savenkov, Eugene Agichtein, and Alina Dubatovka. 2017. What do you mean exactly? analyzing clarification questions in cqa. In *Proceedings of the 2017 Conference on Conference Human Information Interaction and Retrieval*, CHIIR '17, page 345–348, New York, NY, USA. Association for Computing Machinery.

Nicolas Carion, Francisco Massa, Gabriel Synnaeve, Nicolas Usunier, Alexander Kirillov, and Sergey Zagoruyko. 2020. End-to-end object detection with transformers. In *European conference on computer vision*, pages 213–229. Springer.

Ta-Chung Chi, Minmin Shen, Mihail Eric, Seokhwan Kim, and Dilek Hakkani-tur. 2020. Just ask: An interactive learning framework for vision and language navigation. In *Proceedings of the AAAI Conference on Artificial Intelligence*, volume 34, pages 2459–2466.

Javier Chiyah-Garcia, Alessandro Suglia, Arash Eshghi, and Helen Hastie. 2023. ‘what are you referring to?’evaluating the ability of multi-modal dialogue models to process clarificational exchanges. In *Proceedings of the 24th Annual Meeting of the Special Interest Group on Discourse and Dialogue*, Prague, Czech Republic. Association for Computational Linguistics.

Herbert H Clark. 1992. *Arenas of language use*. University of Chicago Press.

Herbert H Clark. 1996. *Using language*. Cambridge university press.

Herbert H Clark. 2002. Speaking in time. *Speech communication*, 36(1-2):5–13.

Yang Deng, Wenqiang Lei, Lizi Liao, and Tat-Seng Chua. 2023. Prompting and evaluating large language models for proactive dialogues: Clarification, target-guided, and non-collaboration. *arXiv preprint arXiv:2305.13626*.

Jacob Devlin, Ming-Wei Chang, Kenton Lee, and Kristina Toutanova. 2019. BERT: Pre-training of deep bidirectional transformers for language understanding. In *Proceedings of the 2019 Conference of the North American Chapter of the Association for Computational Linguistics: Human Language Technologies, Volume 1 (Long and Short Papers)*, pages 4171–4186, Minneapolis, Minnesota. Association for Computational Linguistics.

Malte Gabsdil. 2003. Clarification in spoken dialogue systems. In *Proceedings of the 2003 AAAI Spring Symposium. Workshop on Natural Language Generation in Spoken and Written Dialogue*, pages 28–35.

Xiaofeng Gao, Qiaozi Gao, Ran Gong, Kaixiang Lin, Govind Thattai, and Gaurav S Sukhatme. 2022. Dialfred: Dialogue-enabled agents for embodied instruction following. *IEEE Robotics and Automation Letters*, 7(4):10049–10056.

Spandana Gella, Aishwarya Padmakumar, Patrick Lange, and Dilek Hakkani-Tur. 2022. Dialog acts for task driven embodied agents. In *Proceedings of the 23rd Annual Meeting of the Special Interest Group on Discourse and Dialogue*, pages 111–123, Edinburgh, UK. Association for Computational Linguistics.

Felix Gervits, Antonio Roque, Gordon Briggs, Matthias Scheutz, and Matthew Marge. 2021. How should agents ask questions for situated learning? an annotated dialogue corpus. In *Proceedings of the 22nd Annual Meeting of the Special Interest Group on Discourse and Dialogue*, pages 353–359, Singapore and Online. Association for Computational Linguistics.

Phil Hayes. 1980. Expanding the horizons of natural language interfaces. In *18th Annual Meeting of the Association for Computational Linguistics*, pages 71–74, Philadelphia, Pennsylvania, USA. Association for Computational Linguistics.

Phil Hayes and Raj Reddy. 1979. Graceful interaction in man-machine communication. In *Proceedings of the 6th international joint conference on Artificial intelligence-Volume 1*, pages 372–374.

Philip J Hayes and D Raj Reddy. 1983. Steps toward graceful interaction in spoken and written man-machine communication. *International Journal of Man-Machine Studies*, 19(3):231–284.

Kaiming He, Xiangyu Zhang, Shaoqing Ren, and Jian Sun. 2015. Deep residual learning for image recognition. *CoRR*, abs/1512.03385.

JL Hodges Jr. 1958. The significance probability of the smirnov two-sample test. *Arkiv för matematik*, 3(5):469–486.

Xiang Hu, Zujie Wen, Yafang Wang, Xiaolong Li, and Gerard de Melo. 2020. Interactive question clarification in dialogue via reinforcement learning. In *Proceedings of the 28th International Conference on Computational Linguistics: Industry Track*, pages 78–89, Online. International Committee on Computational Linguistics.

Ryan Blake Jackson and Tom Williams. 2018. Robot: Asker of questions and changer of norms. *Proceedings of ICRES*.

Ryan Blake Jackson and Tom Williams. 2019. Language-capable robots may inadvertently weaken human moral norms. In *2019 14th ACM/IEEE International Conference on Human-Robot Interaction (HRI)*, pages 401–410. IEEE.

Kimiya Keyvan and Jimmy Xiangji Huang. 2022. How to approach ambiguous queries in conversational search: A survey of techniques, approaches, tools, and challenges. *ACM Computing Surveys*, 55(6):1–40.

Baber Khalid, Malihe Alikhani, and Matthew Stone. 2020. Combining cognitive modeling and reinforcement learning for clarification in dialogue. In *Proceedings of the 28th International Conference on Computational Linguistics*, pages 4417–4428, Barcelona, Spain (Online). International Committee on Computational Linguistics.

Baber Khalid and Matthew Stone. 2023. Investigating reinforcement learning for communication strategies in a task-initiative setting. *arXiv preprint arXiv:2308.01479*.

Jin-Hwa Kim, Nikita Kitaev, Xinlei Chen, Marcus Rohrbach, Byoung-Tak Zhang, Yuandong Tian, Dhruv Batra, and Devi Parikh. 2019. CoDraw: Collaborative drawing as a testbed for grounded goal-driven communication. In *Proceedings of the 57th Annual Meeting of the Association for Computational Linguistics*, pages 6495–6513, Florence, Italy. Association for Computational Linguistics.

Diederik P. Kingma and Jimmy Ba. 2015. Adam: A method for stochastic optimization. In *3rd International Conference on Learning Representations, ICLR 2015, San Diego, CA, USA, May 7-9, 2015, Conference Track Proceedings*.

Julia Kiseleva, Alexey Skrynnik, Artem Zholus, Shrestha Mohanty, Negar Arabzadeh, Marc-Alexandre Côté, Mohammad Aliannejadi, Milagro Teruel, Ziming Li, Mikhail Burtsev, et al. 2022. Iglu 2022: Interactive grounded language understanding in a collaborative environment at neurips 2022. *arXiv preprint arXiv:2205.13771*.

Satwik Kottur, Seungwhan Moon, Alborz Geramifard, and Babak Damavandi. 2021. SIMMC 2.0: A task-oriented dialog dataset for immersive multimodal conversations. In *Proceedings of the 2021 Conference on Empirical Methods in Natural Language Processing*, pages 4903–4912, Online and Punta Cana, Dominican Republic. Association for Computational Linguistics.

Lorenz Kuhn, Yarin Gal, and Sebastian Farquhar. 2022. Clam: Selective clarification for ambiguous questions with large language models. *arXiv preprint arXiv:2212.07769*.

Vaibhav Kumar and Alan W Black. 2020. ClarQ: A large-scale and diverse dataset for clarification question generation. In *Proceedings of the 58th Annual Meeting of the Association for Computational Linguistics*, pages 7296–7301, Online. Association for Computational Linguistics.

Staffan Larsson. 2017. User-initiated sub-dialogues in state-of-the-art dialogue systems. In *Proceedings of the 18th Annual SIGdial Meeting on Discourse and Dialogue*, pages 17–22, Saarbrücken, Germany. Association for Computational Linguistics.

Haeju Lee, Oh Joon Kwon, Yunseon Choi, Minho Park, Ran Han, Yoonhyung Kim, Jinhyeon Kim, Youngjune Lee, Haebin Shin, Kangwook Lee, and Kee-Eung Kim. 2022. Learning to embed multimodal contexts for situated conversational agents. In *Findings of the Association for Computational Linguistics: NAACL 2022*, pages 813–830, Seattle, United States. Association for Computational Linguistics.

Haau-Sing (Xiaocheng) Li, Mohsen Mesgar, André Martins, and Iryna Gurevych. 2023. Python code generation by asking clarification questions. In *Proceedings of the 61st Annual Meeting of the Association for Computational Linguistics (Volume 1: Long Papers)*, pages 14287–14306, Toronto, Canada. Association for Computational Linguistics.

Brielen Madureira and David Schlangen. 2023a. "Are you telling me to put glasses on the dog?" Content-grounded annotation of instruction clarification requests in the CoDraw dataset. *arXiv preprint arXiv:2306.02377*.

Brielen Madureira and David Schlangen. 2023b. Instruction clarification requests in multimodal collaborative dialogue games: Tasks, and an analysis of the CoDraw dataset. In *Proceedings of the 17th Conference of the European Chapter of the Association for Computational Linguistics*, pages 2303–2319, Dubrovnik, Croatia. Association for Computational Linguistics.

Bodhisattwa Prasad Majumder, Sudha Rao, Michel Galley, and Julian McAuley. 2021. Ask what's missing and what's useful: Improving clarification question generation using global knowledge. In *Proceedings of the 2021 Conference of the North American Chapter of the Association for Computational Linguistics: Human Language Technologies*, pages 4300–4312, Online. Association for Computational Linguistics.

So Yeon Min, Hao Zhu, Ruslan Salakhutdinov, and Yonatan Bisk. 2022. Don't copy the teacher: Data and model challenges in embodied dialogue. In *Proceedings of the 2022 Conference on Empirical Methods in Natural Language Processing*, pages 9361–9368, Abu Dhabi, United Arab Emirates. Association for Computational Linguistics.

Shrestha Mohanty, Negar Arabzadeh, Julia Kiseleva, Artem Zholus, Milagro Teruel, Ahmed Awadallah, Yuxuan Sun, Kavya Srinet, and Arthur Szlam. 2023. Transforming human-centered ai collaboration: Redefining embodied agents capabilities through interactive grounded language instructions.

Shrestha Mohanty, Negar Arabzadeh, Milagro Teruel, Yuxuan Sun, Artem Zholus, Alexey Skrynnik, Mikhail Burtsev, Kavya Srinet, Aleksandr Panov, Arthur Szlam, Marc-Alexandre Côté, and Julia Kiseleva. 2022. Collecting interactive multi-modal datasets for grounded language understanding.

Anjali Narayan-Chen, Prashant Jayannavar, and Julia Hockenmaier. 2019. Collaborative dialogue in Minecraft. In *Proceedings of the 57th Annual Meeting of the Association for Computational Linguistics*, pages 5405–5415, Florence, Italy. Association for Computational Linguistics.

Kata Naszad, Michiel Van Der Meer, Kim Taewoon, and Putra Manggala. 2022. Learning to ask timely questions in a collaborative grounded language understanding task. unpublished two-page abstract.

Khanh Nguyen and Hal Daumé III. 2019. Help, anna! visual navigation with natural multimodal assistance via retrospective curiosity-encouraging imitation learning. In *Proceedings of the 2019 Conference on Empirical Methods in Natural Language Processing and the 9th International Joint Conference on Natural Language Processing (EMNLP-IJCNLP)*, pages 684–695, Hong Kong, China. Association for Computational Linguistics.

Khanh X Nguyen, Yonatan Bisk, and Hal Daumé Iii. 2022. A framework for learning to request rich and contextually useful information from humans. In *International Conference on Machine Learning*, pages 16553–16568. PMLR.

Aishwarya Padmakumar, Jesse Thomason, Ayush Shrivastava, Patrick Lange, Anjali Narayan-Chen, Spandana Gella, Robinson Piramuthu, Gokhan Tur, and Dilek Hakkani-Tur. 2022. Teach: Task-driven embodied agents that chat. In *Proceedings of the AAAI Conference on Artificial Intelligence*, volume 36, pages 2017–2025.

Steven T Piantadosi, Harry Tily, and Edward Gibson. 2012. The communicative function of ambiguity in language. *Cognition*, 122(3):280–291.

Matthew Purver, Jonathan Ginzburg, and Patrick Healey. 2001. On the means for clarification in dialogue. In *Proceedings of the Second SIGdial Workshop on Discourse and Dialogue*.

Matthew Purver, Jonathan Ginzburg, and Patrick Healey. 2003. On the means for clarification in dialogue. In *Current and new directions in discourse and dialogue*, pages 235–255. Springer.

Hossein A. Rahmani, Xi Wang, Yue Feng, Qiang Zhang, Emine Yilmaz, and Aldo Lipani. 2023. A survey on asking clarification questions datasets in conversational systems. In *Proceedings of the 61st Annual Meeting of the Association for Computational Linguistics (Volume 1: Long Papers)*, pages 2698–2716, Toronto, Canada. Association for Computational Linguistics.

Sudha Rao and Hal Daumé III. 2018. Learning to ask good questions: Ranking clarification questions using neural expected value of perfect information. In *Proceedings of the 56th Annual Meeting of the Association for Computational Linguistics (Volume 1: Long Papers)*, pages 2737–2746, Melbourne, Australia. Association for Computational Linguistics.

Verena Rieser and Oliver Lemon. 2006. Using machine learning to explore human multimodal clarification strategies. In *Proceedings of the COLING/ACL 2006 Main Conference Poster Sessions*, pages 659–666, Sydney, Australia. Association for Computational Linguistics.

Kepa Joseba Rodríguez and David Schlangen. 2004. Form, intonation and function of clarification requests in german task-oriented spoken dialogues. In *Proceedings of Catalog (the 8th workshop on the semantics and pragmatics of dialogue; SemDial04)*.

Robin Rojowiec, Jana Götze, Philipp Sadler, Henrik Voigt, Sina Zarrieß, and David Schlangen. 2020. From "before" to "after": Generating natural language instructions from image pairs in a simple visual domain. In *Proceedings of the 13th International Conference on Natural Language Generation*, pages 316–326, Dublin, Ireland. Association for Computational Linguistics.

Philipp Sadler and David Schlangen. 2023. Pento-DIARef: A diagnostic dataset for learning the incremental algorithm for referring expression generation from examples. In *Proceedings of the 17th Conference of the European Chapter of the Association for Computational Linguistics*, pages 2106–2122, Dubrovnik, Croatia. Association for Computational Linguistics.

David Schlangen. 2004. Causes and strategies for requesting clarification in dialogue. In *Proceedings of the 5th SIGdial Workshop on Discourse and Dialogue at HLT-NAACL 2004*, pages 136–143, Cambridge, Massachusetts, USA. Association for Computational Linguistics.

David Schlangen. 2021. Targeting the benchmark: On methodology in current natural language processing research. In *Proceedings of the 59th Annual Meeting of the Association for Computational Linguistics and the 11th International Joint Conference on Natural Language Processing (Volume 2: Short Papers)*, pages 670–674, Online. Association for Computational Linguistics.

Julian Schlöder and Raquel Fernández. 2014. Clarification requests at the level of uptake. In *Proceedings of the 18th Workshop on the Semantics and Pragmatics of Dialogue - Poster Abstracts*, Edinburgh, United Kingdom. SEMDIAL.

Michael F Schober and Herbert H Clark. 1989. Understanding by addressees and overhearers. *Cognitive psychology*, 21(2):211–232.

Burr Settles. 2012. *Active Learning. Synthesis Lectures on Artificial Intelligence and Machine Learning.* Springer Cham.

Omar Shaikh, Kristina Gligorić, Ashna Khetan, Matthias Gerstgrasser, Diyi Yang, and Dan Jurafsky. 2023. Grounding or guesswork? large language models are presumptive grounders. *arXiv preprint arXiv:2311.09144*.

Ravi Shekhar, Tim Baumgärtner, Aashish Venkatesh, Elia Bruni, Raffaella Bernardi, and Raquel Fernandez. 2018. Ask no more: Deciding when to guess in referential visual dialogue. In *Proceedings of the 27th International Conference on Computational Linguistics*, pages 1218–1233, Santa Fe, New Mexico, USA. Association for Computational Linguistics.

Zhengxiang Shi, Yue Feng, and Aldo Lipani. 2022. Learning to execute actions or ask clarification questions. In *Findings of the Association for Computational Linguistics: NAACL 2022*, pages 2060–2070, Seattle, United States. Association for Computational Linguistics.

Zhengxiang Shi, Jerome Ramos, To Eun Kim, Xi Wang, Hossein A Rahmani, and Aldo Lipani. 2023. When and what to ask through world states and text instructions: Iglu nlp challenge solution. *arXiv preprint arXiv:2305.05754*.

Svetlana Stoyanchev, Alex Liu, and Julia Hirschberg. 2013. Modelling human clarification strategies. In *Proceedings of the SIGDIAL 2013 Conference*, pages 137–141, Metz, France. Association for Computational Linguistics.

Jesse Thomason, Michael Murray, Maya Cakmak, and Luke Zettlemoyer. 2020. Vision-and-dialog navigation. In *Conference on Robot Learning*, pages 394–406. PMLR.

Ashish Vaswani, Noam Shazeer, Niki Parmar, Jakob Uszkoreit, Llion Jones, Aidan N Gomez, Łukasz Kaiser, and Illia Polosukhin. 2017. Attention is all you need. *Advances in neural information processing systems*, 30.

Yijun Xiao and William Yang Wang. 2019. Quantifying uncertainties in natural language processing tasks. In *Proceedings of the AAAI conference on artificial intelligence*, volume 33, pages 7322–7329.

Ziyu Yao, Yu Su, Huan Sun, and Wen-tau Yih. 2019. Model-based interactive semantic parsing: A unified framework and a text-to-SQL case study. In *Proceedings of the 2019 Conference on Empirical Methods in Natural Language Processing and the 9th International Joint Conference on Natural Language Processing (EMNLP-IJCNLP)*, pages 5447–5458, Hong Kong, China. Association for Computational Linguistics.

C Lawrence Zitnick and Devi Parikh. 2013. Bringing semantics into focus using visual abstraction. In *Proceedings of the IEEE Conference on Computer Vision and Pattern Recognition*, pages 3009–3016.

A Additional Analysis

Here we present additional analysis. Figure 4 illustrates the distribution of the number of actions per turn. Table 4 presents the average precision for each type of action, which are aggregated in Table 2. Figure 5 show the boxplots for the distribution of certainty scores, to aid visualising that they have different shapes in each sample.

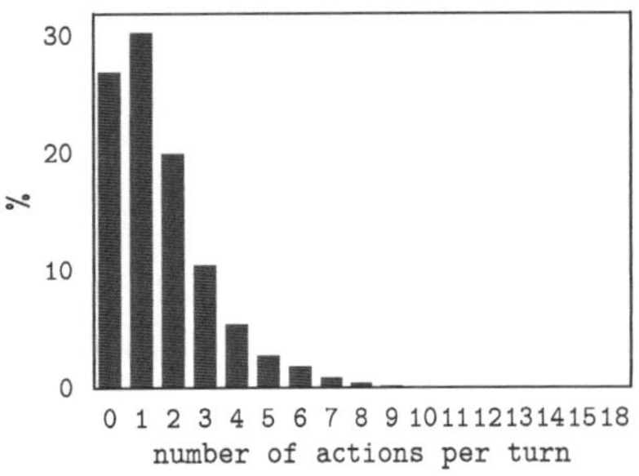

Figure 4: Empirical distribution of the number of actions per turn in the CoDraw dataset.

	add/del	move	flip	resize
Action-Taker G, D	.875	.617	.367	.531
iCR-Action-Taker G, D	.865	.600	.398	.539
Action-Detecter G, D, $S_{a,b}$	.976	.644	.414	.636
iCR-Action-Detecter G, D, $S_{a,b}$	.974	.642	.423	.626

Table 4: Detailed performance of the Action-Takers and Action-Detecters for *when to ask*. Values are the average precision for each type of action in the test set.

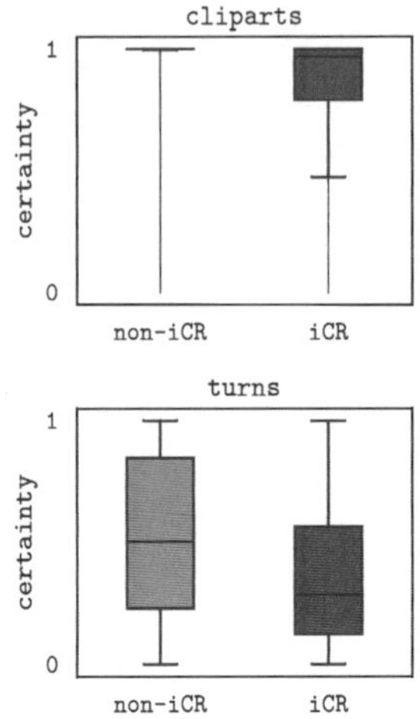

Figure 5: Empirical distribution of the certainty of taking actions for each clipart (top) and the minimum by turn (bottom).

B Reproducibility

In this section, we provide details of our data preprocessing and implementation. For precise details, please check the available code. Here, we provide a brief overview of each component and the justification of some decisions.

B.1 Data

We used the annotation released in the file `codraw-icr-v2.tsv`[13] to identify iCRs and mentioned cliparts. We followed the train-val-test splits as in the original CoDraw data. The *ambiguity classes* introduced by the authors were treated as follows: If an iCR was about an ambiguous but concrete class, we assigned the positive iCR label to all objects in the gallery that belong to that class. For instance, for `hat_group`, all hats in the gallery were treated as positive cases. The general ambiguity class, used for unclear cases, was ignored in our labelling. This occured in 318 iCRS. The whole dataset was used in all experiments, except for the

[13] `https://osf.io/gcjhz/files/osfstorage`

tasks of *what to ask* about, for which only the turns containing iCRs were included for all splits.

The gallery and scene representation was constructed using features in a similar fashion as the original paper. Each clipart was assigned integers for its identifier, size (three categories), orientation (two categories), presence in the current scene (a binary feature), pose (seven categories) and facial expression (5 categories), as well as five features for its position (x and y coordinates of its centre, width, height and area in the canvas). We set features (except pose and facial expression) to a special category 0 for objects that are not in the scene. All boy and girl cliparts were collapsed into one class for each, and their facial expressions and poses were turned into features in the symbolic representation, as in original paper. Other cliparts were assigned a "not-applicable" class for these two features. To define bounding boxes, we rescaled sizes according to the AbstractScenes documentation.

Actions were defined as either addition/deletion or edits. Edits meant flip, resize and move. If a clipart was added or deleted, we did not consider changes to its orientation, position and size with respect to the gallery (in order to avoid that the model only learnt the edits that occur due to an addition or deletion). Actions were defined by comparing the state of the gallery in a turn in relation to its state in the previous turn. For initial turns and some cases where the scene string was not available in the dataset, we set the scene to empty and use the gallery in adjacent turns (since the gallery should remain the same across the game). We also introduced an "acted upon" action that is positive whenever any type of action occurs upon a clipart.

Text embeddings were retrieved from `bert-base-uncased`, licensed under Apache 2.0. Following Shi et al. (2022), we concatenate the IG and IF utterances using special tokens before each speaker. Special tokens `<TELLER>` and `<DRAWER>` were appended before the instruction giver and follower, respectively. The last utterance from the instruction follower was appended to the beginning of the utterance of the instruction giver, so that potential previous iCRs are encoded with their responses, if given immediately. Embedding sequences were padded with zeros to the right to an empirical length of 80 tokens. When context is used, the previous turns are appended to the left of the last instruction and, if necessary, padded with zeros to the left, so that the most recent turn is always at the same position in the input.

B.2 Implementation

The models were implemented with Python (v3.10.12), PyTorch[14] (v1.13.1) and Pytorch Lightning[15] (v2.0.8), in Linux 5.4.0-99-generic with processor x86_64 on an NVIDIA GeForce GTX 1080 Ti GPU with CUDA (v11.6). The pre-trained ResNet model was retrieved from torchvision[16] (v0.14.1) and the pre-trained BERT came from HuggingFace transformers[17] (v4.29.2).

Optimisation was done with the Adam algorithm (Kingma and Ba, 2015), using `BCEWithLogitsLoss` with `reduction` set to sum and the argument `pos_weight` to 2 for each task. The total loss used for backpropagation was a sum of all task losses. Early stopping was implemented using a patience of 8 epochs and the minimum delta of 0.001 for maximisation of a monitored metric. Metrics were computed using torchmetrics[18] (v0.11.4). The monitored metric varied according to the task: If iCRs were predicted, we tracked the binary average precision of iCR labels; otherwise, we tracked the binary average precision of the meta-action class. The maximum number of epochs was set to 30. The checkpoint that lead to best performance in the validation set was saved and loaded to run the tests. Comet[19] was used to manage experiments and to perform hyperparameter search.

Hyperparameter search was performed with the base model (*i.e.* an Overhearer that gets only the dialogue and the gallery representation as input and predicts only *when to ask* iCRs). We used comet's Bayes algorithm as well as a few manual selections of hyperparameters, and opted for the model with highest iCR binary average precision in the validation set. Table 5 shows the final hyperparameter configuration used in all experiments.

We did not keep records of all experiments during development. For the final run, we run 43 experiments during tuning and 102 for the analysis. The duration varied from 5 minutes (the random baseline) to 06h16m (the iCR-Action-Detecter using the full Transformer), without including the time for data preparation. The number of parameters varied according to the model. The turn-

[14]`https://pytorch.org/`

[15]`https://lightning.ai/pytorch-lightning`

[16]`https://pytorch.org/vision/stable/models.html`

[17]`https://huggingface.co/bert-base-uncased`

[18]`https://torchmetrics.readthedocs.io/en/latest/`

[19]`https://www.comet.com`

hyperparameter	type	options	selected
accumulate gradient	discrete	1, 2, 5, 10, 25	1
batch size	discrete	16, 32, 64, 128, 256	32
clipping	discrete	0, 0.25, 0.5, 1, 2.5, 5	1
context length	integer	min=1, max=5	3
dropout	discrete	0.1, 0.2, 0.3	0.1
d_model	discrete	128, 256, 512	256
hidden_dim	discrete	32, 64, 128, 256, 512, 1024	256
hidden_dim_trf	discrete	256, 512, 1024	2048
learning rate	discrete	0.1, 0.01, 0.001, 0.0001, 0.003, 0.0003, 0.00001, 0.0005	0.0001
lr scheduler	bool	True, False	False
lr step	integer	min=1, max=10	-
n heads	discrete	1, 2, 4, 8, 32	16
n layers	float	min=1, max=6	3
n reload datasets	float	min=1, max=10	1
pos weight	float	min=0.8, max=3	2
pre-trained text embeddings	categorical	bert-base-uncased, roberta-base, distilbert-base-uncased	bert-base-uncased
random seed	integer	min=1, max=54321	12345
weight decay	discrete	1, 0.1, 0.01, 0.001, 0.0001	0.
weighted loss	bool	True, False	False

Table 5: Hyperparameters: Investigated options and selected values. Note that the search did not extensively cover all possibilities for each hyperparameter.

level Overhearer without scenes had 5,008,923 and with both scenes 29,054,299 (5,546,267 learnable). The turn-level iCR-Action-Taker without scenes had 5,339,168, and the iCR-Action-Detecter had 29,384,544 (5,876,512 learnable).

To enable reproducibility, we set the use of use deterministic algorithms to `True` in PyTorch and used Lightning's `seed_everything` method with a fixed random seed. Despite this, according to the documentation, some methods cannot be forced to be deterministic in PyTorch when using CUDA.[20]

B.3 Model

In this section, we explain in more detals how we address five of the limitations of the baseline model (iCR-baseline) by Madureira and Schlangen (2023b), some of them already acknowledged by the authors. We also refer to the original CoDraw model (CoDraw-orig) by Kim et al. (2019), which, however, did not include the instruction follower's utterances in the game.

Incorporating the gallery The gallery is an informative source in CoDraw (*e.g.* if it contains just one of the three tree cliparts, it is less likely that disambiguation is needed). iCR-baseline does not include the available objects as input, whereas CoDraw-orig uses a symbolic representation assuming all 58 objects are available at any time. Both approaches do not correspond to reality, as players only see 28 cliparts. We follow a similar symbolic approach to represent the objects' attributes (presence in the scene, orientation, position, size, pose, facial expression), but only for those at play. The cliparts' features and bounding boxes are projected to a higher-dimensional space following Sadler and Schlangen (2023).

Using contextual word embeddings iCR-baseline relies only on two sentence-level embeddings, one to encode the whole dialogue context and one for the last utterance, both not optimised for the game. To allow the policy to access more fine-grained linguistic information, we make all token-level contextual embeddings available to the player, constructed by a pretrained language model.

Enhancing scene representations iCR-baseline uses a pretrained image encoder. It is unlikely that off-the-shelf encoders fit well to clipart scenes without fine-tuning. Here, we follow the approach in DETR (Carion et al., 2020), employing a ResNet (He et al., 2015) backbone with learnable positional encodings to extract scene features, followed by a trainable convolutional layer to reduce the number of channels. The sequence of image features is then used as part of the input.

Transforming The iCR predictions rely only on pretrained embeddings with a feed forward neural network in iCR-baseline, and CoDraw-orig did not employ Transformers (Vaswani et al., 2017) as a trainable component. Given its leading perfor-

[20] `https://pytorch.org/docs/1.13/generated/torch.use_deterministic_algorithms.html#torch.use_deterministic_algorithms`

mance in several scenarios, we bring them more explicitly to the scene, in an approach similar to DETR (Carion et al., 2020). We feed the clipart representations to the decoder, to allow self-attention to build up embeddings of the state of the gallery and scene, without positional encoding due to the arbitrary order of the cliparts. Here, we also rely on the findings by Chiyah-Garcia et al. (2023) that encoding relations between objects and their locations is helpful for CRs. Then, it performs cross-attention with the scene and text. We make text and scene available as one sequence like Lee et al. (2022). Since cross-attention between modalities is a cornerstone in current CR models (Shi et al., 2022, 2023), we also run experiments using the encoder to let text and scene attend to each other. We then end up with a multimodal representation of each clipart in the current context, which is then passed to classifier layers for each prediction.

Action-taking via multi-task learning iCR-baseline is an Overhearer, modelling only the policy of *when to ask* iCRs. To test our hypotheses, we implement (iCR-)Action-Takers that predict the game actions (or detect them, if the updated image is used) via multi-task learning. Note that this is not yet a full-fledged Action-Taker. For each object in the gallery, it makes high level binary classification on which actions are needed (add/delete, move, resize, flip); a full model would also make the subsequent fine-grained decision of exact positions and sizes. We take inspiration from Shi et al. (2022) and train a joint encoding for multiple classifiers. We let the action logits (or the real actions via teacher forcing) be part of the input to the iCR decoder. To facilitate evaluation, we add an additional meta-action prediction which is 1 whenever *any* action is made to a clipart.

Components Let d_model be the dimension used for the Transformer. First of all, an embedding of the gallery and scene state is constructed. Embedding layers are used for a clipart's identifier, orientation, presence, size, face and pose states with dimensions d_model-100, 10, 10, 10, 20 and 20, respectively. The position is embedded with a linear layer that maps its centre coordinates, area, width and height to 30 dimensions. All embedded features are concatenated so as to create a representation with dimensions 28 (number of cliparts) by d_model. We used only the decoder of the Transformer, which gets the gallery representation as "target" and the instruction tokens (whose dimensions were reduced with a linear layer and, if applicable, the sequence was concatenated to the scene features) summed to positional encodings as "memory". The decoder performs self-attention in the gallery and then cross-attention with the memory. Scenes are encoded following Carion et al. (2020)'s implementation, but we first preprocess the scene according to the pretrained model's documentation. The scene is then fed into a pre-trained ResNet50 followed by a trainable convolutional layer that reduces the number of channels to the same dimension used for the Transformer. Then, the height and width dimensions are flattened and the result is added to learnable position embeddings, with a dropout layer. The probabilities (for iCRs or actions) are predicted by taking each output of the Transformer (*i.e.* one representation for each clipart in the gallery) and passing it through a feed-forward network with the following sequential layers: leaky ReLU, dropout, linear, leaky ReLU and linear. For predicting turn-level iCRs, the representations of all cliparts are averaged. If the action-taking logits or teacher forcing is used, they are appended to the input. The output logits are converted to probabilities using the sigmoid function.

B.4 Evaluation

The threshold for the F1-Scores was set to 0.5. We did not include the meta-action label in the main results for taking actions to avoid inflating the performance; it was only used for the analysis for H2, done on the Action-Taker+G, D. Metrics for the evaluation were computed with sklearn[21] (v1.0.2) and the plots were generated with seaborn (v0.12.2) and matplotlib[22] (v3.7.1). The hypothesis test was done with SciPy[23] (v1.11.1) `stats.ks_2samp` method with a two-sided alternative.

C CoDraw Examples

Figures 6-9 exemplify strategies of crowdworkers, showing various levels of commitment to playing the game well. The images are generated with the CoDraw Dataset Visualizer, developed by @jnhwkim at `https://github.com/facebookresearch/CoDraw`. Scenes at the top are the state of the reconstructions at the highlighted turns.

[21] `https://scikit-learn.org/stable/index.html`

[22] `https://matplotlib.org/`

[23] `https://docs.scipy.org/doc/scipy/reference/generated/scipy.stats.ks_2samp.html`

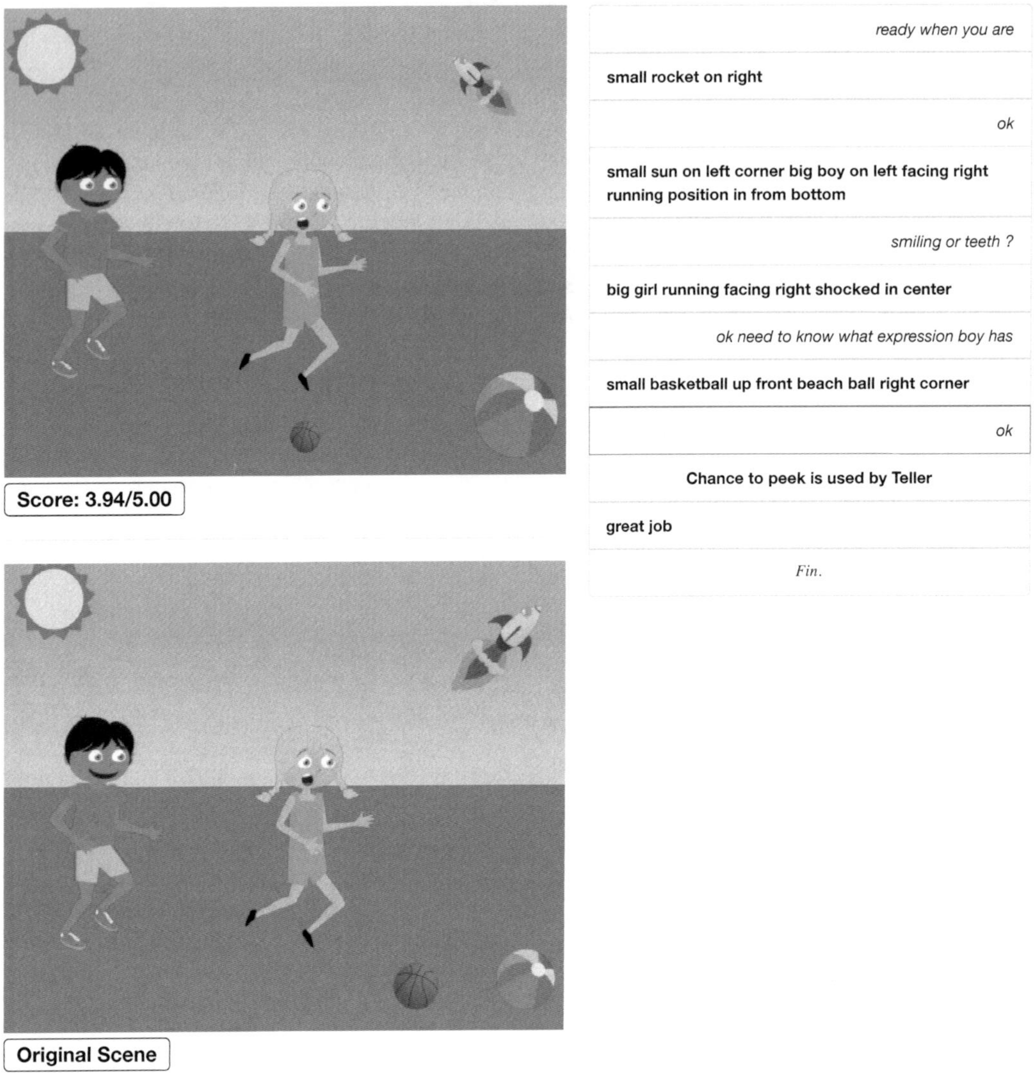

Figure 6: Even peeking, the instruction giver does not inform the instruction follower that the reconstruction is not totally correct: The orientation of the rocket is wrong, as well as the position of the basketball and the size of the two balls. From: CoDraw dialogue game 488, CC BY-NC 4.0, scene from Zitnick and Parikh (2013).

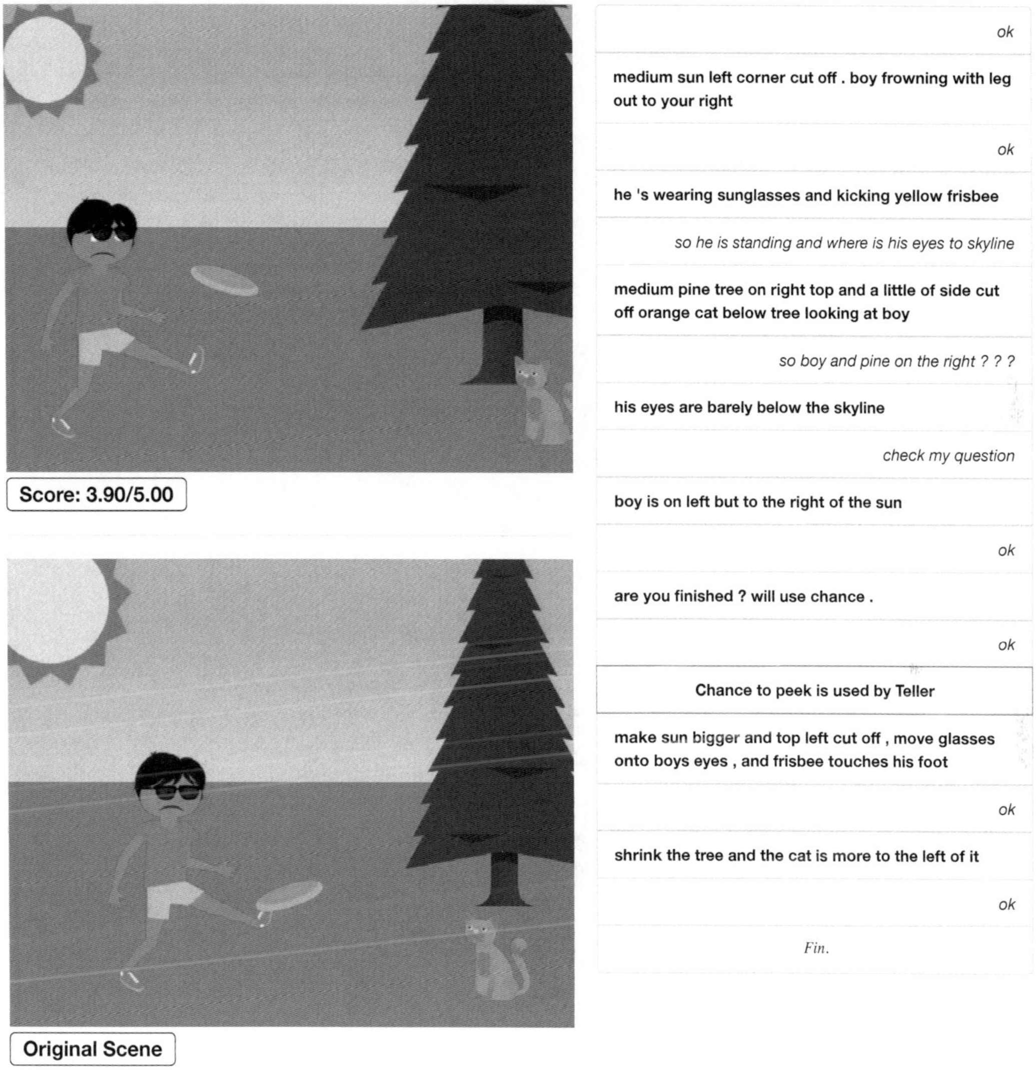

Figure 7: A more careful instruction giver uses two turns to try to repair even minor details after the peek, like the slightly wrong position of the sunglasses. From: CoDraw dialogue game 198, CC BY-NC 4.0, scene from Zitnick and Parikh (2013).

Figure 8: The instruction follower gets underspecified instructions at the first turn (for instance, nothing is said about the orientation of the boy and his position with respect to the bucket), but acts even so without asking for clarification. From: CoDraw dialogue game 3835, CC BY-NC 4.0, scene from Zitnick and Parikh (2013).

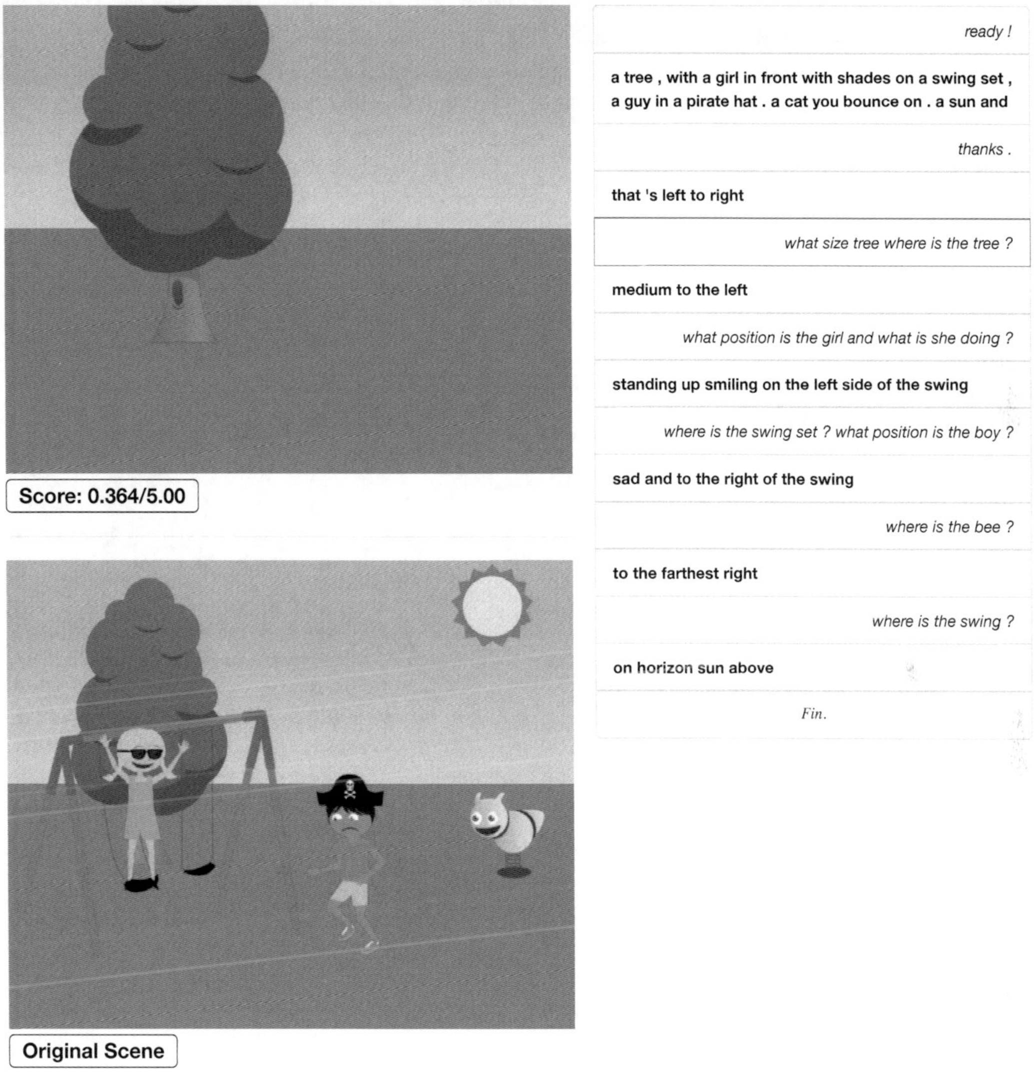

Figure 9: The instruction giver provides underspecified instructions at the first turn. Instead of taking all actions immediately, the instruction follower does many rounds of clarification. From: CoDraw dialogue game 4286, CC BY-NC 4.0, scene from Zitnick and Parikh (2013).

More Labels or Cases?
Assessing Label Variation in Natural Language Inference

Cornelia Gruber[*1♠] **Katharina Hechinger**[*1♠] **Matthias Aßenmacher**[1,2♠]
Göran Kauermann[1♠] **Barbara Plank**[2,3♣]
[1] Department of Statistics, LMU Munich, Germany
[2] Munich Center for Machine Learning (MCML), Munich, Germany
[3] Center for Information and Language Processing (CIS), LMU Munich, Germany
♠{cornelia.gruber, katharina.hechinger, matthias, goeran.kauermann}@stat.uni-muenchen.de
♣bplank@cis.uni-muenchen.de

Abstract

In this work, we analyze the uncertainty that is inherently present in the labels used for supervised machine learning in natural language inference (NLI). In cases where multiple annotations per instance are available, neither the majority vote nor the frequency of individual class votes is a trustworthy representation of the labeling uncertainty. We propose modeling the votes via a Bayesian mixture model to recover the data-generating process, i.e., the posterior distribution of the "true" latent classes, and thus gain insight into the class variations. This will enable a better understanding of the confusion happening during the annotation process. We also assess the stability of the proposed estimation procedure by systematically varying the numbers of i) instances and ii) labels. Thereby, we observe that few instances with many labels can predict the latent class borders reasonably well, while the estimation fails for many instances with only a few labels. This leads us to conclude that multiple labels are a crucial building block for properly analyzing label uncertainty.

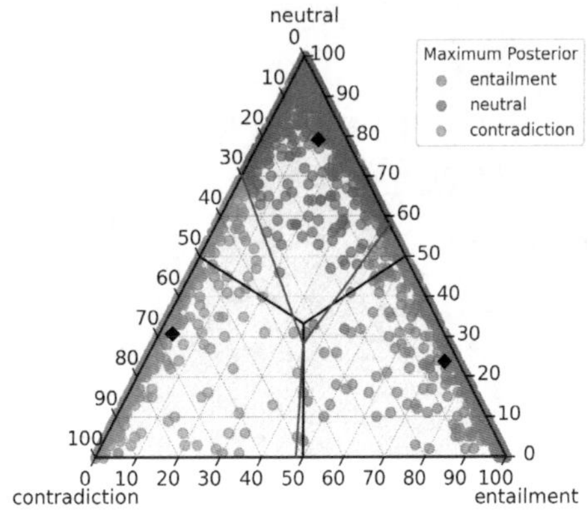

Figure 1: Scatter plot of the vote distribution of ChaosSNLI. Each point represents one instance. Its location is determined by the vote distribution. Corner points represent 100 votes for the respective class, i.e., *entailment*, *neutral*, *contradiction* for the bottom right, top, and bottom left, respectively. Solid black lines represent the border of class membership by majority vote. The color of the points is determined by the estimated latent class given by our model. Black diamonds describe the center points of the latent classes. Solid red lines represent the borders of latent class membership.

1 Introduction

Commonly, binary or multi-class classification settings in machine learning assume that a single gold label—representing the "true" class of an instance—can easily be acquired via human annotation. However, there are numerous examples where remarkable variations between different annotators exist, challenging the validity of this assumption (Uma et al., 2021). This issue is especially prevalent in datasets relating to the difficult task of perceiving human language, such as natural language inference (NLI). In NLI, the textual entailment of two sentences is to be determined. There exists an increasing body of work documenting inherent disagreement in labeling for NLI (Pavlick and Kwiatkowski, 2019; Nie et al., 2020; Zhang and de Marneffe, 2021; Jiang et al., 2023). Such human label variation can be caused by context dependency and subjectivity, amongst others, and is ubiquitous (Plank, 2022). Moreover, human label variation is different from annotation errors, as plausible, linguistic reasons for such variation exist (Jiang and de Marneffe, 2022).

To provide new grounds to study human variation in labeling, Nie et al. (2020) collected the ChaosNLI (Collective HumAn OpinionS on Natural Language Inference) dataset. ChaosNLI comprises 100 labels per instance from quality-controlled annotators for each of the ambiguous

Proceedings of the Third Workshop on Understanding Implicit and Underspecified Language, pages 22–32
March 21, 2024 ©2024 Association for Computational Linguistics

instances from multiple NLI-related datasets. In this paper, we analyze ChaosSNLI, a sub-dataset of ChaosNLI based on the Stanford Natural Language Inference (SNLI) data (Bowman et al., 2015). Several works on NLI (Pavlick and Kwiatkowski, 2019; Nie et al., 2020) show that many instances exhibit high human disagreement or uncertainty, i.e., human labelers do not agree on a single class, resulting in a high spread of the annotators' votes among multiple classes. Less work has looked at label variation and stability from a data-generating process viewpoint in light of uncertainty.

Uncertainty in machine learning and NLP is, however, gaining increased attention recently (Hüllermeier and Waegeman, 2021; Gruber et al., 2023; Baan et al., 2023). Different lines of research study sources of uncertainty in various parts of machine learning, such as the data itself, the model choice, the estimation procedure, and model deployment (Gruber et al., 2023). Early works characterize uncertainty in terms of reducible and irreducible randomness (Hüllermeier and Waegeman, 2021), while some works argue that this line is fuzzy (Gruber et al., 2023; Baan et al., 2023).

Variation in labels is part of the uncertainty in the data and is ubiquitous given the inherent ambiguity of language (Zhang et al., 2021). Yet, understanding the uncertainty in labels enables us to not only empirically investigate human confusion in annotated data, but also to gain insights on the classification task itself. For example, the complexity of detecting certain classes or the composition of class structures can be derived from voting patterns—this information can provide useful insights into task characteristics.

Therefore, in order to analyze the uncertainty in the label vote distribution of ChaosSNLI, we model the data-generating process and analyze the stability of the resulting estimation. To do so, we employ a Bayesian mixture model and recover the latent "true" class label, see also Hechinger et al. (2024). More precisely, we obtain the posterior probability for each of the classes and can thus assess the certainty for the class labels given the votes.

Our results could further be incorporated into a machine learning pipeline, e.g., by fitting a model on our latent classes instead of majority vote classes or class frequencies. This is, however, beyond the scope of this paper. In this work, we focus on the fundamental step of quantifying labeling uncertainty instead. We propose an estimation procedure and analyze its *stability* for different amounts of i) instances and ii) labels. Our work shows that more labels are more beneficial for stable estimation of uncertainty, while only a few instances already suffice. We also suggest new tools for *visual assessment* of the uncertainty in labels for three-way classification tasks (see Fig. 1).

Contributions With this paper, we contribute to a better understanding of label variation via a deep assessment of trustworthiness by 1) quantifying labeling uncertainty with Bayesian mixture models, 2) providing a novel visual tool for a better assessment of labeling uncertainty, and 3) deriving practical guidance for labeling tasks. We identify the benefit of using fewer cases with many labels rather than the other way around.[1]

2 Related Work

The need to analyze diverse human opinions in natural language inference is discussed by works including Pavlick and Kwiatkowski (2019) and Nie et al. (2020). Nie et al. (2020) show that some state-of-the-art models (including BERT, RoBERTa, XLNET, AL- BERT, DistilBERT, and BART) are neither designed nor able to capture human variation in labels and are therefore not appropriate. Their work also states that predicting the majority vote and predicting the human label distribution are distinct and seemingly conflicting objectives. In their benchmark study, all considered models performed consistently worse on examples with low human agreement. This indicates that analyzing label variation is of significant relevance for a more complete understanding of natural language inference.

Hovy et al. (2013) already advocated that majority voting might be the simplest but not most appropriate strategy for finding the correct label and, that modeling the votes leads to improved predicted label accuracy. The authors propose a method to separately model annotations from spamming and non-spamming annotators. Our methods differ in the way variation in labels is modeled. Hovy et al. (2013) explicitly model the behavior of annotators and assumes non-spamming annotators always provide the correct label, while votes by spamming annotators are drawn from a multinomial distribution. In contrast, our approach models human confusion in the annotation process, assuming equal levels of annotation skills. This is a reasonable assumption

[1]Code and data available at: https://github.com/corneliagru/label-variation-nli

for ChaosSNLI as all annotators undergo strict quality control, see Nie et al. (2020) for details. Nevertheless, both methods share the goal of estimating the distribution of the data-generating process and its parameters via an expectation-maximization (EM) algorithm.

Paun et al. (2018) compare various Bayesian approaches for modeling annotation. Based on their taxonomy, we employ a pooled model, i.e., assuming equal quality of the annotators. They conclude that such pooled models underperform, as the assumption that all annotators share the same ability is inappropriate in typical crowdsourcing settings. However, when information on individual annotators is unavailable, as is the case for the investigated ChaosSNLI dataset, pooling is inevitable.

The benefits of harnessing multiple labels are presented in Zhang et al. (2021). They demonstrate that improvements in accuracy can be achieved by varying the number of annotations for some examples within a given annotation budget. Our findings show a more nuanced picture supporting their claims, as we show the necessity of multiple annotations but a flattening value curve (see section 5).

3 Dataset and Problem Setting

We examine label uncertainty in NLI, a task for which textual entailment of two sentences is typically classified as either *entailment*, *neutral*, or *contradiction*. In ChaosSNLI (Nie et al., 2020), *multiple* annotations for *each* instance are provided. Example sentences of ChaosSNLI with their respective votes are shown in Table 1. Since those annotators do not necessarily agree with each other, we face a high degree of (human) label uncertainty. We chose this dataset as it provides a unique ground to explore label variation. Having access to a high amount of labels per instance is particularly valuable, but unfortunately not a common setting.

Our analysis is based on $N = 1,514$ instances with $J = 100$ labels, each, that originate from the development set of the SNLI dataset (Bowman et al., 2015). The original SNLI development set was generated by a multistep procedure, where first an initial annotator provides a text description of an image, i.e., generating the *premise*. Second, a different annotator constructs three *hypotheses* as an entailing, neutral, and contradicting description of the premise. Third, four more annotators, independent of the first two steps, provide labels for the premise-hypothesis pairs, i.e., classify the pairs into *entailment, neutral* or *contradiction*. This procedure yields five annotations per instance in total. In ChaosSNLI, examples, where only three out of those five annotators agree, are then relabeled by 100 quality-controlled annotators. For details on the quality control procedure, we refer to Nie et al. (2020). This relabeling procedure leads to a dataset, where instances with a high degree of uncertainty are overrepresented. Such a biased sample is valuable, as our main interest lies in understanding exactly those uncertain and hard-to-classify cases.

In the dataset, we observe that the most common class according to majority voting is *neutral*, with 53.7% of all examples, while *entailment* and *contradiction* amount to 27.8% and 18.5%, respectively. This already suggests that identifying *neutral* seems to be more challenging than discerning the other classes, as human annotators do not agree on those especially challenging examples that were collected for ChaosSNLI.

To gain a better understanding of label uncertainty in NLI, we analyze the annotations for the premise-hypothesis pairs available in ChaosSNLI. In order to detect hidden structures and comprehend label variation, we follow a statistical approach for modeling the label distribution. It is thus distinct from classical machine learning, where models are optimized for predictive power. However, our approach can ultimately be incorporated as a preprocessing step for predictive models. A precise description of our methodology can be found in section 4.

4 Modeling Approach

The main goal of this work is to explore the uncertainty inherent in the (multiple) labels of the sentence pairs in ChaosSNLI which is expressed by the distribution of the annotations. In order to formally describe the dataset with its multiple annotations and to assess label uncertainty, we use tools from statistical modeling. The multinomial mixture model provides the possibility to put multiple annotations into a distributional framework and subsequently estimate the associated parameters. Based on these parameters, a latent ground truth label can be derived for each instance, incorporating the uncertainty expressed by the distributions of the annotations over all instances. We follow the methodology proposed in Hechinger et al. (2024) for modeling multiple annotations via a Bayesian

Context/Premise	Statement/Hypothesis	[E, N, C]
A boy in an orange shirt sells fruit from a street cart.	A boy is a street vendor.	[90, 10, 0]
A woman wearing a red hat and black coat.	The woman is asleep.	[0, 87, 13]
People walk amongst a traffic jam in a crowded city.	The cars are zooming past the people.	[3, 15, 82]
A woman holding a child in a purple shirt.	The woman is asleep at home.	[1, 53, 46]

Table 1: Examples of ChaosSNLI. Annotators answered the question: "Given a context, a statement can be either: definitely correct (Entailment); or definitely incorrect (Contradiction); or neither (Neutral). Your goal is to choose the correct category for a given pair of context and statement."

mixture model.

First, let us introduce a formal description of the data. Each instance is a pair of $(X^{(i)}, \boldsymbol{Y}^{(i)}), i = 1, \ldots, N$, where $X^{(i)}$ denotes the sentence pair of premise and hypothesis and $\boldsymbol{Y}^{(i)}$ denotes the corresponding vote distribution. For this work, our focus lies on the latter exclusively, i.e., we only consider the vector of annotations for each instance. To explicitly represent votes for K possible classes by J different annotators, $\boldsymbol{Y}^{(i)}$ is set to $\boldsymbol{Y}^{(i)} = (Y_1^{(i)}, \ldots, Y_K^{(i)})$ with $Y_k^{(i)} = \sum_{j=1}^{J} \mathbb{1}(V_j^{(i)} = k)$. Here, $V_j^{(i)}$ denotes the individual vote for instance i by annotator j. In ChaosSNLI we do not have access to individual annotator-specific votes, but observe $\boldsymbol{Y}^{(i)}$ directly. As mentioned above, we model the uncertainty inherent in the labels, so we omit $X^{(i)}$ and only analyze $\boldsymbol{Y}^{(i)}$. It is worth mentioning that incorporating the actual text is still possible for downstream tasks, but is out of the scope of this work.

In order to make use of the multinomial mixture model, we assume that each instance is associated with one true label, i.e., there exists an unambiguous ground truth. However, due to the inherent uncertainty in the perception of language, annotators are not easily capable of recovering the ground truth and they might vote for different classes. We denote the latent ground truth of each instance $X^{(i)}$ with $Z^{(i)} \in \{1, \ldots, K\}$. Again, to match our notation with the definition of a multivariate variable, we define $\boldsymbol{Z}^{(i)}$ as a one-hot encoded vector indicating the latent class, i.e., $\boldsymbol{Z}^{(i)} = (\mathbb{1}\{Z^{(i)} = 1\}, \ldots, \mathbb{1}\{Z^{(i)} = K\})$.

In the context of this particular dataset, as described in section 3, there exists a clearly defined ground truth that annotators should recover. This is due to the fact, that the annotator had one specific class in mind while inventing the hypothesis. Thus, the assumption of exactly one underlying "true" label is justified. However, this methodology can be applied beyond scenarios with known ground truth. In cases where no such information is available, the distributions of votes can serve as a valuable tool for deducing the latent labels.

Model Framework Let us now proceed to the analysis of the voting distribution $\boldsymbol{Y}^{(i)}$, which carries information about the latent true labels. We employ the following Bayesian modeling framework. First, considering the ground truth labels to be unobserved (or unobservable), they are assumed to follow a multinomial distribution

$$\boldsymbol{Z}^{(i)} \sim Multi(\boldsymbol{\pi}, 1) \text{ i.i.d.},$$

where $\boldsymbol{\pi} = (\pi_1, \ldots, \pi_K)$ denote the prior probabilities for all classes. This distribution is also called the *prior* distribution. Given the true classes, the annotations are also assumed to be distributed multinomially, i.e.,

$$\boldsymbol{Y}^{(i)} | Z^{(i)} \sim Multi(\boldsymbol{\theta}_p, J). \quad (1)$$

This multinomial distribution describes the data *likelihood* conditional on Z. Here, the parameter vector $\boldsymbol{\theta}_p$ depends on the latent true class $Z^{(i)}$, i.e., the multinomial probabilities vary based on what we consider to be the true label. Hence, this parameter describes the probability of voting for a class given the true label. We can summarize the multinomial probability vectors of each latent, true class into a matrix $\boldsymbol{\Theta} = (\theta_{pk}, p, k = 1, \ldots, K)$, which can be interpreted as a confusion matrix. Formally, θ_{pk} describes the probability of an annotator voting for class k given the instance has the true class p, i.e., using the notation in Eq. (1) we have $\boldsymbol{\theta}_p = (\theta_{p1}, \theta_{p2}, \ldots, \theta_{pK})$.

The key component of the model is the *posterior* distribution, i.e., the probabilities for an instance to truly belong to each of the classes given the observed annotations. These probabilities are calculated as

$$\begin{aligned}\tau_p^{(i)} &= P(Z^{(i)} = p|\boldsymbol{Y}^{(i)}; \boldsymbol{\pi}, \boldsymbol{\Theta}) \\ &= \frac{P(Z^{(i)} = p; \boldsymbol{\pi})P(\boldsymbol{Y}^{(i)}|Z^{(i)} = p; \boldsymbol{\Theta})}{P(\boldsymbol{Y}^{(i)}; \boldsymbol{\pi}, \boldsymbol{\Theta})} \\ &= \frac{\pi_p P(\boldsymbol{Y}^{(i)}; \boldsymbol{\theta}_p)}{\sum_{p'=1}^{K} \pi_{p'} P(\boldsymbol{Y}^{(i)}; \boldsymbol{\theta}_{p'})}.\end{aligned}$$

The class with the maximal posterior serves as an estimate for the latent ground truth, it is however also possible to use $\boldsymbol{\tau}$ in downstream tasks directly, i.e., for training a classifier on the probabilities instead of discrete class labels and thus directly incorporate the label uncertainty.

It is important to note that the prior modeling assumption of a single ground truth does not dictate the reality to be discrete, much more it enables us to compute the posterior distribution and quantify the evidence for each class, given the vote distribution. It thus allows us to model settings with ambiguous labels.

Estimation Procedure The model above includes unknown parameters, which we suggest estimating through maximum likelihood. As we are in the latent variable framework, straightforward estimation of the model parameters via maximum likelihood is, however, not possible. Instead, we apply an iterative estimation procedure to obtain parameter estimates. With the help of the expectation-maximization (EM) algorithm as introduced by Dempster et al. (1977), we can replace the latent class label $\boldsymbol{Z}^{(i)}$ with its expectation for each voting distribution. The expected latent class is thereby calculated given the data and the current parameter estimates and can be used afterward to update the estimates, leading to an iterative procedure that is performed until convergence. The algorithm can be outlined as follows, with additional details available in Hechinger et al. (2024) and in Appendix A. For the current parameter values at estimation iteration (t), $\boldsymbol{\Theta} = \boldsymbol{\Theta}_{(t)}$ and $\boldsymbol{\pi} = \boldsymbol{\pi}_{(t)}$, one iterates over the two steps:

1. **E-Step:** Calculate the expectation of the full data likelihood given the data and the current estimates. Applying Bayes' rule, this simplifies to the computation of the expected latent class, given by posterior probabilities $\tau_p^{(i)}$, $i = 1, ..., N$ and $p = 1, ..., K$.

2. **M-Step:** Update the parameters $\boldsymbol{\Theta} = \boldsymbol{\Theta}_{(t+1)}$ and $\boldsymbol{\pi} = \boldsymbol{\pi}_{(t+1)}$ based on the posterior $\boldsymbol{\tau}$.

The final estimates are denoted as $\hat{\boldsymbol{\Theta}}$ and $\hat{\boldsymbol{\pi}}$. Our modeling approach harnesses the information retrieved from the annotations from all instances, as in every EM-step all instances are used for recalculating the estimates. This enables our method to incorporate knowledge about all annotation uncertainties and provide a comprehensive and holistic view of label variation.

Label Switching The classes obtained through mixture models are subject to label switching, i.e., their numbering is arbitrary and does not correspond to the original order anymore. This is a common issue in mixture models and can be resolved in various ways depending on the specific application at hand, as outlined by Stephens (2000). In this case, we apply a simple heuristic permutation to the latent classes. The original classes *entailment, contradiction, neutral*, denoted with index $k = 1, 2, 3$, are assigned to the respective latent classes $p = 1, 2, 3$ based on the diagonal entries of the estimated confusion matrix $\boldsymbol{\Theta}$. E.g., the class *entailment* is assigned to the mixture component, where the highest voting probability is *entailment*. This corresponds to the permutation $\sigma^{-1}(p) = \arg\max_k(\hat{\boldsymbol{\theta}}_p)$ and the latent classes are re-ordered accordingly.

To summarize, by allowing for human uncertainty, i.e., human confusion while labeling a certain instance, we can recover information on a latent class Z. The posterior distribution of the latent class is then a more trustworthy representation of the "true" class an instance belongs to, since all information contained in the full dataset is used for estimation, and not only the specific label distribution.

5 Results

5.1 Introspection by Visualization

As described earlier, the dataset ChaosSNLI (Nie et al., 2020) consists of $J = 100$ annotations for $K = 3$ classes. We propose to analyze human label variation in NLI with a novel visualization tool, to help gain insights into labeling. Figure 1 illustrates the distribution of votes present in ChaosSNLI, which we then contrast to the majority vote and our model's estimated class membership votes.

Each point in Figure 1 represents one instance, where its location is determined by the empirical distribution of votes. It is clearly visible by the density of dots that most instances cluster around the top of the plot, i.e., with many votes for *neutral*.

This is consistent with the distribution of majority votes (with *neutral* being observed 53.7% of times, as discussed in section 3). Furthermore, we observe that there is little confusion between *contradiction* and *entailment*, as almost no points lie close to the lower horizontal line or the vertical line starting in the center. This observation is intuitively plausible, due to the contrasting nature of the two labels of *entailment* vs. *contradiction*. Interestingly, this visualization tool helps us to quickly identify that there are cases in the datasets where many labels for both *entailment* and *contradiction* were observed.

In order to analyze our modeling result in relation to majority voting, we examine the borders between the three classes. Figure 1 shows the borders of the majority voting as solid black lines, which connect the center points of the axes, i.e., 50:50 votes for two of the classes, to the center, i.e., 33.33 votes for all three classes.

The borders between the latent classes are shown as red lines. To calculate these borders between two latent classes, we determine the vote combinations that lead to equal posterior probabilities. That is, we calculate the specific vote distribution $\boldsymbol{Y}^{(i)}$ such that $\tau_k = \tau_j$ for two classes $k, j \in \{1, 2, 3\}, k \neq j$, while there are no votes for the third class. This gives us the critical points lying on the axis connecting classes k and j. For the middle point, i.e., the connection between all three classes, the equation $\tau_1 = \tau_2 = \tau_3$ is solved for the corresponding vote distribution. This results in four critical points. By connecting the points on the axes to the center, we obtain the new borders of the latent classes, which are now based on posterior probability estimates and not just on the empirical distribution of the votes for one instance. In other words, they are estimated by taking all data into account. The exact border points are described in Appendix A.

In Figure 1, for all instances that lie between the black and red borders, the latent class label does not agree with the majority vote. It is especially evident that the latent class *neutral* comprises a smaller fraction of vote distributions than it would have by majority voting (black line). More precisely, considering all cases with a majority vote for *neutral*, our model agrees for 83.3%, however, *entailment* is estimated for 6.9% of cases and *contradiction* for the remaining 9.8%, i.e., 16.7% of the majority vote *neutral* are assigned a different label by our model. This is however desirable, as many votes for one of the more informative classes (*entailment* or *contradiction*) strongly speak for exactly those classes, even if there is no majority. For example, having 40 votes for *contradiction*, 60 for *neutral*, and none for *entailment*, indicates that *entailment* is unlikely. Likewise, if *neutral* would be the "true" latent class, at least some votes for entailment are expected. Thus, in this setting, a latent *contradiction* is most probable. Analogous reasoning can be applied for instances with many votes for *entailment*, without *entailment* as the majority. Further, we argue that negative votes by the annotators can be regarded as a stronger signal for the instance actually being *contradiction* as fewer of them are required for our model to assign the label *contradiction*, compared to *entailment*. This becomes evident from Figure 1 as the red border between *neutral* and *contradiction* is much closer to the *neutral* corner compared to its counterpart between *neutral* and *entailment*.

To summarize, the model especially refines the class *neutral* and alleviates the issue that the majority class *neutral* does not only contain true neutral statements, but might also be conflated with examples where the annotators were indecisive or had conflicting interpretations (Nighojkar et al., 2023).

5.2 Stability Analysis

Having provided a visualization tool that allows valuable insights into the dataset, we are now interested in the *stability* of the modeling procedure. One common approach to assess the estimation uncertainty and stability of the resulting parameter estimates is to employ a resampling method, like bootstrapping (Efron, 1979). We therefore analyze the stability of the estimation procedure in relation to three aspects:

1. overall stability,
2. stability in the number of instances, N,
3. stability in the number of labels, J.

Overall stability In order to assess the uncertainty of the estimation procedure itself, we employ a classical bootstrap. That is, we sample from the data with replacement[2] and subsequently estimate the model parameters. Repeating this multiple times allows us to assess how the estimation would change if we had different datasets coming from the same distribution as the initial one.

[2] i.e., the same instance can be present multiple times, while other instances might not be included at all.

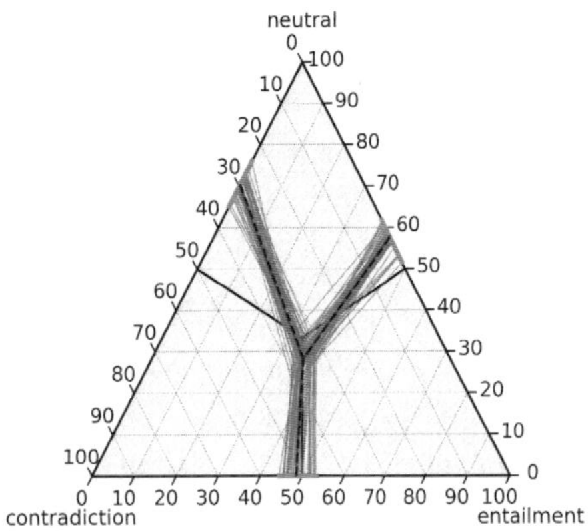

Figure 2: The ternary plot contains the decision borders between the three classes calculated based on $B = 50$ bootstrapped estimates as gray lines. The range of the gray lines is outlined in orange. The blue dashed line indicates the mean of the bootstrapped versions and the red line shows the original borders for comparison.

We run B bootstrap iterations, producing bootstrapped versions of the parameter estimates $\boldsymbol{\pi}$ and $\boldsymbol{\Theta}$. Based on these values, the borders of the latent classes can be recalculated B times. Figure 2 shows the estimated borders for $B = 50$ bootstrap replicates in gray alongside the borders computed based on the full dataset in red (cf. Fig. 1). This leads us to conclude that the estimation of the parameters and, therefore, the latent classes is stable for the full dataset. Due to the high number of instances in the dataset, this result is not surprising. However, the question arises whether stable estimation is also possible with a smaller dataset. Reducing N, the number of multiple annotated instances on the one hand, and reducing J, the number of annotations for the instances on the other hand, could lead to substantially reduced labeling effort. Hence, these aspects will be analyzed in the following.

Stability of Number of Instances In many real-world applications, the number of instances that can be annotated multiple times is often limited to a couple of hundred instances (as an example, the earlier multi-annotated NLI dataset from Pavlick and Kwiatkowski (2019) contained five annotations for less than 500 instances as available in ChaosNLI). Therefore, it is worthwhile to examine the stability of the estimation procedure and the resulting estimates for a smaller dataset in terms of sample size (less than 1.5k instances). Specifically, we are interested in the location of the decision borders regarding the latent classes and their stability for fewer instances.

Therefore, we employ a bootstrap again but this time randomly sample smaller datasets, i.e., $N < 1,514$ with replacement to artificially reduce the sample size. Figure 3 shows $B = 50$ bootstrapped borders of the latent classes for various numbers of samples N with fixed $J = 100$. While the bootstrapped borders still show quite some variation for very small sample sizes (e.g., $N = 50$), the average of all bootstrapped borders already aligns quite well with the original borders. For a sample size of $N = 100$, the variation has already decreased noticeably, and for even larger samples, like $N = 500$, which is only one-third of the original sample size, almost no differences to the original results are visible. Hence, we conclude that reducing the sample size leads to reasonably good and stable estimation results if a certain minimum of instances is kept.

Stability of Number of Labels While this work focuses on the ChaosSNLI dataset with $J = 100$ annotations, the original SNLI development dataset only contains five labels per instance. In practice, annotating instances many times is costly and might seem inefficient. Hence, we are also interested in the stability of the estimation procedure in terms of the number of labels as well as the *minimal* number of labels needed per instance for stable parameter estimates.

Again, we draw bootstrap samples from the original dataset. This time, the sample size is kept constant at $N = 1000$ but the number of annotations per sample is reduced. Therefore, we randomly choose $J < 100$ annotations from the original ones. The resulting bootstrapped borders are shown in Figure 3. As expected, only using $J = 5$ annotations leads to large variations and unstable results. For $J = 25$ annotations, the procedure is already quite stable. For more than $J = 50$ annotations, the results show diminishing returns: they depict similar behavior to the original ones with the double amount of J, i.e., $J = 100$ (see Fig. 2). Therefore, we note that acquiring a smaller number of labels for each instance is possible, but a sufficient amount of annotations is needed for stable estimation. Particularly, the number of annotations seems to be more crucial for the stability of the results than the sample size. Additional results for simultaneously varying the amount of N and J that further support this finding can be found in Figure 4, Appendix A.

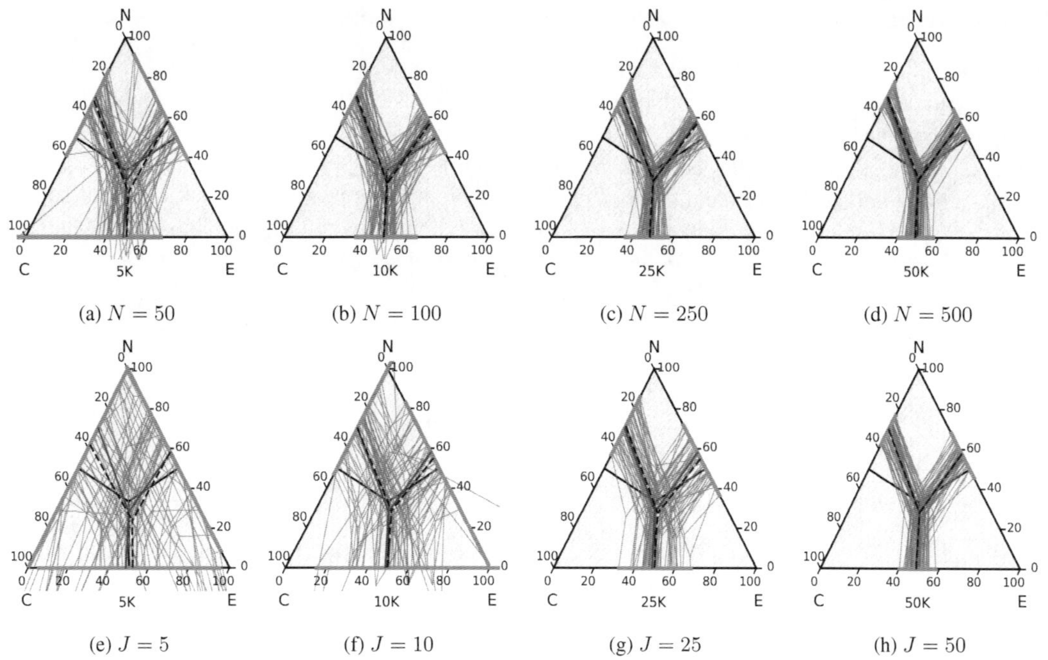

(a) $N = 50$ (b) $N = 100$ (c) $N = 250$ (d) $N = 500$

(e) $J = 5$ (f) $J = 10$ (g) $J = 25$ (h) $J = 50$

Figure 3: The ternary plots show the bootstrapped latent class borders as gray lines, the range of the gray lines in orange, the mean of the bootstrapped as blue dashed lines, and for comparison, the original borders as red lines for various sample sizes and annotations. In the top row J is set to $J = 100$ and $N \in \{50, 100, 250, 500\}$. In the bottom row, we set $N = 1000$ and $J \in \{5, 10, 25, 50\}$. The total number of annotations, i.e., $N \cdot J$, is below each plot.

6 Discussion

Reliable and correct labels are crucial for classification models. While it is common practice to gather multiple annotations to ensure high-quality labels, these are often summarized into one single final label via a majority vote (Paun et al., 2018). However, this strategy leads to a major loss of information and uncertain ground truth labels in applications where a high degree of label variation is present. The statistical approach pursued in this work offers the possibility to condense information, given in multiple labels through the whole dataset, into a single ground truth label. To evaluate the results, we compared the borders between the classes, i.e., we examined the voting combinations where the ground truth label changes for an instance. By choosing the estimated latent ground truth instead of the majority vote, these borders shifted reasonably, from a semantic perspective.

Additionally, we showed that the parameters of the model and, hence, the borders can be estimated reliably based on the available instances and annotations. However, in many realistic applications, the data basis might be smaller in terms of both aspects. Hence, we also conducted a stability analysis for random subsets of the number of instances (N) and the number of votes per instance (J) of the dataset. The results show that stable estimation is already possible for a smaller dataset and that human labeling effort can be decreased, without loss of information. The quantity of accessible labels proves to be more important for ensuring a stable model performance than the sample size. We assume that this is because the annotations bear the majority of the inherent uncertainty. Therefore, acquiring multiple labels, particularly for uncertain instances, i.e., instances where label variation is expected, is advisable.

While the results and decision borders obtained via the proposed model in this work showcase the problem of label uncertainty, future directions of research could include the incorporation of this information into the ML pipeline or the development of a quantitative measure for label uncertainty. This could then lead to a detailed strategy for acquiring labels efficiently. Though these questions are highly relevant and should be tackled in the future, they are beyond the scope of the current work.

7 Conclusion

In conclusion, by analyzing ChaosSNLI we showcase the suitability of Bayesian mixture models to recover the true data-generating process of annotation tasks with access to multiple labels. Our work provides a framework to deal with multi-annotation settings in classification and is applicable regardless of the underlying task, i.e., NLI. Furthermore, our results suggest that in the annotation process, the focus should lie on increasing the number of labels per instance, instead of more instances in total, as this promotes capturing the labeling uncertainty.

Limitations

Our proposed method analyzes uncertainty in labels for a three-way classification task. However, since the concept of *uncertainty* is by definition vague and fuzzy, it is important to determine which aspects of uncertainty *should be* or *can be* specified. In our work, we focus on modeling the annotation process. If other aspects of uncertainty are of relevance, our method might not be the most appropriate anymore. This points to the individuality of dealing with uncertainty and that no one-fits-all approach exists.

Further limitations might arise upon the application of the model to other datasets. 1) Multiple annotations per instance are needed. 2) Visual assessment of class memberships (c.f. Fig 1) or the stability of class borders (c.f. Fig 3) works reasonably well for up to three classes. Analyzing datasets with labels of higher dimensions is straightforward, as shown by Hechinger et al. (2024) for the classification of ambiguous images. However, assessing the stability of class borders needs to be done quantitatively, e.g., by computing confidence intervals of the bootstrapped borders. 3) In case annotator IDs are available, we recommend extending our approach in order to incorporate all available information. This could be done by determining the impact of individual annotators or a general annotator effect on the results, e.g., by discarding votes by certain annotators and re-estimating the model, see Hechinger et al. (2024).

Our work contributes to the understanding of NLI tasks and provides guidance for the early stage of data collection. Therefore, analyzing the impact on the full machine learning pipeline, i.e., improvements on the predictive power of classifiers is beyond the scope of this paper, but is open for future work.

Acknowledgements

CG is supported by the DAAD program Konrad Zuse Schools of Excellence in Artificial Intelligence, sponsored by the Federal Ministry of Education and Research. KH is supported by the Helmholtz Association under the joint research school HIDSS-006 - Munich School for Data Science@Helmholtz, TUM&LMU. MA has been partially funded by the Deutsche Forschungsgemeinschaft (DFG, German Research Foundation) as part of BERD@NFDI - grant number 460037581. BP is supported by European Research Council (ERC) grant agreement No. 101043235.

References

Joris Baan, Nico Daheim, Evgenia Ilia, Dennis Ulmer, Haau-Sing Li, Raquel Fernández, Barbara Plank, Rico Sennrich, Chrysoula Zerva, and Wilker Aziz. 2023. Uncertainty in natural language generation: From theory to applications.

Samuel R. Bowman, Gabor Angeli, Christopher Potts, and Christopher D. Manning. 2015. A large annotated corpus for learning natural language inference. In *Proceedings of the 2015 Conference on Empirical Methods in Natural Language Processing*, pages 632–642, Lisbon, Portugal. Association for Computational Linguistics.

Arthur P Dempster, Nan M Laird, and Donald B Rubin. 1977. Maximum likelihood from incomplete data via the em algorithm. *Journal of the royal statistical society: series B (methodological)*, 39(1):1–22.

B. Efron. 1979. Bootstrap methods: Another look at the jackknife. *The Annals of Statistics*, 7(1):1 – 26.

Cornelia Gruber, Patrick Oliver Schenk, Malte Schierholz, Frauke Kreuter, and Göran Kauermann. 2023. Sources of Uncertainty in Machine Learning – A Statisticians' View. ArXiv:2305.16703 [cs, stat].

Katharina Hechinger, Xiao Xiang Zhu, and Göran Kauermann. 2024. Categorising the world into local climate zones: towards quantifying labelling uncertainty for machine learning models. *Journal of the Royal Statistical Society Series C: Applied Statistics*, 73:143–161.

Dirk Hovy, Taylor Berg-Kirkpatrick, Ashish Vaswani, and Eduard Hovy. 2013. Learning Whom to Trust with MACE. In *Proceedings of the 2013 Conference of the North American Chapter of the Association for Computational Linguistics: Human Language Technologies*, pages 1120–1130, Atlanta, Georgia. Association for Computational Linguistics.

Eyke Hüllermeier and Willem Waegeman. 2021. Aleatoric and epistemic uncertainty in machine learning: an introduction to concepts and methods. *Machine Learning*, 110(3):457–506.

Nan-Jiang Jiang and Marie-Catherine de Marneffe. 2022. Investigating reasons for disagreement in natural language inference. *Transactions of the Association for Computational Linguistics*, 10:1357–1374.

Nan-Jiang Jiang, Chenhao Tan, and Marie-Catherine de Marneffe. 2023. Ecologically valid explanations for label variation in NLI. In *Findings of the Association for Computational Linguistics: EMNLP 2023*, pages 10622–10633, Singapore. Association for Computational Linguistics.

Yixin Nie, Xiang Zhou, and Mohit Bansal. 2020. What Can We Learn from Collective Human Opinions on Natural Language Inference Data? ArXiv:2010.03532 [cs].

Animesh Nighojkar, Antonio Laverghetta Jr., and John Licato. 2023. No strong feelings one way or another: Re-operationalizing neutrality in natural language inference. In *Proceedings of the 17th Linguistic Annotation Workshop (LAW-XVII)*, pages 199–210, Toronto, Canada. Association for Computational Linguistics.

Silviu Paun, Bob Carpenter, Jon Chamberlain, Dirk Hovy, Udo Kruschwitz, and Massimo Poesio. 2018. Comparing Bayesian Models of Annotation. *Transactions of the Association for Computational Linguistics*, 6:571–585.

Ellie Pavlick and Tom Kwiatkowski. 2019. Inherent Disagreements in Human Textual Inferences. *Transactions of the Association for Computational Linguistics*, 7:677–694. Place: Cambridge, MA Publisher: MIT Press.

Barbara Plank. 2022. The 'Problem' of Human Label Variation: On Ground Truth in Data, Modeling and Evaluation. ArXiv:2211.02570 [cs].

Matthew Stephens. 2000. Dealing with label switching in mixture models. *Journal of the Royal Statistical Society: Series B (Statistical Methodology)*, 62(4):795–809.

Alexandra N. Uma, Tommaso Fornaciari, Dirk Hovy, Silviu Paun, Barbara Plank, and Massimo Poesio. 2021. Learning from Disagreement: A Survey. *Journal of Artificial Intelligence Research*, 72:1385–1470.

Shujian Zhang, Chengyue Gong, and Eunsol Choi. 2021. Learning with Different Amounts of Annotation: From Zero to Many Labels. ArXiv:2109.04408 [cs].

Xinliang Frederick Zhang and Marie-Catherine de Marneffe. 2021. Identifying inherent disagreement in natural language inference. In *Proceedings of the 2021 Conference of the North American Chapter of the Association for Computational Linguistics: Human Language Technologies*, pages 4908–4915, Online. Association for Computational Linguistics.

A Appendix

Details on Model and Estimation

The EM algorithm is initialized with $\boldsymbol{\pi}_{(0)} = (\frac{1}{3}, \frac{1}{3}, \frac{1}{3})$, and $\boldsymbol{\Theta}_{(0)}$ is drawn from a Dirichlet distribution where $\boldsymbol{\alpha}$ is set to be a vector with K entries, where each value is $2 \cdot K$. In this case $\boldsymbol{\alpha} = (6, 6, 6)$.

The model estimated on the full dataset (i.e., $N = 1514, J = 100$), which is also depicted in Figure 1, results the following final parameter estimates:

$$\hat{\boldsymbol{\pi}} = (0.314, 0.448, 0.238)$$

$$\hat{\boldsymbol{\Theta}} = \begin{pmatrix} \hat{\boldsymbol{\theta}}_{entailment} \\ \hat{\boldsymbol{\theta}}_{neutral} \\ \hat{\boldsymbol{\theta}}_{contradiction} \end{pmatrix} = \begin{pmatrix} 0.73 & 0.24 & 0.03 \\ 0.14 & 0.79 & 0.07 \\ 0.03 & 0.31 & 0.66 \end{pmatrix}$$

In both parameters, the order of entries/columns is *entailment, neutral, contradiction*.

Based on the estimated parameters obtained via the procedure described in section 4 the decision borders are defined by connecting the points ([E, N, C]):

- center point: $[35.98, 28.15, 35.86]$
- EC axis: $[48.46, 0.0, 51.54]$
- EN axis: $[42.03, 57.97, 0.0]$
- NC axis: $[0.0, 70.13, 29.87]$

Combined Stability Analysis

Figure 4 shows the estimation results and their bootstrapped stability for various sample sizes and numbers of annotations. Reducing N and J simultaneously leads to unstable results for very small datasets. However, this visualization supports the earlier finding that a sufficient number of annotations is more crucial than a large sample for stable and reliable estimation.

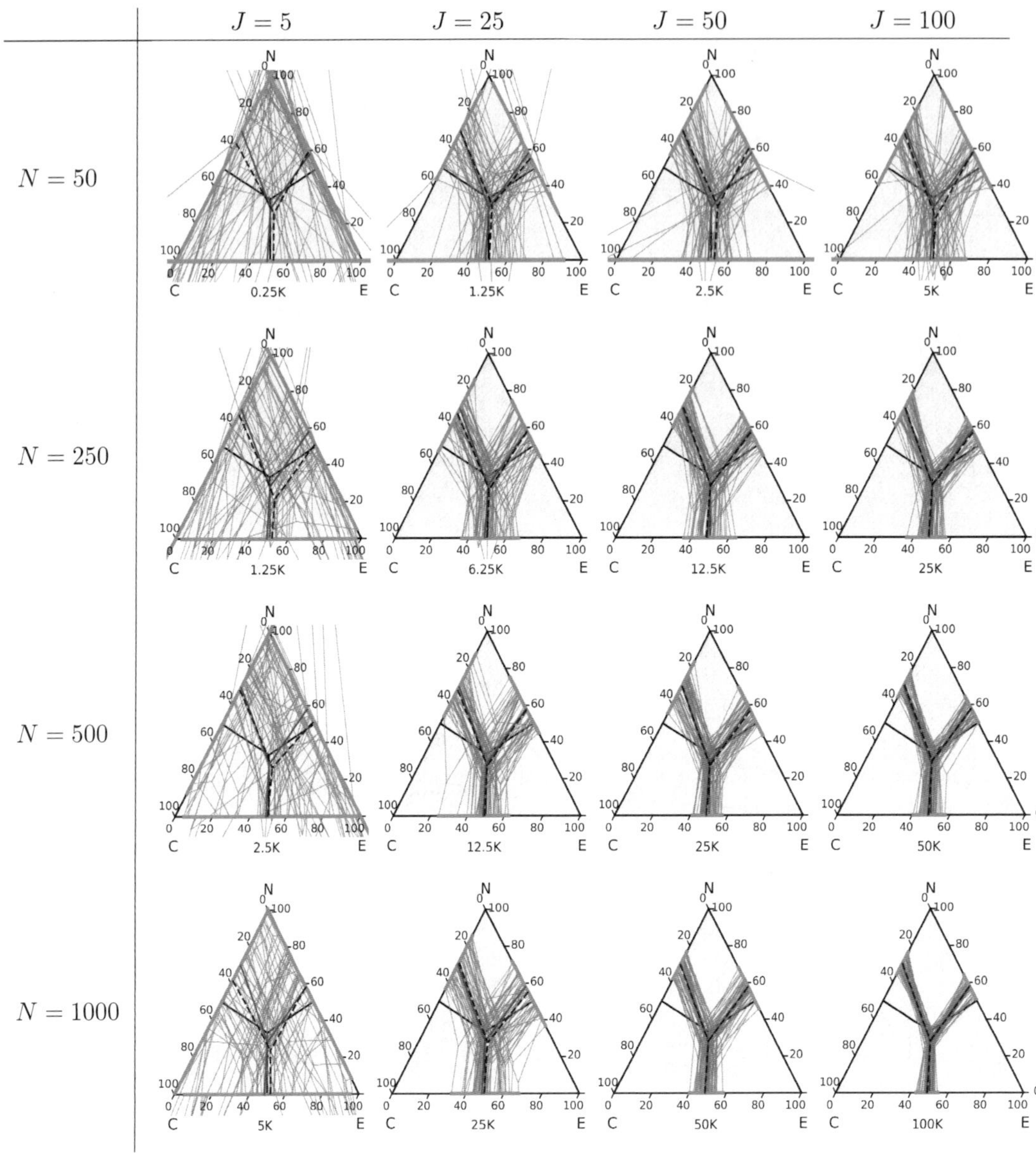

Figure 4: The Figure shows the bootstrapped latent class borders as gray lines, the range of the gray lines in orange, the mean of the bootstraps as blue dashed lines and the original borders as red lines for different values of N and J. The total number of annotations, i.e., $N \cdot J$, is below each plot.

Resolving Transcription Ambiguity in Spanish: A Hybrid Acoustic-Lexical System for Punctuation Restoration

Xiliang Zhu*, **Chia-Tien Chang***, **Shayna Gardiner**, **David Rossouw**, **Jonas Robertson**
Dialpad Canada Inc.
{xzhu, karol.chang, sgardiner, davidr, jonas}@dialpad.com

Abstract

Punctuation restoration is a crucial step after Automatic Speech Recognition (ASR) systems to enhance transcript readability and facilitate subsequent NLP tasks. Nevertheless, conventional lexical-based approaches are inadequate for solving the punctuation restoration task in Spanish, where ambiguity can be often found between unpunctuated declaratives and questions. In this study, we propose a novel hybrid acoustic-lexical punctuation restoration system for Spanish transcription, which consolidates acoustic and lexical signals through a modular process. Our experiment results show that the proposed system can effectively improve F1 score of question marks and overall punctuation restoration on both public and internal Spanish conversational datasets. Additionally, benchmark comparison against LLMs (Large Language Model) indicates the superiority of our approach in accuracy, reliability and latency. Furthermore, we demonstrate that the Word Error Rate (WER) of the ASR module also benefits from our proposed system.

1 Introduction

Automatic Speech Recognition (ASR) systems are applied in a variety of industry applications such as voice assistance and conversation analysis. However, typical ASR systems avoid producing punctuation marks in the transcripts, which leads to poor readability and causes ambiguity in the context (Jones et al., 2003). Therefore, a post-processing step to restore punctuation marks in transcripts is critical for speech-based commercial products.

Lexical-based approaches have been extensively studied in punctuation restoration tasks (Păiș and Tufiș, 2021). One major advantage of using lexical features is the availability of a massive amount of text data that is often well punctuated, such as Wikipedia. Most of the existing work on punctuation restoration focuses on English. Spanish is little studied, although it is the world's second largest mother tongue and even has more native speakers than English. Although a handful of work has addressed Spanish punctuation restoration using BERT-based approaches in recent years (González-Docasal et al., 2021; Zhu et al., 2022a), one major challenge in restoring punctuation marks for languages like Spanish has not been fully tackled: the rich morphology of Spanish allows speakers to omit subject pronouns and order words in sentences more freely than in English, which forces Spanish speakers to rely more on prosodic features when distinguishing questions from declarative sentences. These characteristics present a unique challenge from an NLP perspective when written transcripts are the main source of information for models.

In order to address the challenges in predicting Spanish question marks and improve the overall punctuation restoration accuracy, we introduce a hybrid punctuation restoration system leveraging both acoustic and lexical signals for Spanish conversations. While previous work on multimodal methodologies often requires large-scale, parallel audio-text data (Klejch et al., 2017), or additional audio encoding and fusion steps (Sunkara et al., 2020), our approach employs the conventional modular ASR-NLP setup in industry applications with no additional computational cost. Moreover, our system allows independent training of ASR and NLP modules, eliminating the need for massive parallel training resources. The main contributions of this paper are as follows:

1. Evaluate the impact of including punctuation in Spanish ASR training data on Word Error Rate (WER).

2. Propose a hybrid system for Spanish punctuation restoration leveraging ASR and NLP sequentially.

*These authors contributed equally to this work

Proceedings of the Third Workshop on Understanding Implicit and Underspecified Language, pages 33–41
March 21, 2024 ©2024 Association for Computational Linguistics

3. Demonstrate the effectiveness of our system by achieving up to a 2.1% relative reduction in Word Error Rate (WER) for the Spanish ASR decoder, improving question mark prediction F1 score by over 4% absolute, and consequently enhancing overall punctuation restoration accuracy on internal and public datasets from the Linguistic Data Consortium (LDC) (Graff et al., 2010a,b), also outperforming top LLMs (Large Language Model) in terms of accuracy, reliability and latency.

2 Background

2.1 Related Work

Punctuation restoration is often formulated as a sequence labeling task, where punctuation marks are predicted at appropriate positions in a sequence of words. Early studies used lexical-based methods such as n-gram language models (Gravano et al., 2009) and Conditional Random Fields (CRF) (Lu and Ng, 2010). More recently, long short-term memory (LSTM) (Hochreiter and Schmidhuber, 1997) and pre-trained large language models have been used (Xu et al., 2016; Devlin et al., 2019; Fu et al., 2021). Some works (Guan, 2020; O'Neill et al., 2021) proposed a speech recognition system with direct punctuation output, but it is unclear whether this approach is more effective than a traditional lexicon-based approach. For Spanish, a multilingual LSTM-based approach was studied in (Li and Lin, 2020). (Zhu et al., 2022a) proposed a transformer-based architecture with transfer learning to overcome the Spanish resource limitation and (González-Docasal et al., 2021) integrated silence embedding into BERT; however, as far as we are aware, no study has yet investigated the use of a hybrid approach incorporating acoustic input for the task of Spanish punctuation restoration.

Recent advances in LLMs such as ChatGPT[1], GPT4[2] and PaLM2[3] have reshaped the approaches for many NLP tasks. (Qin et al., 2023) found that ChatGPT performs well on tasks favouring reasoning capabilities while still faces challenges in sequence tagging tasks. (Lai et al., 2023) studied the multilingual capability of ChatGPT and found that it shows less optimal performance compared to task-specific models in different languages. However, the application of LLM in punctuation restoration task has not been studied yet to the best of our knowledge.

2.2 Ambiguity in Unpunctuated Spanish Text

Identifying Spanish questions from unpunctuated text is a challenging task. There are three relevant sociolinguistic features to consider for question identification in Spanish.

First, declarative sentences can occasionally become questions on intonation and context alone; e.g. *ustedes no pueden mandar un cheque con la orden* can be either a declarative or a question. This is true even for its English counterpart – both *Can't you send a cheque with the order?* and *You can't send a cheque with the order?* are well-formed – but the phenomenon is extremely common in Spanish (Brown and Rivas, 2011; Raymond, 2015; Cuza, 2016). In fact, in Caribbean Spanish, it is becoming increasingly more common to see questions like *¿ustedes no pueden mandar un cheque con la orden? (You can't send a cheque with the order?)*, which has typical declarative syntax, rather than *¿no pueden ustedes mandar un cheque con la orden? (Can't you send a cheque with the order?)*, which uses subject-verb inverted order (Brown and Rivas, 2011).

Second, Spanish morphosyntax also allows the reverse to occur: that is, declarative sentences can have subject-verb inversion too (Mackenzie, 2021), meaning that the question *no pueden ustedes mandar un cheque con la orden* above is also a perfectly well-formed declarative sentence.

Third, Spanish is a pro-drop language: due to richly-inflected morphology, it is possible to drop a subject pronoun entirely, using a verb's suffix alone to identify its subject – and removing the possibility of subject-verb inversion. For instance, the above example could easily become *no pueden mandar un cheque con la orden* or *¿no pueden mandar un cheque con la orden?*. In a small survey of our own data, we reviewed 200 utterances, in which there were 180 questions, of which 125 (69%) were pro-dropped – leaving only 55 questions with a fully realized subject noun or pronoun.

These facts make subject-verb inversion a much less helpful tool for definitively identifying questions in Spanish than it is for English, which consequently limits the performance of lexical-based NLP models in the Spanish punctuation restoration task. We also know that Spanish speakers them-

[1]https://openai.com/blog/chatgpt

[2]https://openai.com/gpt-4

[3]https://blog.google/technology/ai/google-palm-2-ai-large-language-model/

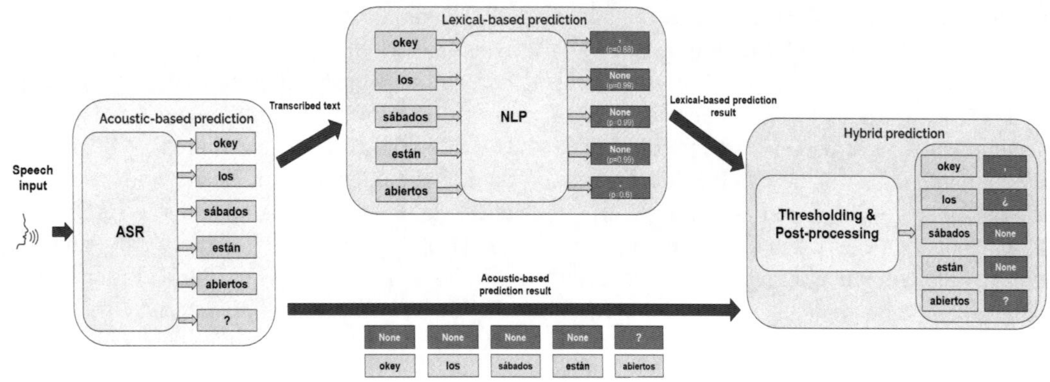

Figure 1: Overview of our hybrid punctuation restoration system, showing the example of an ambiguous unpunctuated utterance "*okey los sábados están abiertos*" (can be interpreted as "OK, they are open on Saturdays." or "OK, are they open on Saturdays?") processed as "*Okey, ¿los sábados están abiertos?*"

selves do not rely on lexical information alone to distinguish questions from declaratives: evidence suggests that acoustic features are measurably different when the speaker intends an utterance as a question rather than a declarative, and that this is true across many varieties of Spanish (Face, 2005; Willis, 2007; Lee and M.A., 2010; Armstrong, 2017).

3 Method

3.1 System Overview

Our hybrid punctuation restoration system is used in a Spanish call center product. In the real-time system pipeline, the audio from customer support phone calls is first transcribed by the ASR module, then text output is fed into the downstream NLP module. Instead of adding an extra acoustic encoder and combining it with a lexical encoder as proposed in (Sunkara et al., 2020; Zhu et al., 2022b), we directly train the ASR decoder to predict target punctuation marks. The ASR punctuation predictions (acoustic-based) are combined with the NLP module predictions (lexical-based) via a probability thresholding process. A heuristic-based post-processing step is then applied to make corrections in the prediction as the final step. Our system is illustrated in Figure 1. The set of Spanish punctuation marks predicted by the system are: OPEN_QUESTION (¿)[4], CLOSE_QUESTION (?), COMMA (,), PERIOD (.), and NONE (for tokens that have no associated punctuation marks).

3.2 Acoustic-based Prediction

Acoustic features, including intonation and prosody, play an important role in distinguishing declarative and interrogative sentences in Spanish, as described in section 2.2. In order to leverage our ASR module to directly predict punctuation marks from the speech signal, we keep each target punctuation mark in our ASR training data and treat it as an individual token by separating it from surrounding words; an example of predicting CLOSE_QUESTION is shown in Figure 1. Note that we omit OPEN_QUESTION from the training data since it can mostly be restored by heuristics in the following post-processing step.

We use an End-to-End based ASR system provided by the Nemo toolkit (Kuchaiev et al., 2019). The applied Conformer-CTC architecture is slightly different from the original Conformer architecture (Gulati et al., 2020), where the LSTM decoder is replaced with a linear decoder. The encoder uses CTC (Connectionist Temporal Classification) loss (Graves et al., 2006) instead of RNNT (RNN-Transducer) (Graves, 2012) which makes it a non-autoregressive model. For word prediction, we use an in-house streaming decoder with language model shallow fusion.

3.3 Lexical-based Prediction

The lexical-based approach is capable of predicting all supported punctuation marks outlined in section 3.1, which consumes unpunctuated transcribed text emitted from the ASR module as shown in Figure 1. For the NLP module utilized in this lexical-based prediction, we follow the similar structure as uti-

[4]An open question mark (¿) is used at the start position of a question in Spanish

lized in (Zhu et al., 2022a) and (Fu et al., 2021), which is a fine-tuned mBERT (multilingual BERT) (Devlin et al., 2019) with an additional token classification head. The output of the prediction indicates the appropriate punctuation marks to be attached to the corresponding input token. Additionally, a probability score (illustrated as p in Figure 1) is also computed for each token using a softmax layer on top of the prediction logits, which reflects the confidence of each predicted punctuation mark in the lexical-based prediction.

Algorithm 1 Thresholding algorithm

```
Input:
Pred_a: acoustic-based prediction
Pred_l: lexical-based prediction
P_l: probability score of Pred_l
T_question & T_declarative: hyperparameters
Output:
Pred_c: consolidated prediction
Where:
C_Q: CLOSE_QUESTION

if Pred_a == C_Q and Pred_l in {PERIOD, COMMA}
then
    if P_l ≤ T_declarative then
        Pred_c ← C_Q
    else
        Pred_c ← Pred_l
    end if
else if Pred_a != C_Q and Pred_l == C_Q then
    if P_l ≤ T_question then
        Pred_c ← PERIOD
    else
        Pred_c ← C_Q
    end if
else
    Pred_c ← Pred_l
end if
```

3.4 Hybrid Prediction

To consolidate the results from both acoustic-based and lexical-based predictions, we introduce a probability thresholding step based on the probability score generated by the lexical-based prediction. Our approach focuses on improving Spanish question prediction, which employs a set of threshold values $T_{question}$ and $T_{declarative}$ as hyperparameters. These thresholds represent the minimal probability score the lexical-based prediction needs to have when conflicting with acoustic-based prediction. The detailed thresholding algorithm is illustrated in Algorithm 1. The optimal values of $T_{question}$ and $T_{declarative}$ are identified through grid search towards the development dataset in our experiment[5].

[5]We found [0.7, 0.8] is usually a reasonable range to start with for both $T_{question}$ and $T_{declarative}$ in our experiments.

A heuristic-based post-processing step (details in Appendix A.1) is also applied after probability thresholding to mitigate the error caused by unmatched OPEN_QUESTION and CLOSE_QUESTION in the prediction. For example, as illustrated in the hybrid prediction result in Figure 1, an OPEN_QUESTION is added on the first token of the word chunk *los sábados están abiertos?* after an unmatched CLOSE_QUESTION is created after the thresholding process.

4 Experiment

4.1 Datasets

We conduct our experiment using a variety of data resources. Since the proposed system is used in our call center product, the in-domain data resource is our internal audio recording and human-annotated transcripts from real customer support calls in Spanish. This internal data resource consists of 50 hours of audio and around 10,000 rows of corresponding transcribed utterances (more statistical detail is available in Appendix A.2). Apart from our internal dataset, Linguistic Data Consortium (LDC) Spanish Fisher corpora (Graff et al., 2010a,b) is also added as a supplementary resource for real-life human conversations, which has approximately 160 hours of audio with 130,000 rows of transcribed utterances from Spanish telephone conversations. Out of both LDC and our internal data, we leave out 10% and 5% as test and development sets respectively in our experiments. Note that in order to evaluate the performance of our system on reference transcripts, we leverage Levenshtein distance to align punctuation marks from each ASR hypothesis to reference transcript in acoustic-based prediction during our evaluation process on the test set.

Additionally, the open-sourced Spanish datasets from Openslr (Guevara-Rukoz et al., 2020; Kolobov et al., 2021) and Common-voice (Ardila et al., 2019) are used in ASR training as well, which collectively provide 1200 hours of audio. A subset of 80,000 utterances were also randomly sampled from the Spanish OpenSubtitle corpus (Lison and Tiedemann, 2016) and added as an extra text-only dataset into the NLP module training process to improve the accuracy of lexical-based prediction. All text-based resources are also used in the language model for the in-house streaming ASR decoder.

	Baseline	ASR w/ C_Q	ASR w/ all
Public	15.77	**15.44 (-2.1%)**	16.53 (+4.8%)
Internal	26.81	**26.36 (-1.7%)**	27.95 (+4.3%)

Table 1: WER and relative changes compared to the baseline on public (LDC) and internal datasets, where the *Baseline* performance is evaluated by the ASR module trained without punctuation. *ASR w/ C_Q*: ASR module trained with only CLOSE_QUESTION; *ASR w/ all*: ASR module trained with CLOSE_QUESTION, PERIOD and COMMA.

	Reliability	Latency (s)
ChatGPT-few	92.4%	1.13
ChatGPT-zero	87.9%	1.10
PaLM2-few	28.7%	0.56
PaLM2-zero	28.6%	0.49
Our system (excl. ASR)	-	**0.04**

Table 2: Reliability and Latency comparison between LLM APIs (with both zero- and few- shot prompting) and our system (excluding ASR latency), averaged over all internal and public test samples. Latency shown as "seconds per input utterance".

4.2 Experiment Setup

For the ASR module, we use the Nemo (Kuchaiev et al., 2019) Spanish model `STT_Es_Conformer_CTC_Large` as the pre-trained model. The presented model is fine-tuned for 20 epochs, with the Adam optimizer (Kingma and Ba, 2014) and no weight decay. The Noam learning scheduler (Vaswani et al., 2017) is used with a warmup of 100 steps and a learning rate of 0.01.

In consideration of the real-time inference speed, we take only the bottom 6 layers of `bert-base-multilingual-cased` from Hugging Face (Wolf et al., 2020) library as the backbone of our NLP module. The 6-layer mBERT is then fine-tuned through a token classification task using all lexical training data described in section 4.1. The NLP module is trained using the Adam optimizer with 4 epochs and a learning rate of 3e-5.

In the subsequent sections, all assessments are performed utilizing a single Intel Xeon 2.20GHz CPU, 1.5G memory and under identical network connection condition.

5 Results

5.1 Evaluation on Speech Recognition

We first evaluate the performance impact by introducing CLOSE_QUESTION prediction in our ASR module. Word-Error-Rate (WER) is a standard metric for the ASR system. A lower word error rate shows superior accuracy in speech recognition, compared with a higher word error rate. To accurately determine the word error rate of the ASR module, free from punctuation interference, we exclude all punctuation marks in both the ASR hypothesis and reference transcripts while evaluating. Table 1 shows WER on both test sets. Compared to our baseline, the ASR module trained only with CLOSE_QUESTION shows 2.1% and 1.7% WER improvement in public (LDC) and the internal test set respectively, which indicates that our ASR module can learn better acoustic features of Spanish interrogative sentences by keeping CLOSE_QUESTION in training data. In addition to predicting CLOSE_QUESTION, we also conduct a second experiment to keep all CLOSE_QUESTION, COMMA and PERIOD in the ASR module, but this unexpectedly increases the WER by up to 4.8%, which is not a tolerable performance deterioration for our production use. Therefore, we only focus on CLOSE_QUESTION prediction from the ASR module in our design.

5.2 Evaluation on Punctuation Restoration

In order to assess the comprehensive proficiency of our system in restoring Spanish punctuation, we conduct a benchmark test against some leading LLMs available on the market. First, we evaluate and compare the runtime performance of producing Spanish punctuation marks from unpunctuated transcripts between (a) utilizing commercial LLM APIs (ChatGPT and PaLM2) and (b) executing our proposed system. Our evaluation criteria for this analysis include two metrics: (1) *Reliability*: the percentage of the results where the original input words can be extracted without any modification or reordering (except casing changes), to measure the impact of the LLM hallucination or other undesired outcomes. (2) *Latency*: the elapsed time to receive responses from API calls for ChatGPT and PaLM2, as well as the total execution time of our lexical and hybrid prediction (excluding ASR latency), under the same environment setting as stated in section 4.2. Table 2 presents the *Reliability* and *Latency* comparison, it is clear that except our proposed system, all LLM APIs exhibit various levels of reliability concerns. Additionally, our system shows much lower latency compared to API calls. It is also noteworthy that *Reliability* of PaLM2 stands at a mere 28% in both zero- and few- shot prompting, suggesting that it is not suitable for the Spanish punctuation restoration task. Details on the API call setup and prompts are listed in Appendix A.3 and A.4.

Table 3 presents the comprehensive F1 score

	Public (LDC) data					Internal data				
	Lexical	Acoustic	ChatGPT-zero	ChatGPT-few	Hybrid	Lexical	Acoustic	ChatGPT-zero	ChatGPT-few	Hybrid
C_Q	54.0	51.5	13.5	13.9	**58.2**	47.3	28.2	24.4	28.6	**51.7**
O_Q	50.6	-	11.1	11.7	**52.7**	44.5	-	22.9	25.4	**47.0**
COMMA	**60.8**	-	43.5	51.0	60.7	68.9	-	47.2	60.4	**69.0**
PERIOD	87.7	-	58.6	58.8	**88.0**	83.6	-	59.5	72.4	**83.8**
Overall[1]	74.49	-	44.92	49.57	**74.83**	72.29	-	48.04	61.20	**72.61**

[1]Micro average of all punctuation

Table 3: F1 score comparison over all punctuation marks with different approaches. *C_Q*: CLOSE_QUESION; *O_Q*: OPEN_QUESTION; *Lexical*: lexical-based prediction; *Acoustic*: acoustic-based prediction; *Hybrid*: our proposed hybrid system with consolidated prediction; *ChatGPT-few/zero*: ChatGPT with few/zero-shot prompting, details in Appendix A.

	Public (LDC) data				Internal data			
	Lexical	Acoustic	Union	Threshold	Lexical	Acoustic	Union	Threshold
Precision	48.0	**65.3**[2]	47.0	53.1	63.7	**98.4**[3]	66.0	66.1
Recall	61.7	44.1	**71.1**	64.3	37.7	16.4	42.1	**42.4**
F1	54.0	51.5	56.5	**58.2**	47.3	28.2	51.4	**51.7**

[2]19.3% of the True Positive prediction is ambiguous in unpunctuated text, and not identified as questions by Lexical.
[3]32.3% of the True Positive prediction is ambiguous in unpunctuated text, and not identified as questions by Lexical.

Table 4: F1, precision and recall comparison on **CLOSE_QUESTION** using different approaches. *Lexical*: lexical-based prediction; *Acoustic*: acoustic-based prediction; *Union*: the union of CLOSE_QUESTION predictions from both lexical and acoustic prediction; *Threshold*: our proposed thresholding process to consolidate lexical and acoustic predictions.

performance of our punctuation restoration system and LLM API[6] on both public and internal datasets. Note that we also show the performance of the standalone lexical module which represents the conventional BERT-based lexical-only structure used in recent punctuation restoration studies (Zhu et al., 2022a; Fu et al., 2021). It is clear that both lexical and hybrid predictions demonstrate a substantial accuracy advantage over ChatGPT. Moreover, the hybrid approach, enhanced by the improvements in CLOSE_QUESTION of up to 4.4%, exhibits varied degrees of F1 score improvement for all other punctuation marks after our thresholding and post-processing step outlined in section 3.4. Consequently, our proposed hybrid system outperforms the lexical-only approach by 0.34% and 0.32% absolute in overall F1 score respectively on public and internal datasets.

To better illustrate the enhancement on CLOSE_QUESTION from our hybrid system, we additionally provide precision, recall and F1 score details on CLOSE_QUESTION in Table 4. Although with a lower F1 score, acoustic-based prediction exhibits a higher precision in predicting CLOSE_QUESTION compared to lexical prediction in both testing datasets. In addition, up to 32.3% of True Positives from the acoustic prediction is ambiguous in unpunctuated text and does not overlap with that in lexical prediction. In order to demonstrate the effectiveness of our proposed thresholding process to consolidate acoustic and lexical predictions as described in section 3.4, we compare it with a naive union of the two on CLOSE_QUESTION. Table 4 shows that *Thresholding* consistently outperforms *Union* in both datasets. As a result, with our thresholding approach, the F1 score for CLOSE_QUESTION is noticeably improved by 4.2% and 4.4% compared to lexical-only prediction across public and internal datasets respectively.

[6]Only reliable outcomes from ChatGPT are evaluated. PaLM2 is left out in this evaluation as it cannot produce reliable results of a large enough size to establish a meaningful comparison, due to its low *Reliability*.

6 Future Work

From the evaluation result in section 5.1, contrary to the WER improvement when predicting only CLOSE_QUESTION by the ASR module, we discovered a WER deterioration when adding COMMA and PERIOD to the prediction. Future work may focus on establishing a possible cause for this change. In addition, lexical ambiguity between questions and declarations exists beyond Spanish; thus, a natural next step would be evaluating our system in other human languages.

7 Conclusion

In this study, we propose a hybrid acoustic-lexical punctuation restoration system for Spanish conversational transcripts, with a focus to address the ambiguity in unpunctuated Spanish questions. The proposed system leverages an ASR decoder to make direct predictions of Spanish question marks, which are later consolidated with lexical predictions from an NLP module. We evaluate the system on both internal and public datasets and show that it can effectively enhance Spanish question marks prediction, and consequently improve the overall punctuation restoration accuracy. Additional benchmark indicates that our proposed system outperforms some top LLMs in accuracy, latency and reliability. Furthermore, we demonstrate that keeping question marks in the ASR decoder vocabulary results in an improved WER of the ASR module alone.

8 Ethical Considerations

During our internal data collection process, we implement a data retention policy for all our users, such that user consent is obtained prior to any data collection. In addition, we have ensured that all the annotators involved in the transcription process of our internal dataset are paid with adequate compensation. Moreover, to protect the privacy and confidentiality of individuals, the dataset underwent further processing to remove any sensitive, personal, or identifiable information.

References

Rosana Ardila, Megan Branson, Kelly Davis, Michael Henretty, Michael Kohler, Josh Meyer, Reuben Morais, Lindsay Saunders, Francis M. Tyers, and Gregor Weber. 2019. Common Voice: A Massively-Multilingual Speech Corpus.

Meghan E. Armstrong. 2017. Accounting for intonational form and function in puerto rican spanish polar questions. *Probus*, 29(1):1–40.

Esther Brown and Javier Rivas. 2011. Subject-verb word order in spanish interrogatives: A quantitative analysis of puerto rican spanish. *Spanish in Context*, 8.

Alejandro Cuza. 2016. The status of interrogative subject–verb inversion in spanish-english bilingual children. *Lingua*, 180.

Jacob Devlin, Ming-Wei Chang, Kenton Lee, and Kristina Toutanova. 2019. BERT: Pre-training of deep bidirectional transformers for language understanding. In *Proceedings of the 2019 Conference of the North American Chapter of the Association for Computational Linguistics: Human Language Technologies, Volume 1 (Long and Short Papers)*, pages 4171–4186, Minneapolis, Minnesota. Association for Computational Linguistics.

Timothy L. Face. 2005. F0 peak height and the perception of sentence type in castilian spanish. *Revista Internacional de Lingüística Iberoamericana*, 3:49–65.

Xue-Yong Fu, Cheng Chen, Md Tahmid Rahman Laskar, Shashi Bhushan, and Simon Corston-Oliver. 2021. Improving punctuation restoration for speech transcripts via external data. In *Proceedings of the Seventh Workshop on Noisy User-generated Text (W-NUT 2021)*, pages 168–174, Online. Association for Computational Linguistics.

Ander González-Docasal, Aitor García-Pablos, Haritz Arzelus, and Aitor Álvarez. 2021. Autopunct: A BERT-based Automatic Punctuation and Capitalisation System for Spanish and Basque. *Procesamiento del Lenguaje Natural*, 67(0):59–68.

David Graff, Shudong Huang, Ingrid Cartagena, Kevin Walker, and Christopher Cieri. 2010a. Fisher Spanish - Transcripts LDC2010T04. Web Download. Philadelphia: Linguistic Data Consortium.

David Graff, Shudong Huang, Ingrid Cartagena, Kevin Walker, and Christopher Cieri. 2010b. Fisher Spanish Speech LDC2010S01. Web Download. Philadelphia: Linguistic Data Consortium.

Agustin Gravano, Martin Jansche, and Michiel Bacchiani. 2009. Restoring punctuation and capitalization in transcribed speech. In *2009 IEEE International Conference on Acoustics, Speech and Signal Processing*, pages 4741–4744.

A. Graves, S. Fernandez, F. Gomez, and J. Schmidhuber. 2006. Connectionist temporal classification: Labelling unsegmented sequence data with recurrent neural nets. In *ICML '06: Proceedings of the International Conference on Machine Learning*.

Alex Graves. 2012. Sequence transduction with recurrent neural networks. *CoRR*, abs/1211.3711.

Yushi Guan. 2020. End to End ASR System with Automatic Punctuation Insertion.

Adriana Guevara-Rukoz, Isin Demirsahin, Fei He, Shan-Hui Cathy Chu, Supheakmungkol Sarin, Knot Pipatsrisawat, Alexander Gutkin, Alena Butryna, and Oddur Kjartansson. 2020. Crowdsourcing Latin American Spanish for Low-Resource Text-to-Speech. In *Proceedings of The 12th Language Resources and Evaluation Conference (LREC)*, pages 6504–6513, Marseille, France. European Language Resources Association (ELRA).

Anmol Gulati, James Qin, Chung-Cheng Chiu, Niki Parmar, Yu Zhang, Jiahui Yu, Wei Han, Shibo Wang, Zhengdong Zhang, Yonghui Wu, and Ruoming Pang. 2020. Conformer: Convolution-augmented Transformer for Speech Recognition.

Sepp Hochreiter and Jürgen Schmidhuber. 1997. Long Short-term Memory. *Neural computation*, 9:1735–80.

Douglas Jones, Florian Wolf, Edward Gibson, Elliott Williams, Evelina Fedorenko, Douglas Reynolds, and Marc Zissman. 2003. Measuring the readability of automatic speech-to-text transcripts.

Diederik P. Kingma and Jimmy Ba. 2014. Adam: A Method for Stochastic Optimization.

Ondřej Klejch, Peter Bell, and Steve Renals. 2017. Sequence-to-sequence models for punctuated transcription combining lexical and acoustic features. In *2017 IEEE International Conference on Acoustics, Speech and Signal Processing (ICASSP)*, pages 5700–5704.

Rostislav Kolobov, Olga Okhapkina, Andrey Platunov Olga Omelchishina, Roman Bedyakin, Vyacheslav Moshkin, Dmitry Menshikov, and Nikolay Mikhaylovskiy. 2021. MediaSpeech: Multilanguage ASR Benchmark and Dataset.

Oleksii Kuchaiev, Jason Li, Huyen Nguyen, Oleksii Hrinchuk, Ryan Leary, Boris Ginsburg, Samuel Kriman, Stanislav Beliaev, Vitaly Lavrukhin, Jack Cook, et al. 2019. Nemo: a toolkit for building ai applications using neural modules. *arXiv preprint arXiv:1909.09577*.

Viet Dac Lai, Nghia Trung Ngo, Amir Pouran Ben Veyseh, Hieu Man, Franck Dernoncourt, Trung Bui, and Thien Huu Nguyen. 2023. Chatgpt beyond english: Towards a comprehensive evaluation of large language models in multilingual learning.

Su Ar Lee and B.A.and M.A. 2010. Absolute interrogative intonation patterns in Buenos Aires Spanish.

Xinxing Li and Edward Lin. 2020. A 43 Language Multilingual Punctuation Prediction Neural Network Model. In *Proc. Interspeech 2020*, pages 1067–1071.

Pierre Lison and Jörg Tiedemann. 2016. OpenSubtitles2016: Extracting large parallel corpora from movie and TV subtitles. In *Proceedings of the Tenth International Conference on Language Resources and Evaluation (LREC'16)*, pages 923–929, Portorož, Slovenia. European Language Resources Association (ELRA).

Wei Lu and Hwee Tou Ng. 2010. Better Punctuation Prediction with Dynamic Conditional Random Fields. In *Proceedings of the 2010 Conference on Empirical Methods in Natural Language Processing*, pages 177–186, Cambridge, MA. Association for Computational Linguistics.

Ian Mackenzie. 2021. The linguistics of spanish.

Patrick K. O'Neill, Vitaly Lavrukhin, Somshubra Majumdar, Vahid Noroozi, Yuekai Zhang, Oleksii Kuchaiev, Jagadeesh Balam, Yuliya Dovzhenko, Keenan Freyberg, Michael D. Shulman, Boris Ginsburg, Shinji Watanabe, and Georg Kucsko. 2021. SPGISpeech: 5,000 hours of transcribed financial audio for fully formatted end-to-end speech recognition.

Vasile Păiș and Dan Tufiș. 2021. Capitalization and punctuation restoration: a survey. *Artificial Intelligence Review*, 55:1681 – 1722.

Chengwei Qin, Aston Zhang, Zhuosheng Zhang, Jiaao Chen, Michihiro Yasunaga, and Diyi Yang. 2023. Is chatgpt a general-purpose natural language processing task solver?

Chase Wesley Raymond. 2015. Questions and responses in spanish monolingual and spanish–english bilingual conversation. *Language and Communication*, 42:50–68.

Monica Sunkara, Srikanth Ronanki, Dhanush Bekal, Sravan Bodapati, and Katrin Kirchhoff. 2020. Multimodal Semi-supervised Learning Framework for Punctuation Prediction in Conversational Speech.

Ashish Vaswani, Noam Shazeer, Niki Parmar, Jakob Uszkoreit, Llion Jones, Aidan N Gomez, Łukasz Kaiser, and Illia Polosukhin. 2017. Attention is all you need. In *Advances in Neural Information Processing Systems*, pages 5998–6008.

Erik Willis. 2007. Utterance signaling and tonal levels in dominican spanish declaratives and interrogatives. *Journal of Portuguese Linguistics*, 6:179.

Thomas Wolf, Lysandre Debut, Victor Sanh, Julien Chaumond, Clement Delangue, Anthony Moi, Pierric Cistac, Tim Rault, Remi Louf, Morgan Funtowicz, Joe Davison, Sam Shleifer, Patrick von Platen, Clara Ma, Yacine Jernite, Julien Plu, Canwen Xu, Teven Le Scao, Sylvain Gugger, Mariama Drame, Quentin Lhoest, and Alexander Rush. 2020. Transformers: State-of-the-art natural language processing. In *Proceedings of the 2020 Conference on Empirical Methods in Natural Language Processing: System Demonstrations*, pages 38–45, Online. Association for Computational Linguistics.

Kaituo Xu, Lei Xie, and Kaisheng Yao. 2016. Investigating LSTM for punctuation prediction. In *2016 10th International Symposium on Chinese Spoken Language Processing (ISCSLP)*, pages 1–5.

Xiliang Zhu, Shayna Gardiner, David Rossouw, Tere Roldán, and Simon Corston-Oliver. 2022a. Punctuation restoration in Spanish customer support transcripts using transfer learning. In *Proceedings of the Third Workshop on Deep Learning for Low-Resource Natural Language Processing*, pages 80–89, Hybrid. Association for Computational Linguistics.

Yaoming Zhu, Liwei Wu, Shanbo Cheng, and Mingxuan Wang. 2022b. Unified Multimodal Punctuation Restoration Framework for Mixed-Modality Corpus.

A Appendix

A.1 Heuristic-based post-processing

As mentioned in 3.4, we apply the following heuristic-based steps to post-process the prediction result:

1. Convert all unmatched OPEN_QUESTION to NONE in the prediction.

2. For all unmatched CLOSE_QUESTION, change the prediction of the first token in the continuous word chunk (the longest continuous word sequence where no punctuation is predicted in-between) to OPEN_QUESTION.

A.2 Description of our internal dataset

Our internal data is collected from audio recordings of Spanish customer support conversations, covering a large range of domains such as retail, technology, automotive and professional services. Our primary focus lies within the North American region, including both Mexican and American accents. The audio duration of the dataset totals around 50 hours. For ASR training purposes, each individual audio clip is broken down into segments based on audio silence, with a maximum of 2 minutes and averaging approximately 18 seconds. Audio clips are also transcribed by the annotators to create text data for NLP training. We provide the statistical summary on the length of the transcribed utterances in Table 5.

	mean	medium	min	max	std
num of words	43.4	38.0	1.0	231.0	25.4

Table 5: Statistical summary on length of the utterances in our internal dataset.

A.3 API call setup

We use `gpt-3.5-turbo` for ChatGPT and `text-bison@001` for PaLM2 in API calls. For both models, *temperature* is set as 0.2 while the maximum token length of output (named as *max_tokens* in ChatGPT and *maxOutputTokens* in PaLM2) is configured as 1024.

A.4 Prompt

The following prompts are used in our experiments when calling LLM APIs:

Few-shot prompting:

```
Without any explanation or modification,
add punctuation to the following Spanish
transcript from human conversations, use
only punctuation marks from this list:
comma(,), period(.), open_question(¿)
and close_question(?). Return the punc-
tuated utterance only. Here are some
examples:

### Input: {Unpunctuated Spanish Utter-
ance 1}
### Output: {Punctuated Spanish Utter-
ance 1}

### Input: {Unpunctuated Spanish Ut-
terance 2}
### Output: {Punctuated Spanish Utter-
ance 2}

### Input: {Unpunctuated Spanish Ut-
terance 3}
### Output: {Punctuated Spanish Utter-
ance 3}

Now, add punctuation marks to:
### Input: {text}
### Output:
```

Zero-shot prompting:

```
Without any explanation or modification,
add punctuation to the following Spanish
transcript from human conversations, use
only punctuation marks from this list:
comma(,), period(.), open_question(¿)
and close_question(?). Return the punc-
tuated utterance only.
Add punctuation marks to:
### Input: {text}
### Output:
```

where we put the unpunctuated test utterance in the **text** field. Note that in all of our experiments, we use three in-context examples for few-shot prompting. In addition, we make sure to sample utterances with presence of all targeted punctuation marks in these three in-context examples. Note that both zero-shot and few-shot prompting are used in the evaluation results as presented in Table 3 and Table 4.

Assessing the Significance of Encoded Information in Contextualized Representations to Word Sense Disambiguation

Deniz Ekin Yavas
Heinrich Heine University Düsseldorf
deniz.yavas@hhu.de

Abstract

The similarity of representations is crucial for WSD. However, a lot of information is encoded in the contextualized representations, and it is not clear which sentence context features drive this similarity and whether these features are significant to WSD. In this study, we address these questions. First, we identify the sentence context features that are responsible for the similarity of the contextualized representations of different occurrences of words. For this purpose, we conduct an explainability experiment and identify the sentence context features that lead to the formation of the clusters in word sense clustering with CWEs. Then, we provide a qualitative evaluation for assessing the significance of these features to WSD. Our results show that features that lack significance to WSD determine the similarity of the representations even when different senses of a word occur in highly diverse contexts and sentence context provides clear clues for different senses.

1 Introduction

Contextualization is a powerful tool as it enables us to capture sentence context. This is crucial especially in word sense disambiguation (WSD) because sentence context provides valuable information for resolving lexical ambiguity in both NLP and human language processing.

The similarity of representations is crucial for WSD. With contextualization, we expect the representations of different occurrences of the same sense to be similar to each other. This is based on the assumption that different senses of a word occur in different contexts and sentence context contains explicit clues that signal one of the senses of the word. Consider the sentences in (1) that demonstrate two senses of 'bank'. In both sentences, some words successfully signal each sense of the word; in (1-a), the words 'money' and 'withdraw' and in (1-b), the words 'picnic' and 'river'.

(1) 'bank' (homonymy):
  a. *financial institution:*
  I went to the **bank** to withdraw money.
  b. *geographical feature:*
  They had a picnic by the river **bank**.

(2) 'pass' (polysemy):
  a. *go across or through:*
  She **passed** through towns.
  b. *move past:*
  She **passed** the bakery on her way.

However, in practice, we lack clarity on which specific sentence context features are responsible for the similarity of the contextualized representations. It has been shown that a wide variety of information is encoded in the contextualized representations (Sajjad et al., 2022) and using contextualized word embeddings (CWEs) of pre-trained language models alone does not achieve good performance in unsupervised settings (Yenicelik et al., 2020).

The purpose of this study is to investigate which sentence context features determine the similarity of the representations of different occurrences of words and whether these features are significant to WSD. By doing so, we aim to provide a clearer understanding of contextualized representations in terms of their ability to capture different meanings of words. For this purpose, we conduct an explainability experiment. We focus on word sense clustering with CWEs of BERT (Devlin et al., 2019) and identify sentence context features that lead to the formation of the clusters. This way, we determine which features drive the similarity of the representations.

Our cluster explainability method follows several steps and is depicted in Figure 1. We start by performing word sense clustering with CWEs and cluster the sentences of a word. Our aim is essentially to reverse the word sense clustering process

Proceedings of the Third Workshop on Understanding Implicit and Underspecified Language, pages 42–53
March 21, 2024

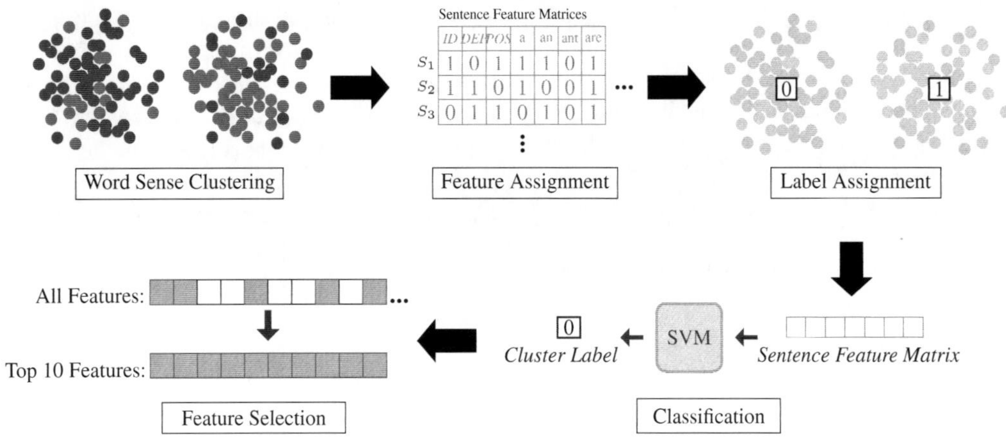

Figure 1: Cluster Explainability Method: i) Perform Word Sense Clustering with CWEs, ii) Represent each sentence with sentence context features, iii) Assign each sentence a label based on the cluster it belongs to, iv) Train a classifier to predict the clusters that sentences belong to based on their sentence context features, v) Apply feature selection to determine the sentence context features responsible for the performance of the classifier.

and recreate the clusters with a classification task. For this purpose, we represent each sentence with its sentence context features and assign it a label based on the cluster that it belongs to. Then, we train a classifier to predict the cluster labels of the sentences based on their sentence context features. As the final step, we apply a feature selection algorithm to the classifier to determine which features are the most relevant for the performance of the classifier. This tells us which sentence context features lead to the formation of the clusters. We use this method to identify the features that lead to the clusters for each word in our dataset. Finally, we assess the significance of these features to WSD for each word through qualitative evaluation.

In this study, we distinguish two types of lexical ambiguity; homonymy and polysemy. The most distinctive feature that distinguishes these two types is the semantic relatedness of their senses (Klepousniotou, 2002; Klepousniotou and Baum, 2007; Klepousniotou et al., 2008, 2012). Homonyms have less semantically related senses compared to polysemes. As a result, homonyms occur in more diverse contexts. Consider the examples in (1) and (2). The provided senses of 'bank' are homonymous, whereas those of 'pass' are polysemous. The senses of 'bank' are not related semantically and the noun co-occurs with semantically different words in its different senses ('money', 'withdraw' vs. 'river', 'picnic'). However, this is not true for 'pass'. The meaning difference between the senses of 'pass' is less clear and the verb co-occurs with words that are similar in meaning in its different senses, specifically words that are related to a location.

Their inherent differences also result in differences in NLP performance. For example, WSD performance is better with homonyms (Nair et al., 2020; Haber and Poesio, 2021) and contextualization affects homonyms more (Sevastjanova et al., 2021) compared to polysemes. Therefore, it's important to consider that not all words present an equal challenge for WSD. In addition to that, it's important to consider that different lexical ambiguity types have different relations to context, and as a result, the information that is required for their disambiguation might not always be the same. In this study, we expect different results for each type. Considering that homonyms occur in more diverse contexts, we expect sentence context to provide clearer clues for their different senses and the similarity of the representations to be affected by these clues.

Our results show that the sentence context features that are responsible for the similarity of the representations and lead to the formation of clusters lack significance to WSD in most cases. This is true for both lexical ambiguity types. Even with homonyms—where different senses of a word occur in highly diverse contexts and sentence context provides clear clues for different senses—the similarity of the representations does not arise from the significant features.

2 Related Work

Studies have shown that the similarity of the embeddings is primarily influenced by the sentence context rather than the meaning of words. Ethayarajh (2019) have shown that words have different representations based on their contextual variation, rather than their meaning variation. Similarly, Garcia (2021) have shown that the similarity between a word and its synonym is lost when the sentence context is identical for different words; the similarity between a word and a random word is not different from the similarity between a word and its synonym when their sentence contexts are similar.

One reason for this is that a lot of information is encoded in the contextualized representations and they affect the similarity of the representations. Sajjad et al. (2022) have shown that the information encoded in the contextualized representations can be explained to some extent by semantic, morphological, syntactic, and lexical concepts. These concepts include the words' POS tags, CCG super-tags, ngrams, casings, WordNet concepts, and so on. Additionally, Mickus et al. (2020) have shown that the similarity of the representations is affected by the segment embeddings that the model assigns to tokens to indicate their sentences. In this study, this is not an issue because we only use one sentence as an input. However, we aim to investigate whether a similar effect can be found for the positional encoding, resulting words in the same position having similar representations.

Clustering reveals these similarities within the representations. Sajjad et al. (2022) have shown that the clusters of contextualized representations overlap with the concepts that are found to be encoded in the representations. Furthermore, it has been shown that word sense clustering with CWEs of the BERT model doesn't achieve good performance and sentence context similarities have been observed within the clusters (Yenicelik et al., 2020). The effects of the sentence context have been also observed in similarity ranking for WSD with CWEs of BERT (Gessler and Schneider, 2021). However, there hasn't been any effort to systematically explain the relation between sentence context and contextualized representations of different occurrences of the same word and with a focus on WSD. This study aims to fill this gap.

Finally, the studies that distinguish different types of lexical ambiguity have shown that WSD performance with CWEs changes depending on the type and it is easier to disambiguate homonymy than polysemy (Nair et al., 2020; Haber and Poesio, 2021). Similarly, contextualization of BERT affects different types differently and homonyms are affected more by contextualization due to the fact that they occur in more diverse contexts (Sevastjanova et al., 2021). In this study, we also expect the results to be different for each type. In the case of homonymy, we expect sentence context to provide clearer clues for different senses and the similarity of the representations to be affected by these clues.

3 Data

We use SemCor (Miller et al., 1993) which provides sentences that are annotated with WordNet senses for a wide variety of words (Fellbaum, 2010) for English. We restrict our focus to nouns and verbs. A word can be both homonymous and polysemous at the same time because different senses of a word can have different relations, e.g. two senses can be homonymous while another two can be polysemous. Because of this, we don't focus on homonymous or polysemous words but sense groups of words. These sense groups are formed by grouping the senses of a word according to their relations, so we end up with sense groups in which all pairs are homonymous or polysemous to each other.

In order to decide if a sense pair is homonymous or polysemous, we use the data provided in Nair et al. (2020). This data contains semantic relatedness judgment scores for a subpart of WordNet. Semantic relatedness determines where on the homonymy-polysemy continuum a word is (Klepousniotou, 2002; Klepousniotou and Baum, 2007; Klepousniotou et al., 2008, 2012) and semantic relatedness judgments of speakers overlap with different types of lexical ambiguity (Klepousniotou et al., 2008; Nair et al., 2020). In Nair et al. (2020), semantic relatedness judgement scores are collected for each sense pair from several speakers. We use the average of the scores for each sense pair to decide if the word is homonymous or polysemous in those senses. We consider the sense pairs that have a distance over 0.8 as homonymy pairs and a distance below 0.5 as polysemy pairs.[1]

[1]Psycholinguistics studies have shown that some polysemy types show homonymy-like behaviors and have less semantic relatedness (Klepousniotou and Baum, 2007; Klepousniotou et al., 2008). Due to this, we leave a certain range out to avoid these mixed types.

Lexical Ambiguity	Clustering Sense Group #	ARI	Sentence-Feature Classifiers Sense Group #	*WSD* F1	P	R	*Cluster* F1	P	R	*10-Cluster* F1	P	R	*10-Rand.* F1
Homo.	19	0.68	5	0.80	0.80	0.80	**0.87**	0.87	0.87	0.85	0.86	0.85	0.42
Poly.	39	0.36	5	0.72	0.76	0.72	0.78	0.80	0.78	**0.86**	0.86	0.87	0.37
Overall	58	0.52	10	0.76	0.78	0.76	0.82	0.83	0.82	**0.85**	0.86	0.86	0.39

Table 1: Data size and experimental results summary. *WSD* refers to the classifiers that are trained for WSD, *Cluster* for cluster assignment. *10-Cluster* classifiers refer to the classifiers that are trained for cluster assignment with only the top 10 features. *10-Rand.* refers to the classifiers that are trained for cluster assignment with random 10 features. *F1*, *Precision* and *Recall* scores are given. The best F1 score overall and for each type is given in bold.

As our data, we use the sentences of the selected senses from SemCor. We do not include the senses that have less than 10 sentences in SemCor. We balance the number of sentences for each group by random under-sampling. We exclude the words that show inherent and metonymical polysemy because different types of polysemy have different characteristics (Klepousniotou and Baum, 2007; Klepousniotou et al., 2008) and we focus only on irregular polysemy.[2]

4 Method

The goal of this study is to first, identify the sentence context features that determine the similarity of the contextualized representations. For this purpose, we identify the sentence context features that lead to the formation of clusters in word sense clustering with CWEs. Then, we evaluate these features' significance to WSD.

In order to identify these features, we conduct a cluster explainability experiment. First, we perform word sense clustering and cluster the sentences of a word (Section 4.1). As the next step, we aim to determine the sentence context features that are responsible for the formation of the clusters. For this, we try to recreate the clusters using the sentence context information of the sentences alone. We formulate this task as a classification task. We represent each sentence with a set of sentence context features and we assign the sentences to the clusters based on these features using classifiers. These classifiers are trained to predict the cluster labels from the sentence context features of the sentences (referred to as *sentence-feature classifiers*) (Section 4.2).

This gives us the advantage of representing sentences with discrete features, as opposed to contextualized representations which are continuous. This enables us to identify the specific sentence context features that contribute to the classifier performance. For this purpose, we use *recursive feature elimination* and we determine the top 10 features that are most important for the performance of the classifiers. Finally, we qualitatively evaluate the significance of the selected features to WSD (Section 4.3).

4.1 Clustering

As explained in Section 3, we focus on sense groups and each sense group contains several senses of a word. We perform word sense clustering with each sense group, clustering the sentences of senses within each group.

We cluster the sentences using the word's CWEs in these sentences. We extract the CWEs from the English BERT model (*base, cased*)[3] from each layer.[4] In cases where the words are tokenized into subwords, only the first subword's embedding is used.

We use the *K-means* clustering algorithm, selecting k as the number of senses in each group.[5] We evaluate the performance by comparing cluster labels to the sense labels using *Adjusted Rand Index* (ARI). To be able to compare the performance of each lexical ambiguity type, first, we determine the performance for each sense group within a type, then calculate their average and this average represents the performance of each lexical ambiguity type. We compare the performance change across layers and also the performances based on the best-performing layer. We expect homonymy to perform better in word sense clustering based on the

[2]See Appendix B for the list of words and the number of their senses used in this study.

[3]We choose the BERT *cased* model because it encodes more concepts relevant to WSD, such as words' WordNet concepts, compared to the *uncased* model, which encodes more linguistic concepts (Sajjad et al., 2022).

[4]We use the Transformers library (Wolf et al., 2020) for extracting the embeddings.

[5]Sci-kit learn library is used for the implementation (Pedregosa et al., 2011).

findings of the previous studies (Nair et al., 2020; Haber and Poesio, 2021).

4.2 Sentence-Feature Classifiers

We use the resulting clusters from the previous experiments for training and testing the classifiers. We use the last layer's results because this layer performs best in the clustering experiment. For each sense group, we train a classifier for cluster assignment: to predict which cluster a sentence belongs to. We only select the sense groups that have more than 25 sentences in each cluster since this experiment requires data for training. This reduces the number of sense groups we focus on in this experiment. Additionally, even though we do not limit the number of senses in each group, we end up with only two senses per group. See Table 1 for the number of sense groups for each experiment.

Our aim is to predict the cluster that each sentence belongs to based on its sentence context features. First, we represent each sentence with a manually selected sentence context features; bag-of-words, morphological properties of the target word (tense, number, etc.), POS tag of the word's neighbors, the syntactic role of the target word, and the position of the target word in the sentence. We create a sentence feature matrix by binarizing and combining features, resulting in a one-hot representation for each sentence. We select these features to be able to represent the sentences with their context as much as possible. Additionally, we aim to investigate whether the position of the word in the sentence affects the similarity of the representations, considering that positional embeddings are added to the word's representations with the BERT model.[6]

We process the sentences with the spaCy library[7] to automatically extract this information from the sentences. For the morphological properties of the target word, we use the fine-grained POS tag of the word. Similarly, we use the dependency label of the words as their syntactic role.[8] Bag-of-words representations of the sentences are created by first lemmatizing the sentences, also with spaCy.

For each sense group, we use the sentences in all clusters as our training and test data (split by 3:1). We give each cluster a label (0, 1). For each sentence, the input is its sentence feature matrix and the output is the label of its cluster. We use the linear SVM algorithm to train the classifiers because it is ideal in cases where the number of features is larger than the number of samples. Since each sense group contains two senses in this experiment, our task is to do binary classification to assign the correct cluster label.

We evaluate the performance of the classifiers based on lexical ambiguity type. We calculate the average F1 score (as well as precision and recall scores) for all sense groups within a type and consider it as each type's performance. The high performance of the classifiers will be an indication that clusters can be recreated with these features and therefore these features can explain the clusters.

Additionally, we train another type of classifiers: classifiers for WSD. These classifiers are trained similarly to the classifiers for cluster assignment; for each sense group and using sentence features as the input. But this time instead of predicting the cluster labels, the classifiers are tasked to predict the sense labels. We compare the performances of the classifiers trained for cluster assignment and WSD. This way, we aim to understand how helpful these features are for WSD to begin with. If the classifiers for cluster assignment perform better than the classifiers for WSD, this can suggest that the clusters are more distinguishable by the sentence context features than the senses and this is already an indication that clusters are formed by the sentence context features that are insignificant to WSD. Additionally, we expect these classifiers to perform better with homonymy compared to polysemy because sentence context is more helpful for the disambiguation of homonymy.

4.3 Feature Importance

In order to identify the sentence context features that are responsible for the clusters, we need to identify the features that are important for the performance of the classifiers for cluster assignment. For this purpose, we apply *recursive feature elimination* (RFE) on top of the classifiers.[9] RFE functions as a wrapper feature selection algorithm. It assesses the importance of each feature and iteratively removes the least important ones. The model is then re-fitted with the reduced feature set, and this process continues until the desired number of features is achieved.

[6]For detailed information about the size of the data and the feature matrices for each word, see Appendix D.

[7]Available at: `https://spacy.io/`

[8]See Appendix A for the tags used and their desciptions.

[9]Sci-kit learn library is used both for the implementation of RFE and the training of the classifiers.

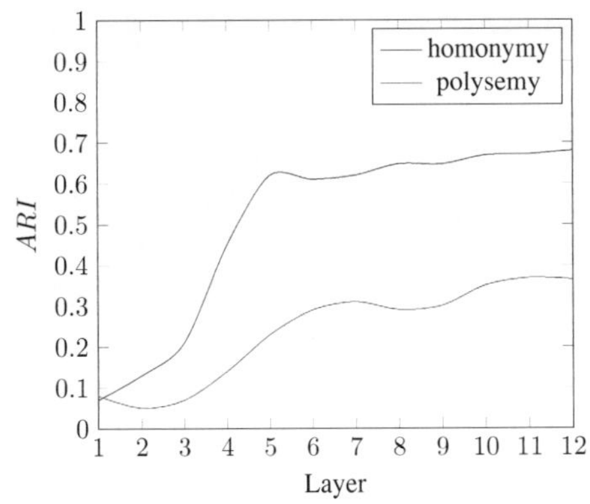

Figure 2: Layer-wise clustering performance with homonymy and polysemy.

We apply RFE to reduce the sentence feature matrix to 10 features. We train the classifiers with RFE using the same training and test datasets as the classifiers trained with the full-sentence feature matrices. By selecting the top 10 features from the sentence feature matrix, we determine which features are important for the correct classification. Then, we evaluate the performance of the classifiers that are trained only with the top 10 features on cluster assignment. Additionally, we train classifiers for cluster assignment with randomly selected 10 features for each sense group in order to establish a baseline. The baseline is determined by averaging the performance of the classifiers across 5 runs for all sense groups. The high performance of the classifiers that are trained with the top 10 features will indicate that these features are responsible for the formation of the clusters.

Finally, we assess the significance of these features to WSD for each word through qualitative evaluation. There are two reasons why we opt for qualitative evaluation. First, there might be coincidental similarities in sentence context within the sentences of one sense that help the clustering process but that are insignificant to WSD. For example, a verb's most past tense occurrences might coincidentally overlap with one sense, and generalizing over this pattern can help the WSD process. However, relying on these patterns is less than ideal. In such cases, performance-based evaluation cannot effectively capture the significance of these features because they might artificially boost performance. Our primary aim is to uncover these features. The second reason is the limited data size. Qualitative evaluation allows for a deeper understanding, even in situations where the data is limited.

5 Results

5.1 Clustering

As shown in Figure 2, the clustering performance improves across the layers, with the highest performance observed in the final layer for both types. Word sense clustering performs better with homonymy than polysemy. In the last layer, ARI score is 0.68 for homonymy and 0.36 for polysemy, as shown in Table 1. Regarding the layer-wise performance of the clustering, the pattern for homonymy and polysemy is different. There is a significant performance improvement observed between the 3rd and 5th layers for homonymy. However, there isn't that steep gain in performance for polysemy overall. This suggests that homonymous senses are mostly disambiguated early in the model layers. Overall, these results are in line with our expectations; the performance with homonymy is higher than with polysemy.

5.2 Sentence-Feature Classifiers

The classifiers for WSD achieve an F1 score of 0.80 for homonymy and 0.72 for polysemy. This difference supports our hypothesis; sentence context features are more useful for the disambiguation of homonymy than polysemy. Regarding the classifiers for cluster assignment, there are also performance differences for each lexical ambiguity type. The performance is better with homonymy (0.87) than with polysemy (0.78). Overall, they achieve an F1 score of 0.82.

The classifiers for cluster assignment show better performance compared to the classifiers for WSD, with an overall increase of 0.06 point. There is an increase for both homonymy (0.07) and polysemy (0.05). This increase suggests that the sentence context features are more prominent in the clusters than the original sense sentences and the clusters are more easily distinguishable by their features compared to the senses. Finally, the overall high performance of the classifiers for cluster assignment suggests that the selected sentence context features are a good starting point for feature selection. The results of the classifier performances can be seen in Table 1.

5.3 Feature Importance

Top 10-Feature Classifiers for Cluster Assignment. The classifiers trained with the top 10 features for cluster assignment achieve good performance with an overall F1 score of 0.85, surpassing

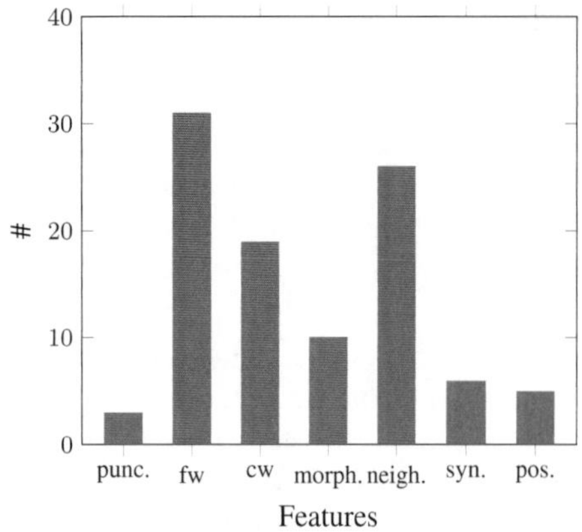

Figure 3: Count of each feature category. The categories are punctuation marks, function words (*fw*), content words (*cw*), neighboring words, the position of the target words in the sentences, and morphological properties and syntactic roles of the target words.

the random baseline (F1: 0.39) by a large margin (see Table 1). This indicates that: *the selected top 10 features are able to recreate the clusters to a great extent.*

Evaluation of the Selected Features. We group the top 10 features selected for all sense groups by their similarities and 6 categories are formed. These categories are punctuation marks, function words, content words, POS tags of neighboring words, morphological properties of the target words, syntactic roles of the target words, and positions of the target words in the sentences. Their counts can be seen in Figure 3.[10]

Punctuation marks ('-', ';', etc.), function words ('if', 'not', etc.), and content words ('river', 'bed', etc.) are the items that are found in the bag-of-words representations of the sentences and are selected as important features. This means that the fact that there are certain items in the sentence determines the decision of the classifiers.

Furthermore, morphological properties of the target word, e.g. whether the verb is in past tense or not, and the syntactic role of the target word, e.g. whether the noun is the direct object of the sentence or not, determine the decision of the classifiers. Similarly, the POS tags of neighboring words also is a determining feature. For example, whether a verb is followed by an adverb or not or whether a verb is followed by a punctuation or not. Finally, the position of the target word is also a determining feature. However, only the 6th, 7th, 8th, 9th and 10th positions are found to be important.

First, without looking at the details, it is apparent that certain feature categories lack significance or have little significance to WSD. These categories include punctuation marks, the position of the target word in the sentence, the syntactic role and the morphological properties of the target words. On the other hand, features such as POS tags of the neighboring words, and the existence of some content words in the sentence can carry more significance. For example, whether a verb is followed by a preposition or not can be a good indicator of a sense. Similarly, the presence of a word in the sentence can signal one sense, as previously shown in (1) for 'bank'.

Yet, a closer examination reveals even more striking results. *In most cases, the important features are insignificant to WSD*, except for a few words and this explains the poor clustering performance. The main issue is that most of the time, *a particular insignificant feature is found in both sense sentences and causes these sentences to cluster together.* The features from all categories affect the performance like this. For example, sentences of different senses of a verb are clustered together because, in all of them, the verb is in the past tense, as illustrated in example (3) with two senses of the verb 'indicate'.

(3) a. *be a signal for or a symptom of:*
"The statistics hardly **indicated** that..."
b. *to state or express briefly:*
"He **indicated** that requests would..."

Other times, *one feature that is not significant to WSD is found only in the sentences of one sense coincidentally and causes these sentences to cluster together.* While this might affect the performance positively, it does so for reasons that are not ideal. This finding aligns with our expectations. For example, the word 'other' is selected as an important feature for the clusters of 'time'. This feature is not significant to the WSD of this word and it is even not found in direct syntactic relation with the target word in the sentences as in example (4).

(4) The debris of his **other** careers was piled everywhere; a pile of wire cages for mice from his **time** as a geneticist and a microscope lying on its side on the window sill...

Finally, we do not observe specific patterns for dif-

[10]A detailed list can be seen in Appendix C.

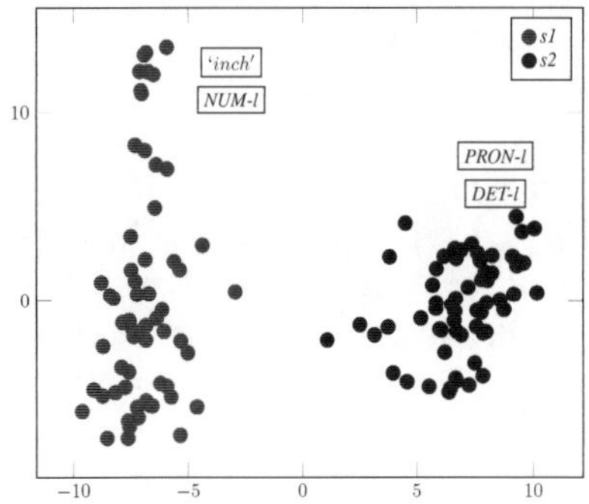

Figure 4: PCA visualization of the embeddings of 'foot' in different sense sentences and important features found in each sentence cluster of the word. The embeddings are extracted from the last layer of the BERT model. The features are 'inch', *NUM-l* (the left neighbor is a numeral), *PRON-l* (the left neighbor is a pronoun) and *DET-l* (the left neighbor is a determiner).

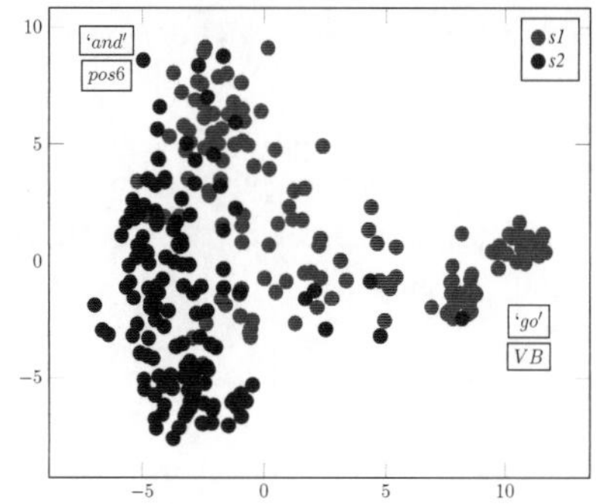

Figure 5: PCA visualization of the embeddings of 'ask' in different sense sentences and important features found in each sentence cluster of the word. The embeddings are extracted from the last layer of the BERT model. The features are 'go', 'and', *VB* (the verb is in base form), and *pos6* (the word is the 6th token in the sentence).

ferent lexical ambiguity types, however, in general, we observe that for some words, there are more clear clues in the sentence context that are helpful for disambiguation.

An Example: 'ask' vs. 'foot'. 'ask' in its first sense means "to request something" as in (5-a) and in its second sense means literally "to ask a question" and in this sense, it is also frequently used with direct speech as in (5-b). 'foot' in its first sense is the *body part* and in its second sense, it is the *measuring unit*, as illustrated in (6).

(5) 'ask':

a. *to request something:* "He **asked** her for recommendation."

b. *to ask a question:* "Don't **ask** a question.", "'Who said that?' he **asked**."

(6) 'foot':

a. *body part:* "He hit his **feet**."

b. *measuring unit:* "She is five **feet** tall."

Even though both of these words are homonymous, there are performance differences between them.[11] Word sense clustering achieves perfect performance with 'foot' (1.0) and bad performance with 'ask' (0.16). However, the sentence-feature classifiers for cluster assignment perform well with both words ('ask': 0.77, 'foot': 1). Looking at the classifier performance, we can conclude that the clusters of both words are distinguishable based on their sentence context features. However, looking at the word sense clustering performance, we can understand that these features are not equally significant to WSD for both words; they are significant in the case of 'foot', but not 'ask'.

The clusters of 'foot' represent each sense well as shown in Figure 4, and features for each cluster are also related to different senses of 'foot'. For the cluster related to the 'measuring unit' sense, the features 'inch', and *NUM-l* (the left neighbor is a numeral, as in "5 feet") are selected as important features. Whereas, for the cluster related to the 'body part' sense, the features *PRON-l* (the left neighbor is a pronoun, as in "his feet"), and the feature *DET-l* (the left neighbor is a determiner, as in "the feet") are selected. These features are indeed good indicators of these senses.

On the other hand, we do not see nicely formed clusters for 'ask' (see Figure 5) and we see that the similarity of the representations is driven by the features that are not significant to WSD. For example, all sentences in which the verb is in base form (*VB*) or the word is the 6th token (*pos6*) or the sentences that have the words 'go' or 'and' are clustered together.

Two senses of 'ask' occur in different sentence structures: the first sense occurs with prepositional objects, as in (5-a), and the second sense with direct speech as in (5-b). It is interesting to see that these distinctions are not captured by the clusters and these features do not determine the similarity of the representations. We also see that the sentence-feature classifier for WSD performs better (0.81) than the sentence-feature classifier for cluster as-

[11] See Appendix D for a performance comparison of all words in the last experiment.

signment (0.77) with 'ask'. This contrasts with the general pattern. This might indicate that the senses are actually distinguishable by their sentence context features, however, not these features but insignificant features are responsible for the formation of the clusters.

6 Discussion

In order to identify the sentence context features that are responsible for the similarity of the contextualized representations, we conducted a cluster explainability study and identified the sentence context features that lead to the formation of the clusters in word sense clustering with CWEs. Our results have shown that features from different categories determine the similarity of the representations; function words, punctuation marks, content words in the sentences, position of the target word in the sentence, neighboring words, morphological properties and the syntactic role of the target word. Our results are in line with Sajjad et al. (2022) who have shown that the CWEs encode both grammatical and semantic properties of the words and the clusters of CWEs reveal these similarities.

Furthermore, we qualitatively evaluated the identified features for each word and have shown that they are mostly insignificant to WSD. We observed that even when different senses of a word occur in diverse contexts and the sentence context provides clear clues for different senses (as in the case with 'ask'), the significant features do not determine the similarity of the representations in most cases. This contradicts our expectations. When the sentence context provides clear clues for different senses, e.g. in the case of homonymy, we expected the similarity of contextualized representations to be determined by these clues. However, this is not the case and there are other features in the sentences that are insignificant to WSD, that affect the similarity of the representations more.

Our analysis also has revealed that insignificant features affect the clustering performance negatively in several ways. Most commonly, some insignificant features occur in the sentences of both word senses and they lead these sentences to cluster together. This explains the poor clustering performance reported previously (Yenicelik et al., 2020) and also in this study. Additionally, in some cases, certain insignificant features occur only in the sentences of one sense by chance and they lead to the formation of clusters. Although these cases don't affect the performance negatively, this shows how the randomness in the data can affect the clustering performance.

In relation to the performance with different lexical ambiguity types, the findings of our study are in line with previous studies (Nair et al., 2020; Haber and Poesio, 2021; Sevastjanova et al., 2021). Clustering performs better with homonymy than polysemy. In addition to previous studies, our results have shown that homonyms are more distinguishable by sentence context features than polysemes and their disambiguation can be more easily achieved with a simple classifier trained with these features. However, contextualized representations' similarity is not consistently determined by the sense-significant features even for homonyms.

7 Conclusion

The information encoded in contextualized representations which determines their similarity is not significant to WSD in most cases. This shows that these representations do not capture the different meanings of words as expected, explaining why using CWEs of pre-trained language models alone does not yield sufficient performance in unsupervised WSD. In the future, we plan to explore possible strategies to create contextualized representations that are more suitable to WSD by limiting the information that is insignificant to WSD encoded in the representations. This way, we aim to enhance unsupervised WSD performance.

8 Acknowledgement

This study is funded by the project "Coercion and Copredication as Flexible Frame Composition" funded by DFG (Deutsche Forschungsgemeinschaft). We would like to thank the anonymous reviewer for their valuable comments. Lastly, special thanks to David Arps for interesting and stimulating discussions.

References

Jacob Devlin, Ming-Wei Chang, Kenton Lee, and Kristina Toutanova. 2019. BERT: Pre-training of deep bidirectional transformers for language understanding. In *Proceedings of the 2019 Conference of the North American Chapter of the Association for Computational Linguistics: Human Language Technologies, Volume 1 (Long and Short Papers)*, pages 4171–4186, Minneapolis, Minnesota. Association for Computational Linguistics.

Kawin Ethayarajh. 2019. How contextual are contextualized word representations? Comparing the geometry of BERT, ELMo, and GPT-2 embeddings. In *Proceedings of the 2019 Conference on Empirical Methods in Natural Language Processing and the 9th International Joint Conference on Natural Language Processing (EMNLP-IJCNLP)*, pages 55–65, Hong Kong, China. Association for Computational Linguistics.

Christiane Fellbaum. 2010. Wordnet. In *Theory and applications of ontology: computer applications*, pages 231–243. Springer.

Marcos Garcia. 2021. Exploring the representation of word meanings in context: A case study on homonymy and synonymy. In *Proceedings of the 59th Annual Meeting of the Association for Computational Linguistics and the 11th International Joint Conference on Natural Language Processing (Volume 1: Long Papers)*, pages 3625–3640, Online. Association for Computational Linguistics.

Luke Gessler and Nathan Schneider. 2021. BERT has uncommon sense: Similarity ranking for word sense BERTology. In *Proceedings of the Fourth BlackboxNLP Workshop on Analyzing and Interpreting Neural Networks for NLP*, pages 539–547, Punta Cana, Dominican Republic. Association for Computational Linguistics.

Janosch Haber and Massimo Poesio. 2021. Patterns of polysemy and homonymy in contextualised language models. In *Findings of the Association for Computational Linguistics: EMNLP 2021*, pages 2663–2676, Punta Cana, Dominican Republic. Association for Computational Linguistics.

Ekaterini Klepousniotou. 2002. The processing of lexical ambiguity: Homonymy and polysemy in the mental lexicon. *Brain and Language*, 81(1):205–223.

Ekaterini Klepousniotou and Shari R. Baum. 2007. Disambiguating the ambiguity advantage effect in word recognition: An advantage for polysemous but not homonymous words. *Journal of Neurolinguistics*, 20(1):1–24.

Ekaterini Klepousniotou, G. Bruce Pike, Karsten Steinhauer, and Vincent Gracco. 2012. Not all ambiguous words are created equal: An eeg investigation of homonymy and polysemy. *Brain and Language*, 123(1):11–21.

Ekaterini Klepousniotou, Debra Titone, and Carolina Romero. 2008. Making sense of word senses: the comprehension of polysemy depends on sense overlap. *Journal of Experimental Psychology: Learning, Memory, and Cognition*, 34(6):1534.

Mitchell P. Marcus, Beatrice Santorini, and Mary Ann Marcinkiewicz. 1993. Building a large annotated corpus of English: The Penn Treebank. *Computational Linguistics*, 19(2):313–330.

Timothee Mickus, Denis Paperno, Mathieu Constant, and Kees van Deemter. 2020. What do you mean, BERT? In *Proceedings of the Society for Computation in Linguistics 2020*, pages 279–290, New York, New York. Association for Computational Linguistics.

George A. Miller, Claudia Leacock, Randee Tengi, and Ross T. Bunker. 1993. A semantic concordance. In *Human Language Technology: Proceedings of a Workshop Held at Plainsboro, New Jersey, March 21-24, 1993.*

Sathvik Nair, Mahesh Srinivasan, and Stephan Meylan. 2020. Contextualized word embeddings encode aspects of human-like word sense knowledge. In *Proceedings of the Workshop on the Cognitive Aspects of the Lexicon*, pages 129–141, Online. Association for Computational Linguistics.

Joakim Nivre, Marie-Catherine de Marneffe, Filip Ginter, Yoav Goldberg, Jan Hajič, Christopher D. Manning, Ryan McDonald, Slav Petrov, Sampo Pyysalo, Natalia Silveira, Reut Tsarfaty, and Daniel Zeman. 2016. Universal Dependencies v1: A multilingual treebank collection. In *Proceedings of the Tenth International Conference on Language Resources and Evaluation (LREC'16)*, pages 1659–1666, Portorož, Slovenia. European Language Resources Association (ELRA).

Fabian Pedregosa, Gaël Varoquaux, Alexandre Gramfort, Vincent Michel, Bertrand Thirion, Olivier Grisel, Mathieu Blondel, Peter Prettenhofer, Ron Weiss, Vincent Dubourg, Jake Vanderplas, Alexandre Passos, David Cournapeau, Matthieu Brucher, Matthieu Perrot, and Édouard Duchesnay. 2011. Scikit-learn: Machine learning in python. *Journal of Machine Learning Research*, 12(85):2825–2830.

Hassan Sajjad, Nadir Durrani, Fahim Dalvi, Firoj Alam, Abdul Khan, and Jia Xu. 2022. Analyzing encoded concepts in transformer language models. In *Proceedings of the 2022 Conference of the North American Chapter of the Association for Computational Linguistics: Human Language Technologies*, pages 3082–3101, Seattle, United States. Association for Computational Linguistics.

Rita Sevastjanova, Aikaterini-Lida Kalouli, Christin Beck, Hanna Schäfer, and Mennatallah El-Assady. 2021. Explaining contextualization in language models using visual analytics. In *Proceedings of the 59th Annual Meeting of the Association for Computational Linguistics and the 11th International Joint Conference on Natural Language Processing (Volume 1: Long Papers)*, pages 464–476, Online. Association for Computational Linguistics.

Thomas Wolf, Lysandre Debut, Victor Sanh, Julien Chaumond, Clement Delangue, Anthony Moi, Pierric Cistac, Tim Rault, Remi Louf, Morgan Funtowicz, Joe Davison, Sam Shleifer, Patrick von Platen, Clara Ma, Yacine Jernite, Julien Plu, Canwen Xu, Teven Le Scao, Sylvain Gugger, Mariama Drame,

Quentin Lhoest, and Alexander Rush. 2020. Transformers: State-of-the-art natural language processing. In *Proceedings of the 2020 Conference on Empirical Methods in Natural Language Processing: System Demonstrations*, pages 38–45, Online. Association for Computational Linguistics.

David Yenicelik, Florian Schmidt, and Yannic Kilcher. 2020. How does BERT capture semantics? a closer look at polysemous words. In *Proceedings of the Third BlackboxNLP Workshop on Analyzing and Interpreting Neural Networks for NLP*, pages 156–162, Online. Association for Computational Linguistics.

Tag	Description
nsubj	nominal subject
pobj	object of a preposition
attr	attribution
xcomp	open clausal complement
npadvmod	noun phrase as adverbial modifier

Table 2: Dependency labels used in this study, from spaCy model *en_core_web_trf*.

Tag	Description
NN	Noun, singular or mass
NNS	Noun, plural
VBD	Verb, past tense
VBP	Verb, non-3rd person singular present
VBZ	Verb, 3rd person singular present
VB	Verb, base form

Table 3: Fine-grained POS tags used in this study, from Penn Tree Bank (Marcus et al., 1993).

Tag	Description
ADP	adposition
PUNCT	punctuation
PART	particle
SCONJ	subordinating conjunction
PRON	pronoun
DET	determiner
ADV	adverb
NUM	numeral

Table 4: POS tags used in this study, from Universal Dependencies (Nivre et al., 2016).

A Feature Tags

The feature tags for the morphological properties of the words, the syntactic role of the words, and the POS tags of neighboring words that are used in this study can be found in Table 2, 3, 4. For the morphological properties of the words, we use their fine-grained POS tag (Table 3). For the syntactic role of the words, we use their dependency label (Table 2). All the labels are obtained by processing the sentences with spaCy.

ask: 1	heart: 2	**life: 5**
begin: 3	produce: 2	point: 5
degree: 3	put: 3	raise: 3
drive: 3	table: 2	**time: 2**
foot: 2	right: 2	**way: 4**
heart: 2	case: 3	**world: 4**
indicate: 2	consider: 4	plane: 2
light: 3	cover: 2	lead: 7
man: 3	**door: 2**	

Table 5: The words that are found in our dataset with their sense counts. All the words are used in the word sense clustering and the bold words are used in the cluster explainability experiment.

B Selected Words

A list of the words that are found in our dataset can be seen in Table 5. All the words and senses are used in the word sense clustering experiment. Only 10 words and 2 sense each are used in the cluster explainability experiment.

C Selected Features List

A detailed list of selected features from each category can be seen in Table 6.

D Performance with Individual Words

The individual performance of each word can be seen in Table 7. Only the performances of the words that are used in the last experiment are reported. Both clustering performance and the performance of the sentence-feature classifiers are reported. The data size (number of sentences) of each word can be also seen in Table 7.

Feature Category	Features
Neighbouring Word (right)	ADP: 3, PUNCT: 2, PART: 2, SCONJ: 1, PRON: 1, DET: 1, ADV: 1
Neighbouring Word (left)	DET: 4, PART: 2, PRON: 2, NUM: 2, ADP: 2, ADJ: 2, PUNCT: 1
Punctuation	'.': 2, '-': 1,
Function Word	'and': 1, 'after': 1, 'can': 1, 'she': 1, 'might': 1, 'the': 3, 'to': 2, 'when': 1, 'my': 1, 'on': 1, 'through': 1, 'no': 1, 'with': 1, 'just': 1, 'a': 1, 'by': 1, 'however': 1, 'in': 1, 'or': 1, ''s': 1, 'each': 2, 'which': 1, 'her': 1 'other': 1, 'their': 1, 'once': 1, 'such': 1
Content Word	'mean': 1, 'nothing': 1, 'high': 1, 'outside': 1, 'see': 1, 'first': 1, 'route': 1, 'Spencer': 1, 'new': 1, 'plan': 1, 'event': 1, 'God': 1, 'three': 1, 'hand': 1, 'go': 1, 'take': 1, 'inch': 1, 'age': 1, 'feel': 1
Syntactic Role	nsubj: 2, pobj: 1, xcomp: 1, attr: 1, npadvmod: 1
Morphological Properties	NNS: 3, VBD: 2, NN: 2, VBP:1, VBZ: 1, VB: 1
Word Position	6th: 1, 7th: 1, 8th: 1, 9th: 1, 10th: 1

Table 6: Selected important features in each category and their counts. POS tags of the word's neighbors are given for neighboring words, the dependency label of the word is given for the syntactic role, and the fine-grained POS tag is given for the word's morphological properties. See Appendix A for the descriptions of the tags used.

Word	Data#	Clustering Performance	Feature#	Sentence-Feature Classifiers								
				WSD			*Cluster*			*10-Cluster*		
				F1	P	R	F1	P	R	F1	P	R
Homonymy												
ask	278	0.16	1668	**0.81**	0.82	0.81	0.77	0.77	0.77	0.77	0.77	0.77
begin	90	0.34	1007	0.87	0.87	0.87	**0.91**	0.93	0.92	0.80	0.80	0.80
foot	119	1	1008	**1**	**1**	**1**	**1**	**1**	**1**	**1**	**1**	**1**
indicate	70	0.12	809	0.62	0.62	0.62	**0.85**	0.86	0.85	**0.85**	0.89	0.85
man	92	0.54	932	0.71	0.71	0.70	0.82	0.83	0.82	**0.85**	0.86	0.85
Polysemy												
life	74	0.34	775	0.59	0.60	0.60	0.81	0.83	0.81	**0.86**	0.86	0.86
man	54	0.16	690	0.66	0.81	0.68	0.84	0.84	0.84	**0.94**	0.95	0.94
time	56	0.69	762	0.71	0.76	0.71	0.84	0.84	0.84	**0.94**	0.95	0.94
way	110	0.55	1179	0.81	0.81	0.81	**0.86**	0.86	0.86	0.73	0.74	0.73
world	56	0.35	692	**0.84**	0.84	0.84	0.53	0.66	0.55	0.83	0.88	0.83

Table 7: Data size and performance details of individual words. *Data#* refers to the number of sentences. Clustering performance is evaluated using ARI. *Feature#* is the size of the sentence feature matrix. *WSD* refers to the classifiers trained for WSD, *Cluster* for cluster assignment. *10-Cluster* classifiers refer to the classifiers trained for cluster assignment with only the top 10 features. *F1*, *Precision* and *Recall* scores are given for each classifier. The best F1 score for each word is given in bold.

Below the Sea (with the Sharks): Probing Textual Features of Implicit Sentiment in a Literary Case-study

Yuri Bizzoni[†]
Center for Humanities Computing
Aarhus University, Denmark
yuri.bizzoni@cc.au.dk

Pascale Feldkamp[†]
Center for Humanities Computing
Aarhus University, Denmark
pascale.moreira@cc.au.dk

Abstract

Literary language presents an ongoing challenge for Sentiment Analysis (SA) due to its complex, nuanced, and layered form of expression. It is often suggested that effective literary writing is evocative, operates beneath the surface and understates emotional expression. To explore features of implicitness in literary expression, this study takes Ernest Hemingway's *The Old Man and the Sea* as a case-study, focusing specifically at implicit sentiment expression in this text. We examine sentences where automatic sentiment scoring shows substantial divergences from human sentiment annotation, and probe these sentences for distinctive traits. We find that sentences where humans perceived a strong sentiment while models did not are significantly lower in arousal and higher in concreteness than sentences where humans and models were more aligned, suggesting the importance of simplicity and concreteness for implicit sentiment expression in literary prose.

1 Introduction

The concept of "implicit" expression is particularly relevant and complex in literary writing. Several theories of literary writing point to the importance of avoiding to present concepts or ideas in an explicit way. For example, the widely known precept of "Show Don't Tell" points at least partly in this direction. As is also made clear by Booth (1983), the distinction between types of narration (showing vs. telling) is not always adequate, though critics often rely on terms like emotional "evocativeness" and "understatement" to describe writing styles (Strychacz, 2002; Daoshan and Shuo, 2014). It is far from clear whether implicit, evocative and expressive strategies can be reliably tracked in text and whether more implicit types of narration display linguistically recognizable marks.

In this study, we use *The Old Man and the Sea*, often considered the exemplary masterpiece of Ernest Hemingway, as a case study for exploring such implicitness.[1] Hemingway's writing style is known for its emotional subtlety and is characterized (also by Hemingway himself) by its "iceberg" (Hemingway, 1996), or "omissive" technique, where: "the emotion is plentiful, though hidden and not exposed" (Daoshan and Shuo, 2014). Moreover, Hemingway's style is direct and limited in use of figurative language (Heaton, 1970). It thus avoids "overt emotional display", presenting actions and situations that *imply* emotions, and leave their inference up to the reader (Strychacz, 2002). As such, it may be that Hemingway's "omissive" writing can be tracked by looking at the amount and intensity of emotion expressions detectable in the text itself, comparing this to how "expressive" the text is perceived by readers.

2 Related works

Literary language may convey emotions in a variety of ways beyond simply using words directly associated with emotional states (e.g., "happy").In the case of Hemingway, the apparent aversion to "emotional display and rhetorical overflow" in his prose has been linked to the Modernists' and New Critics' emphasis on *concreteness* over abstraction (Strychacz, 2002). A key example of this perspective is Brooks and Warren (1976)'s seminal description of poetry as "incorrigibly particular and concrete – not general and abstract". The connection of concreteness to emotional expression is continually formalized in modern literary theory, also with regard to prose, where the most prominent concept is probably that of the *objective correlative* of T.S. Eliot. Eliot defined it as "a set of objects, a situation, a chain of events which shall be the formula of [a] particular emotion" (Eliot, 1948),

[†] The authors contributed equally to this work.

[1] The annotated text is available at: https://github.com/PascaleFMoreira/Annotated_Hemingway

Proceedings of the Third Workshop on Understanding Implicit and Underspecified Language, pages 54–61
March 21, 2024

suggesting a focus on concrete objects and actions over explicit emotion expression as the effective method for communicating emotion in literature. In support of this idea, Auracher and Bosch (2016) indicate that the concreteness of literary language impacts the emotional engagement of readers and their experiences of literary suspense.

We concentrate our study on implicitness in the expression and readers' experience of sentiments in *The Old Man and the Sea*. Sentiment Analysis (SA) has become an increasingly central method for computational literary studies research (Rebora, 2023), often used as a tool to gauge the sentiment arcs of novels (i.e., the consecutive highs and lows of sentiment throughout a narrative)(Jockers, 2014; Reagan et al., 2016) also in connection with assessing reader appreciation (Bizzoni et al., 2023). While divergences between human and model SA scores generally indicate shortcomings in SA methods, we suggest that such divergences may also be informative – both for model improvement and for gaining a deeper understanding of sentiment expression in literary texts – if we test whether certain textual features characterize such instances. First, we seek to find sentences where human sentiment annotation diverges from model scores, the latter of which may not capture implicit or omissive sentiment as well (Zhou et al., 2021; Li et al., 2021). Then, we test whether these sentences of implicit sentiment expression can be told apart from other by certain features, the choice of which are informed by the mentioned literary theory and descriptions of implicitness in Hemingway's style: the mean valence,[2] arousal,[3] and dominance,[4] as well as their mean concreteness.[5]

3 Method

In this preliminary analysis of implicit or omissive writing, we focus on the sentiments in *The Old Man and the Sea*. As noted, the style of the novel is simple and direct. While the feelings of the characters are sometimes stated, their experiences and states of mind are often left to the reader to interpret from similes and object descriptions. For example, the protagonist is introduced as a fisherman who hasn't caught a fish in a long time. Instead of mentioning his feelings, the narrator describes his scars: "`They were as old as erosions in a fishless desert`". This simile can be seen as a case of implicit sentiment as it arguably evokes a sense of despair for the lack of success but without any explicit sentiment expression. The reference to the pain and the fear of the characters is also often powerfully implied without any direct mention: "`'Ay', he said aloud. There is no translation for this word and perhaps it is just a noise such as a man might make, involuntarily, feeling the nail go through his hands and into the wood`". These descriptions, full of concrete objects such as the nail going through the hand, may be seen as a prime example of Eliot's *objective correlative*, where a "set of objects" is set in place to evoke emotion in the reader. Furthermore, when the protagonist is challenged in his final reckoning with the sharks, his fear and tension are rarely stated, but implied in the description of the sharks themselves.

While such passages may appear powerful for the human reader, it is likely that standard SA models would miss their sentimental charge. Words such as "nail" and "hand" gain emotional charge only in the certain composition that Hemingway creates, but will not appear emotionally charged when observed as isolated words. To create a subset of such sentences that appear powerful to human readers but may not be so for automatic annotation systems, we used the distance between SA models' and humans' annotations of sentences. We thus operationalized "implicit sentiment" as those cases in which human readers perceived sentimental charge (whether positive or negative), but where models did not, selecting all such sentences. We proceeded by the following steps:

3.1 Annotation, scoring and selection

1) Two independent human annotators scored each sentence of the novel on a 1-10 sentiment scale. The annotators were instructed to avoid rating how a sentence made them feel but assess the valence of each sentence, without overthinking the story's narrative, reducing – as far as possible – contextual interpretation. We thereafter assigned each sentence of the novel the mean annotator score for each sentence.[6] Both annotators had extensive experience of literary analysis, and hold degrees in

[2]The degree of positiveness or negativeness (/pleasure or displeasure) (Mohammad, 2018).

[3]The degree to which a word prepares for action, captures or focuses attention (Borelli et al., 2018).

[4]The degree of control evoked (Warriner et al., 2013).

[5]The degree to which a word denotes a perceptible entity (Brysbaert et al., 2014).

[6]The Spearman correlation between annotators is 0.65.

literature.[7] Annotators worked independently, not discussing nor changing their scores.

2) There are a variety of SA methods from machine learning to dictionary-based approaches, each displaying advantages and shortcomings (Öhman, 2021). (Reagan et al., 2017). More recent Transformer-based approaches have shown both potential and pitfalls in SA for literary texts (Elkins, 2022), so that an ensemble of models has been suggested (Elkins, 2022). We used several SA models, transformer- and dictionary-based, to score the same book for valence. Our chosen models for annotation on a sentence-base were:
(i) The **VADER dictionary** (Hutto and Gilbert, 2014), arguably the most widespread dictionary-based method for SA.
(ii) The **Syuzhet dictionary** (Jockers, 2014), extracted from 165,000 human coded sentences of contemporary literary novels.[8]
(iii) **roBERTa base**, fine-tuned for SA on tweets (Barbieri et al., 2020).[9]

3) Excluding mid-valued sentences, we selected all the sentences that the human annotators scored as having some sentimental charge (all sentences scoring lower than 5 or higher than 6). Since the human readers did detect some sentiment in these sentences, they are candidates for implicit sentiment expression. This subset accounted for less than half of the sentences of the novel: a total of 835 out of 1923 sentences.

4) Of this subset, we selected only those sentences that did *not* elicit a strong sentiment score from the SA models: we only kept sentences which normalized absolute score was smaller than 0.1 in *all three models*. In short, we selected all sentences that appeared sentiment charged to humans, while being scored as neutral or almost neutral by all three SA systems. This left us with 101 sentences in what we call the "implicit" group (Fig. 1).

5) For comparison, we selected sentences where human and models were more aligned in their sentiment scoring, what we call the "explicit" group (Fig. 1). These are sentences where both humans and models found either a positive or a negative sentiment (above an absolute 0.1), and agree on the sentiment direction (positive/negative).

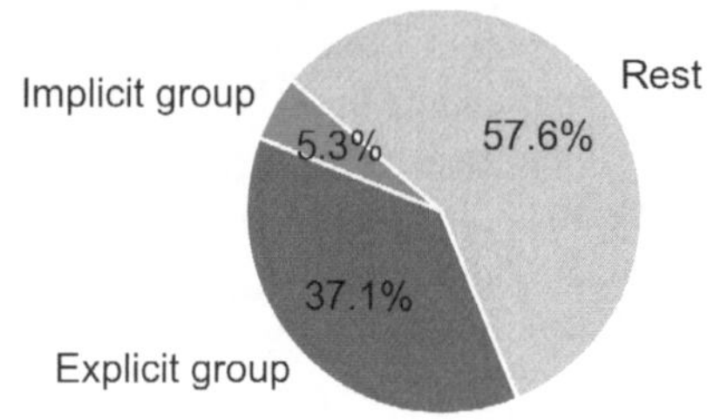

Figure 1: Division of sentences of *The Old Man and the Sea* into groups of: 101 sentences where human and model sentiment scoring diverged significantly, and 714 sentences where it converged.

We then compared the "implicit" group of sentences to the where SA models were neutral but humans were not, to the set of sentences where model and human score were more aligned. We compared the groups in terms of the selected features: valence, arousal, dominance,[10] and concreteness.[11] Finally, we used a Mann-Whitney U test to examine differences between the groups (to further validate our results, we performed additional tests; see the Appendix for an overview of these results).

4 Results

Our selected group of 101 sentences represent a divergence between human and text-based SA systems: humans found them to express some form of sentiment not detected by the three SA models. Notably, the average absolute human score of the "implicit" group was slightly higher (0.23) than the average score of the "explicit" group (0.22). For example, the sentence "`The other watched the old man with his slitted yellow eyes and then came in fast with his half circle of jaws wide to hit the fish where he had already been bitten`" is perceived as negative

[7] Both were academics, male and female, at ages 31 and 34, who were non-native but very proficient English speakers, and who finished a literature degree more than 2 years ago.

[8] Developed by Matthew L. Jockers in the Nebraska Literary Lab (Jockers, 2015).

[9] Note that we converted the categorical Transformer output is to continuous SA scores by using the confidence score of roBERTA's labels as a proxy for sentiment intensity. If the model classifies a sentences as *positive* with a confidence of, for example, 0.89, we interpret it as a valence score of +0.89 for this sentence, and so on. Note that we converted scores of the *neutral* category to 0.0. This procedure of translating SA Transformer output to a continuous scale is detailed in Bizzoni and Feldkamp (2023).

[10] We used the VAD lexicon (Mohammad, 2018) to retrieve the valence, arousal and dominance scores for each word, averaging scores over each sentence: `https://saifmohammad.com/WebPages/nrc-vad.html`

[11] To retrieve concreteness scores of words and lemmatized sentences individually, we used the concreteness lexicon by Brysbaert et al. (2014): `http://crr.ugent.be/archives/1330`

		Valence	Dominance	Arousal	Concreteness
Word-based	Implicit	0.581 ±0.163	0.476 ±0.152	0.379 ±0.155	2.759 ±1.174
	Explicit	0.559 ±0.230	0.482 ±0.170	0.433 ±0.189	2.677 ±1.146
	MWU test	724.263	696.247	582.587*	6196.182*
Sentence-based	Implicit	0.596 ±0.109	0.495 ±0.118	0.401 ±0.106	2.732 ±0.37
	Explicit	0.572 ±0.164	0.494 ±0.110	0.446 ±0.110	2.649 ±0.328
	MWU test	39.308	36.558	25.146*	45.660*

Table 1: Mean and st.d. feature values of the implicit and explicit groups, where features are computed, respectively, on a **word** basis (rows above) and on a **sentence** basis (rows below), as well as the results of the MWU test between the groups in each setup. In the implicit group: sentences perceived non-neutral by humans but neutral by models (below an absolute score of .1); in the explicit group: sentences where human and models were more aligned. * p-value < 0.05.

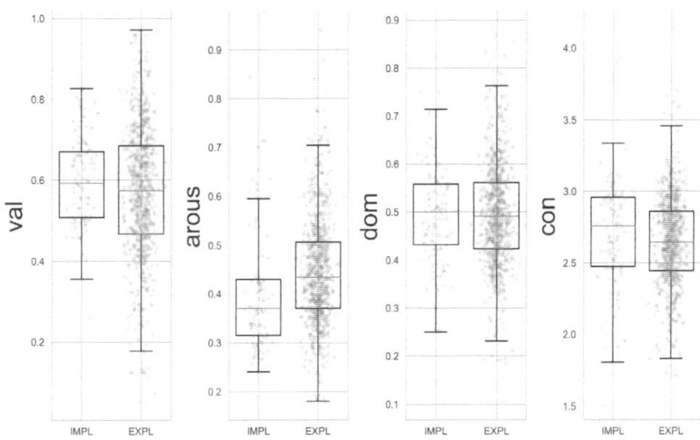

Figure 2: Boxplots comparing implicit (n=101) and explicit (n=714) groups of sentences by scores of each of the four features.

by human annotators, but does not contain any of the explicit expressions of negative emotion that text-based SA models usually pick up on.

We tokenized all the sentences using WordNet's lemmatizer. For each sentence lemmatized, we computed the average Valence, Arousal and Dominance using the NRC-VAD-Lexicon. These measures attempt to position a word in a three-dimensional sentiment space, detailing different aspects of a word's affective semantics. For example, *lion* is higher than *shark* in valence and dominance, but lower in arousal. For concreteness, we used Brysbaert et al. (2014)'s lexicon of English lemmas. This resource complements the elements modelled by the NRC Lexicon, as it attempts to quantify the concreteness of each word independently from its affective aspect, even if it has been suggested that abstract words are connected to a stronger valence than concrete words (Kousta et al., 2011). These dimensions of lexical semantics can appear quite uncorrelated, but their interplay appears evident when looking at many of the "implicit sentiment" sentences from the novel, like the one cited above. We then compared the average valence, arousal, dominance, and concreteness of the words used in the sentences perceived by at least one SA model as having an absolute sentimental intensity stronger than .1 (714 sentences) with those of the words used in the sentences that only humans perceived as sentimentally charged (101 sentences). Using the Mann Whitney U test, we computed which of the differences in textual features between the two groups are significant. Here, we find that while valence and dominance do not show significant differences between the two groups, "implicit sentiment" sentences have a much lower arousal and a slightly higher concreteness, on average, than the set of "explicit" sentence – as can be seen in Table 1. Two of the four feature dimensions appear to be significant in the sentences that implicitly ex-

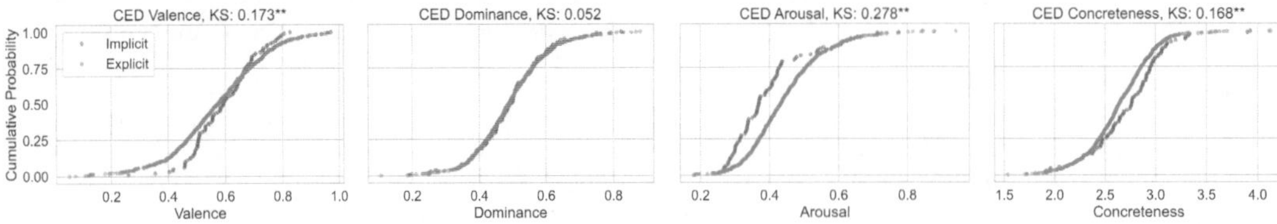

Figure 3: Cumulative Empirical Distribution (CED) of features per group and statistics of the two-sample Kolmogorov-Smirnov test (KS) for goodness of fit (on top). **p-value < 0.01.

press a sentiment: their level of concreteness and their level of arousal.[12] Valence in sentences with lower arousal and higher concreteness appear more detectable to the human eye than to models, pointing to a discrepancy between them. The statistical significance of the two relevant categories is even stronger when they are measured on a sentence- rather than word base (Table 1).

This interplay could be precisely one of the components of the "omissive prose" effect. For example, one sentence which was perceived very positive by human readers and neutral by models also holds high concreteness (2.78): `"The boy took the old army blanket off the bed and spread it over the back of the chair and over the old man's shoulders"`. It seems to exemplify the notion of objective correlative – that is, the literary technique of transmitting sentiment to readers without using emotion associated words, through an exposition of concrete *objects* or *actions*.[13]

To further validate these results, we examined the distribution of our data, performing the The Kolmogorov-Smirnov (KS) test[14] on the empirical cumulative distribution of the groups (Fig. 3). Considering the test values, we may reject the null hypothesis that the two groups are drawn from the same continuous distribution in the case of valence, arousal, and concreteness (see Fig. 3).[15]

5 Conclusions and Future Works

In examining human and model sentiment annotations in *The Old Man and the Sea*, we observed a distinct group of sentences that garnered high human scores but received neutral ratings from our three SA models. Looking into textual features of this group, we found that they can be distinguished by their levels of arousal and concreteness. Because we might assume that humans in these cases pick up on contextual information not available to the models, we find the difference in terms of textual features between the groups particularly interesting. More than just context appear to be giving these sentences an evocative strength that is not captured by the models.

The finding of higher levels of concreteness and lower levels of arousal of this group of sentences aligns with literary theories suggesting that writing styles that employ techniques like "omissive writing" or the *objective correlative* technique evoke a perception of sentiments in human readers without any explicit emotional reference and without using words directly associated to emotional states. Rather, the evocative strength of these sentences relies at least in part on words with a low arousal profile, and higher concreteness levels, managing to be particularly subtle in how sentiment charge is transmitted to the reader. Our findings support supplementing sentiment models with feature detection when dealing with the literary domain, since it may be that fiction texts use language differently than non-fiction, e.g., employing objective correlatives to evoke sentiment in the reader. Further exploration into arousal and concreteness may hold promise for a more comprehensive understanding of sentiment in prose in fiction with that in non-fiction. Finally, broader quantitative studies of fiction would help understanding how concreteness and arousal resonate with readers, particularly regarding their appreciation of implicit sentiments' evocation in prose.

[12]The lack of difference in valence is likely an effect of groups confounding positive and negative sentences.

[13]We only suggest this effect as the method we use – the VAD and concreteness scores – may be considered a relatively crude way of operationalizing this concept.

[14]We used the implementation of this test in the SciPy library: `https://docs.scipy.org/doc/scipy/reference/generated/scipy.stats.ks_2samp.html`.

[15]The significance of valence is predictable, as we have selected the sentences based on their valence. However, it is not picked by all models as it "crosses over" the distribution of explicit sentences. That is, implicit sentences are more positive than the most negative explicit sentences, and more negative than the most positive explicit sentences.

Limitations

We want to underline that the present work is an examination of one work of fiction only, also due to the fact that large-scale annotation of texts is a complex and costly undertaking. Moreover, as this study examined and drew conclusions from what can be considered a particularly "canonical" text of Western literary production, we note that it situates the study in (prestigious) Western literary culture, where certain norms of writing style may prevail. As such, further study is needed to draw more far-reaching conclusions, and the present study should be considered only a step toward a more comprehensive examination of implicit sentiment expression in literary fiction.

References

Jan Auracher and Hildegard Bosch. 2016. Showing with words: The influence of language concreteness on suspense. *Scientific Study of Literature*, 6(2):208–242.

Francesco Barbieri, Jose Camacho-Collados, Luis Espinosa Anke, and Leonardo Neves. 2020. TweetEval: Unified benchmark and comparative evaluation for tweet classification. In *Findings of the Association for Computational Linguistics: EMNLP 2020*, pages 1644–1650, Online. Association for Computational Linguistics.

Yuri Bizzoni and Pascale Feldkamp. 2023. Comparing transformer and dictionary-based sentiment models for literary texts: Hemingway as a case-study. In *Proceedings of the 3rd International Workshop on Natural Language Processing for Digital Humanities*, pages 219–226, Tokyo, Japan. Association for Computational Linguistics.

Yuri Bizzoni, Pascale Moreira, Mads Rosendahl Thomsen, and Kristoffer Nielbo. 2023. Sentimental matters - predicting literary quality by sentiment analysis and stylometric features. In *Proceedings of the 13th Workshop on Computational Approaches to Subjectivity, Sentiment, & Social Media Analysis*, pages 11–18, Toronto, Canada. Association for Computational Linguistics.

Wayne C. Booth. 1983. *The Rhetoric of Fiction*. University of Chicago Press, Chicago.

Eleonora Borelli, Davide Crepaldi, Carlo Adolfo Porro, and Cristina Cacciari. 2018. The psycholinguistic and affective structure of words conveying pain. *PloS one*, 13(6):e0199658.

Cleanth Brooks and Robert Penn Warren. 1976. *Understanding Poetry*. Holt, Rinehart and Winston, New York.

Marc Brysbaert, Amy Beth Warriner, and Victor Kuperman. 2014. Concreteness ratings for 40 thousand generally known English word lemmas. *Behavior Research Methods*, 46(3):904–911.

MA Daoshan and Zhang Shuo. 2014. A discourse study of the Iceberg Principle in *A Farewell to Arms*. *Studies in Literature and Language*, 8(1):80–84.

T.S. Eliot. 1948. *Selected Essays by T. S. Eliot*. Faber & Faber.

Katherine Elkins. 2022. *The Shapes of Stories: Sentiment Analysis for Narrative*. Cambridge University Press.

C. P. Heaton. 1970. Style in *The Old Man and the Sea*. *Style*, 4(1):11–27.

Ernest Hemingway. 1996. *Death in the Afternoon*. Simon & Schuster, New York.

Clayton Hutto and Eric Gilbert. 2014. VADER: A parsimonious rule-based model for sentiment analysis of social media text. In *Proceedings of the international AAAI conference on web and social media*, volume 8, pages 216–225.

Matthew Jockers. 2014. A novel method for detecting plot.

Matthew L. Jockers. 2015. *Syuzhet: Extract Sentiment and Plot Arcs from Text*.

Stavroula-Thaleia Kousta, Gabriella Vigliocco, David P. Vinson, Mark Andrews, and Elena Del Campo. 2011. The representation of abstract words: Why emotion matters. *Journal of Experimental Psychology: General*, 140(1):14–34.

Xiaotao Li, Shujuan You, Yawen Niu, and Wai Chen. 2021. Learning embeddings for rare words leveraging Internet search engine and spatial location relationships. In *Proceedings of *SEM 2021: The Tenth Joint Conference on Lexical and Computational Semantics*, pages 278–287, Online. Association for Computational Linguistics.

Saif Mohammad. 2018. Obtaining reliable human ratings of valence, arousal, and dominance for 20,000 English words. In *Proceedings of the 56th Annual Meeting of the Association for Computational Linguistics (Volume 1: Long Papers)*, pages 174–184, Melbourne, Australia. Association for Computational Linguistics.

Emily Öhman. 2021. The Validity of Lexicon-based Sentiment Analysis in Interdisciplinary Research. In *Proceedings of the Workshop on Natural Language Processing for Digital Humanities*, pages 7–12, NIT Silchar, India. NLP Association of India (NLPAI).

Andrew J. Reagan, Christopher M. Danforth, Brian Tivnan, Jake Ryland Williams, and Peter Sheridan Dodds. 2017. Sentiment analysis methods for understanding large-scale texts: a case for using continuum-scored words and word shift graphs. *EPJ Data Science*, 6(1):1–21.

Andrew J Reagan, Lewis Mitchell, Dilan Kiley, Christopher M Danforth, and Peter Sheridan Dodds. 2016. The emotional arcs of stories are dominated by six basic shapes. *EPJ Data Science*, 5(1):1–12.

Simone Rebora. 2023. Sentiment Analysis in Literary Studies. A Critical Survey. *Digital Humanities Quarterly*, 17(2).

Thomas Strychacz. 2002. "The sort of thing you should not admit": Ernest Hemingway's aesthetic of emotional restraint. In Milette Shamir and Jennifer Travis, editors, *Boys Don't Cry? Rethinking Narratives of Masculinity and Emotion in the U.S.*, pages 141–166. Columbia University Press.

Amy Beth Warriner, Victor Kuperman, and Marc Brysbaert. 2013. Norms of valence, arousal, and dominance for 13,915 English lemmas. *Behavior research methods*, 45:1191–1207.

Deyu Zhou, Jianan Wang, Linhai Zhang, and Yulan He. 2021. Implicit sentiment analysis with event-centered text representation. In *Proceedings of the 2021 Conference on Empirical Methods in Natural Language Processing*, pages 6884–6893, Online and Punta Cana, Dominican Republic. Association for Computational Linguistics.

A Appendix

Test	Valence	Dominance	Arousal	Concreteness
MWU	724.263.0	696.247	582.588**	619.618*
T-test	1.8548	-0.7048	-5.6028**	2.3346*
T(W)-test	2.4353	-0.7703	-6.4615**	2.2885*
T(W)-test, 100 permutations	2.4353	-0.7703	-6.4615**	2.2885**
MWU	39.308	36.558	25.146**	45.660**
T-test	1.4119	0.1118	-3.8562**	2.4327*
T(W)-test	1.8972	0.1148	-3.6547**	2.2209*
T(W)-test, 100 permutations	1.8972	0.1148	-3.6547**	2.2209*

Table 2: Additional test between groups where features were calculated per word (above) and sentence (below). Regarding the t-test, we also ran it without assuming equal population variance, we thus performed a Welch's (W) t-test with and without permutations (n=200). * p-value < 0.05, ** p-value < 0.05. Note that the p-value for concreteness tends to be higher than for arousal (even if in all cases < 0.05, which might indicate that the difference between groups are more strongly distinguished by arousal.

	Constant	Valence	Arousal	Dominance	Concreteness
Coefficient	-2.1609	-3.4922**	-7.2940**	8.9520**	1.1254**

Table 3: The table presents the coefficients and associated p-values resulting from the Ordinary Least Squares (OLS) regression analysis. We performed the regression on the combined "implicit"/"explicit" groups of sentences (n=714+101), using *the difference between human and roBERTa sentiment score* as the dependant variable. The coefficients represent the estimated effect of each independent variable (our four features) on the dependent variable, score divergence. * p-values < 0.01 indicate that all variables have a statistically significant impact on score divergence.

Exposing propaganda: an analysis of stylistic cues comparing human annotations and machine classification

Géraud Faye[1,2], Benjamin Icard[3,4], Morgane Casanova[5], Julien Chanson[6], François Maine[4,7], François Bancilhon[8], Guillaume Gadek[1], Guillaume Gravier[5] and Paul Égré[3]

[1]*Airbus Defence and Space*, France
[2]*Université Paris-Saclay, CentraleSupélec*, MICS, France
[3]*Institut Jean-Nicod*, CNRS, ENS-PSL, EHESS, France
[4]*LIP6*, CNRS, Sorbonne Université, France
[5]*Université de Rennes, CNRS, Inria*, IRISA, France
[6]*Mondeca*, France
[7]*Freedom Partners*, France
[8]*Observatoire des Médias*, France

Abstract

This paper investigates the language of propaganda and its stylistic features. It presents the PPN dataset, standing for Propagandist Pseudo-News, a multisource, multilingual, multimodal dataset composed of news articles extracted from websites identified as propaganda sources by expert agencies. A limited sample from this set was randomly mixed with papers from the regular French press, and their URL masked, to conduct an annotation-experiment by humans, using 11 distinct labels. The results show that human annotators were able to reliably discriminate between the two types of press across each of the labels. We propose different NLP techniques to identify the cues used by the annotators, and to compare them with machine classification. They include the analyzer VAGO to measure discourse vagueness and subjectivity, a TF-IDF to serve as a baseline, and four different classifiers: two RoBERTa-based models, CATS using syntax, and one XGBoost combining syntactic and semantic features.

1 Introduction

In times of warfare as well as in authoritarian regimes, state propaganda is an informational weapon whose aim is to damage the opponents' reputation and to maintain trust in the state's actions (Jowett and O'Donnell, 2019). With the development of the internet and social networks, propaganda has new media to sprawl and to cross borders (Da San Martino et al., 2020a). Current trends on news consumption show an increase in the number of people getting informed on digital device.[1] Internet platforms are a new playground for propagandists, where they can disseminate partisan pieces among news articles and opinions shared on social media.

The rhetorical techniques of propagandists differ and their detection is currently a topic of interest (Da San Martino et al., 2020b; Quaranto and Stanley, 2021). In this paper, we pursue this general line of analysis, by examining the language of propaganda and its stylistic features. More specifically, we propose a comparison between human classification and machine classification of propaganda.

We present the PPN dataset, standing for Propagandist Pseudo-News, a multisource, multilingual, multimodal dataset composed of news articles extracted from websites identified as propaganda sources by Newsguard and Viginum, a French state-backed misinformation and foreign interference surveillance organisation. Composition of the dataset is detailed in Section 2.

To analyse the corpus and deepen our understanding of the language of propaganda, we also conducted a multilabel annotation experiment involving randomly mixing articles from that corpus with a sample of articles from mainstream French newspapers. The experiment is detailed in Section 3, and the results are presented in Section 4, showing that regular press articles and articles from the corpus are recognizably different to annotators, despite sharing topics.

To find the cues characteristic of each corpus, we then used different techniques. In Section 5, we use the expert system VAGO to check on the occurrence of subjective and vagueness markers in either type of corpus, since intentional vagueness (Égré and Icard, 2018) is among recognized techniques of propaganda (Da San Martino et al., 2020b) and its higher prevalence detectable in fake

[1]https://www.pewresearch.org/journalism/fact-sheet/news-platform-fact-sheet/

Proceedings of the Third Workshop on Understanding Implicit and Underspecified Language, pages 62–72
March 21, 2024

news (Guélorget et al., 2021). Then in Section 6, we train machine learning models to detect articles from propagandist sources, three based on text processing and one on stylistic and syntactic features. Explainability capabilities of the models are used to confirm the features learnt by the models and to discuss ways in which they can be improved.

2 The PPN dataset

The proposed PPN dataset is diverse in terms of sources, topics and used languages. The corpus has been extracted from 5 sources (news distribution by source is shown in Table 1), all of which were created after the Russian invasion of Ukraine on February 24, 2022:

- rrn.media: *Reliable Recent News* (previously named *Reliable Russian News*) has the form of a news website publishing articles containing a pro-Russia or anti-Occident stance. The website contains news in 9 languages (Arabic, Chinese, English, French, German, Italian, Russian, Spanish and Ukrainian), which receive a different coverage over time.

- tribunalukraine.info: this website aims at accusing Ukraine of committing war crimes and financially benefiting from the conflict. The writing style is more aggressive than *rrn*, as it aims at damaging Ukraine's reputation. All articles from this source are available in English, French, German, Russian and Spanish.

- waronfakes.com: the counterpart of tribunalukraine, it aims at denying Russian war crimes allegations. It does not publish news articles, but short summaries of allegations, and as such it qualifies as fake news. All *"debunked"* facts are available in Arabic, Chinese, English, French, German and Spanish.

- notrepays.today and lavirgule.news: these French-writing websites publish polarizing news with the aim of damaging trust in Western institutions. Contrarily to the first three sources, which were created at the beginning of the Russian invasion, *notrepays* and *lavirgule* were created one year later, with a related agenda.

Unlike some previous publications (Heppell et al., 2023), we present the propaganda articles in their original language for analysis, but knowing that several of the sites present translations

Source	Number of documents
rrn	12,427
tribunalukraine	4,975
waronfakes	344
notrepays	480
lavirgule	503

Table 1: PPN articles distribution by source.

Language	Number of documents
Arabic	1,079
Chinese	794
English	3,219
French	4,141
German	3,341
Italian	1,796
Russian	1,435
Spanish	2,485
Ukrainian	439

Table 2: PPN articles distribution by language.

in different languages. We share the collected dataset on the following GitHub repository: `https://github.com/hybrinfox/ppn`. The distribution of articles by languages is shown in Table 2.

3 Annotated corpus and labels

To understand how propaganda can be perceived and its characteristics, we conducted an annotation experiment on a subset of the French PPN dataset. In order to balance the dataset, we added articles from five French national newspapers of different political orientations, namely lefigaro.fr, lemonde.fr, marianne.fr, liberation.fr and mediapart.fr. The articles were randomly selected among those sources. They had to be published after the beginning of the Ukraine invasion (February 24, 2022) and to contain at least the mention of Russia or Ukraine. An additional filter, based on article length, was applied to limit bias linked to the length of articles. All annotated articles contained between 1,000 and 10,000 characters (shorter articles belong almost exclusively to the propaganda class and longer articles always belong to the regular class). A total of 48 articles were selected for each type of press, with a maximum of 14 and a minimum of 7 articles by source in the alternative press, and a maximum of 15 vs. a minimum of 1 by source in the regular press, and roughly similar distributions across the two types.

Eleven labels were used for the annotations. Figure 1 presents them in the order in which annotators had to mark them, with a summary of their definition. The 11 labels included 5 labels targeting manipulative content proscribed by the deontology

- **Vague:** the information contained in the article is general with few details or specific facts.
- **Subjective:** the article essentially presents opinions and the explicit or implicit subjective viewpoint of its author.
- **Exaggeration:** the article presents information in an exaggerated or excessive manner.
- **Pejorative:** the article primarily aims to vilify individuals or institutions.
- **Descriptive:** the article essentially reports facts or events rather than opinions.
- **Propaganda:** the article gives a biased presentation of the situation and seems to serve above all the interests of a state or organization.
- **Satirical:** the article is intended to make people laugh and is written in a joking tone.
- **Dishonest Title:** the title reports false or artificially inflated information.
- **Adequate Sources:** the article cites its sources sufficiently and accurately.
- **Fake News:** in your opinion, the article deserves to be called "fake news".
- **False Information:** the article contains at least one false information.

Figure 1: Description of the 11 labels used for the annotation task.

of journalism[2] and the Gricean norms of cooperative discourse (Quality in particular, Grice 1975), namely "Dishonest Title", "Fake News", "False Information", "Exaggeration", and "Propaganda". We also included 2 labels "Satirical" and "Pejorative", targeting jocular and adversarial intention; and finally, 4 labels for features susceptible to be applicable to either type of press, with 2 labels targeting the expression of opinion or its absence, namely "Subjective" and "Descriptive", and 2 labels targeting the quality of justification, namely "Vague" and "Adequate Sources". Each label was explicitly defined and accompanied by examples in the annotation manual, except for "Fake News", which was deliberately left up to the annotator to judge without explicit criteria, in order to find out about its best predictors among the other labels. The label "False Information" was presented last, since the annotators were told they had the option to do some research and fact-checking on each topic if necessary, but in order to minimize the risk of the annotators coming across the source of the articles. The labels were binary (1 for "applies" and 0 for "does not apply") and the annotators forced to choose between them (with the option of giving a free commentary). Some of our labels, finally, overlap with the propaganda techniques listed in Da San Martino et al. (2020a), in particular our label "Pejorative" with their "Name calling" and "Doubt", "Exaggeration" with "Exaggeration/Minimization", "Satirical/Pejorative/Subjective" with their "Loaded language", and "Vague" with their "Obfuscation/Intentional vagueness", except that they define vagueness mostly in terms of confusion and unclarity, whereas our definition targets generality/lack of specificity.

[2]See the 1971 Charter of Munich.

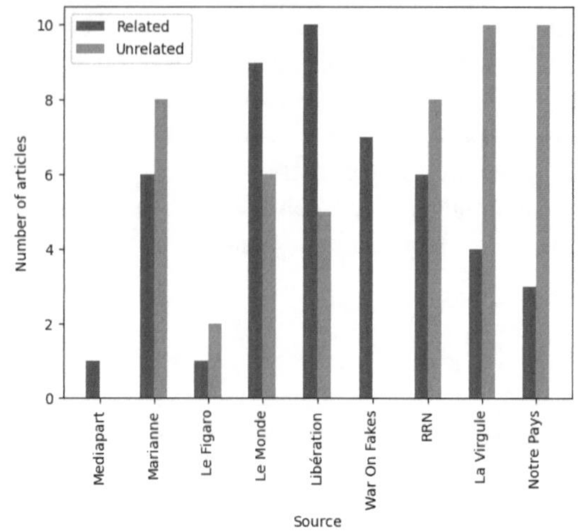

Figure 2: Topic distribution of articles from the annotated corpus.

After the annotation experiment, an additional analysis of the topics was conducted to ensure that regular articles were roughly about the same topics as propaganda articles, in order to validate the experiment results. To this end, we labeled the articles depending on whether they were directly about the armed conflict (labeled *Related*) or about other topics such as economic sanctions or politics (labeled *Unrelated*). The articles' distribution is shown in Figure 2.

Every source, with the exception of *waronfakes* and *mediapart*, had articles in both classes. *mediapart* had only one article meeting our filtering conditions, and *waronfakes* aims at denying war crimes allegations, so it is logical that it only contains articles directly about the armed conflict. Unexpectedly, the sample from *lavirgule* and *notrepays* contained more articles not directly linked to the conflict. Those articles seem to aim at polarizing the public debate not only on the war in Ukraine, but on other topics as well, including French politics. Overall, the annotated dataset is balanced, with 27 *Related* regular articles, 21 *Unrelated* regular articles, 20 *Related* propaganda articles, and 28 *Unrelated* propaganda articles.

4 Analysis of the annotations

The 6 annotators included the designers of the experiment. Only one of them had briefly seen the texts prior to annotating, in order to upload them on the form used for the annotation task, but without verifying their content. The articles were presented in a common random order for all participants. To avoid bias by source, the URL was removed, in contrast to other datasets (viz. ISOT, Ahmed et al. 2018 or Horne and Adali 2017).

One article happened to contain mostly video links, leaving a meta-content description of the journal's policies on cookies: it could not be annotated, and was removed, leaving a total of 48 alternative vs. 47 regular articles for analysis. Among those, five articles (4 regular, 1 alternative) happened to bear an indication of their source by self-citation in their content. Eleven articles were also truncated because they were behind a paywall (ending on the necessity to subscribe in order to access content). We kept them for analysis, but knowing that they might introduce a confound. Importantly, however, post-hoc analyses made after exclusion of those 16 articles show the same main contrasts as reported below.

The combined dataset presents individual annotations grouped by annotator, instead of aggregate data (as PolitiFact and GossipCop, Shu et al. 2018), dropping personal commentaries on the articles to secure anonymity.

In order to assess the quality of the annotations, we calculated the inter-rater agreement based on the percentage of agreement between annotators, rescaled to 0 in a case of equal split between annotators (3:3), and to 1 in case of unanimity (6:0). That is, for each document, we computed the proportion x of 1-answers, rescaled by the function returning the value $|2x - 1|$. For example, a value of 0.4 indicates that 70% of the raters go in the same direction, while a value of .6 or above indicates 80% of agreement or more.

As shown in Figure 3b, for both the regular and the alternative press articles, all labels reached a mean value above .4, indicative of moderate to high agreement. The agreement between annotators increases systematically from the alternative to the regular corpus, meaning that for each label, the

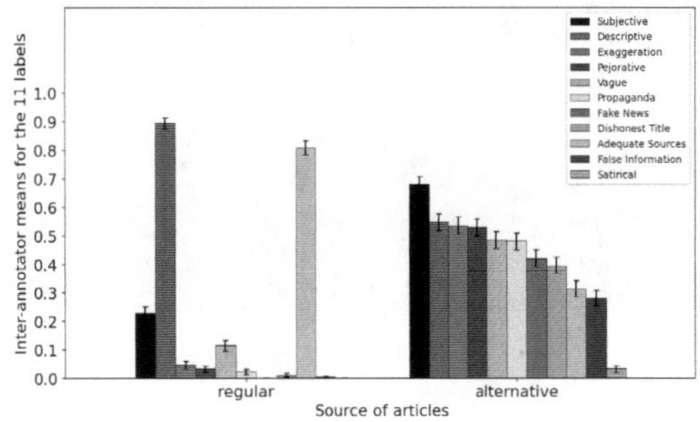

(a) Mean inter-annotator scores per label.

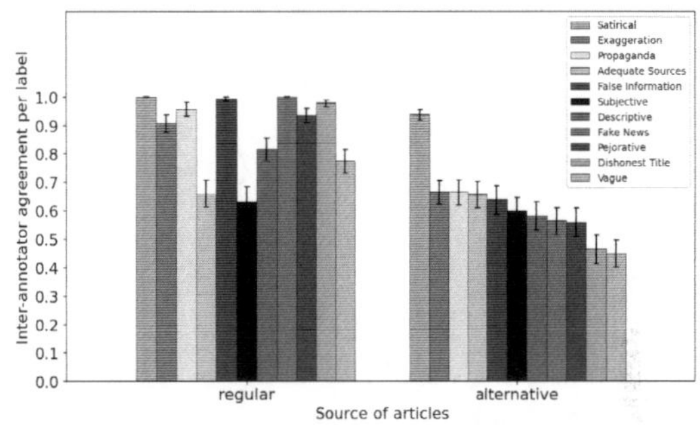

(b) Mean inter-annotator agreement per label.

Figure 3: Mean scores and agreement by label (error bars=standard error of the mean).

agreement is higher in the regular corpus, compared to the alternative corpus.

Regarding the labels themselves, Figure 3a shows a strong contrast between the two types of corpora. Except for the label "Satirical", which is almost never used in either type of corpus, the other 10 labels are used in very distinct proportions in either type of corpora (paired t-tests between the two corpora by label are all significant at the $\alpha = .01$ significance level). While each of the 10 remaining labels is applied to some extent in the alternative corpus, two labels are conspicuously never applied in the case of the regular corpus, namely: "False Information" and "Fake News". The labels "Descriptive" and "Adequate Sources", used for both types of corpora, are used in much higher proportion in the regular case. The labels "Subjective" and "Vague", while occurring for the regular corpus, are much less prevalent in the regular corpus. Finally, all other labels, in particular "Exaggeration", "Propaganda", "Pejorative", "Dishonest Title", are applied only marginally in the regular corpus.

The correlation matrix of the labels is displayed in Figure 4. The label "Satirical" is not corre-

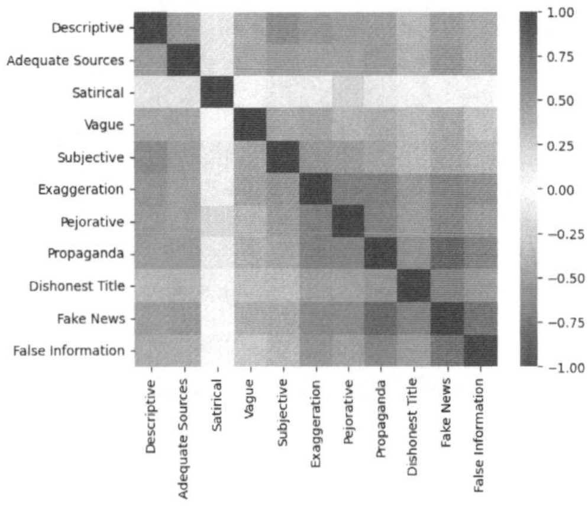

Figure 4: Correlation matrix of the 11 labels used for human annotations.

lated to other labels, due to its low frequency in the annotations (about 1.5% of annotations), and is left out in the remaining of the analysis. Two main groups of labels emerge from the matrix: the labels "Descriptive" and "Adequate Sources" are strongly correlated with each other and inversely with the others, and the remaining labels, including "Vague", "Subjective", etc., are positively correlated to various degrees. Our main label of interest, "Propaganda", correlates most strongly with "Fake News", "Pejorative", and "Exaggeration".

In summary, the annotators were able to reliably discriminate between the two corpora, across each of the dimensions selected by a specific label, and moreover the strong correlation between the labels "Propaganda" and "Exaggeration" legitimizes an analysis in terms of stylistic cues.

5 Analysis with the VAGO tools

To see what textual features might explain the difference between the two classes, we used the lexical database and analyzer VAGO (Icard et al., 2022). For a given text, VAGO calculates three scores: a score of vagueness, a score of opinion, and a score of relative detail (compared to vagueness). To calculate the vagueness score of a text, the system checks for the occurrence of vague expressions, subcategorized into four types: generality V_G (*"some"*, *"or"*), approximation V_A (*"about"*, *"almost"*), one-dimensional vagueness V_D (*"old"*, *"many"*), and multi-dimensional vagueness V_C (*"good"*, *"effective"*). For opinion, VAGO checks for the occurrence of implicit markers of subjectivity (all expressions of type V_D and V_C, including evaluative adjectives and pejorative terms), as well as explicit markers (first-person pronouns, exclamation marks). For detail, finally, the system compares the ratio of named entities to vague terms.

While VAGO does not incorporate any world-knowledge, previous studies on larger corpora have shown that the VAGO scores of vagueness and opinion were positively correlated with the label "biased" in news articles (Guélorget et al., 2021; Icard et al., 2023), and that the score of detail-vs-vagueness was negatively correlated with the label "Satirical" (Icard et al., 2023). Hence, we asked if the VAGO scores of vagueness, opinion, and detail might be good predictors of the human annotations, and in particular of labels such as "Exaggeration", "Pejorative", "Propaganda" and "Dishonest Title".

To investigate this question, we calculated the correlation between the VAGO scores for each article of the corpus and the mean inter-annotator scores for all of the 10 labels ("Satirical" left aside). As shown in Table 3, the labels "Subjective", "Exaggeration" and "Pejorative" turned out to be positively correlated to the VAGO scores of vagueness and opinion, and negatively correlated to the scores of detail-vs-vagueness. Consistent with these results, the scores of vagueness and opinion were also negatively correlated with labels "Descriptive" and "Adequate Sources". By contrast, labels "Propaganda", "Dishonest Title", "Fake News" and "False Information" turned out to be positively correlated to the scores of vagueness only. All these correlations are weak to moderate, but they replicate results found in previous studies, with an even higher order of magnitude in the labels "Subjective" and "Descriptive" connected to VAGO's opinion score, as presented in Figure 5.

Human annotations of the label "Vague" did not correlate with VAGO scores of either vagueness or detail, however, contrary to expectations. We conjecture that this could be due to a discrepancy between the definition given of the label, which targets generality vagueness, and the fact that the VAGO vagueness score is based on more types of vagueness, in particular the semantic vagueness of one-dimensional and multi-dimensional adjectives, which represent 96% of the VAGO lexicon.

Despite that, what Table 3 shows is that the VAGO scores track the clustering of labels found in Figure 4: the polarity of the correlations for the labels "Descriptive" and "Adequate sources" is inverse to that of the other labels. In summary, VAGO scores are correlated with the separating features of the alternative vs. regular press, but they explain only part of the variance in the annotations. In the next section, we examine classification models properly in order to get further insights.

Label	vague	opinion	detail
Vague	0.163	0.188	−0.180
Subjective	0.344*	0.384**	−0.238
Exaggeration	0.282	0.222	−0.225
Pejorative	0.289	0.222	−0.265
Descriptive	−0.371**	−0.367**	0.228
Propaganda	0.249	0.165	−0.152
Dishonest Title	0.257	0.164	−0.206
Adequate Sources	−0.210	−0.210	0.130
Fake News	0.233	0.178	−0.148
False Information	0.214	0.140	−0.099

Table 3: Pearson correlations between the labels' mean scores and the VAGO scores (* and ** indicate p-value $< .05$ and $< .01$), with Bonferroni correction.

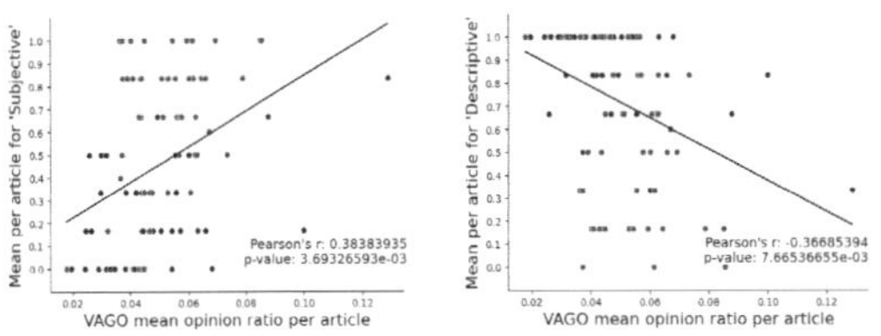

Figure 5: Pearson correlations between the VAGO mean opinion score per article and the mean scores for labels "Subjective" (left) and "Descriptive" (right). Blue data points correspond to regular articles while red data points correspond to alternative press articles.

6 Machine learning for propaganda detection

Propaganda detection (Da San Martino et al., 2020b) from texts can be a difficult task depending on the form of the content. Classifying sentences (Mapes et al., 2019) is harder, even for large language models (LLMs) such as BERT (Devlin et al., 2018). In this section, a methodology for training a propaganda detection model is explained and evaluated. Smaller models with explainability capabilities were also trained in order to identify which parts of the articles the model considers when taking its decision.

6.1 Dataset for detecting propaganda related to the conflict

In order to train a model that could be used to identify propaganda articles, it is required to also collect regular press articles on a related topic. Here, we present the larger corpus of regular press from which the French subset of the previous section was drawn. This larger corpus also contains English articles, since the classification model is supposed to handle classification in French and in English.

English regular articles were collected from 11 reliable news outlets, with constraints of date (being post Ukraine invasion), length (between 1,000 and 10,000 characters), and topic (mention Russia and Ukraine). English regular articles were collected using `news-please` (Hamborg et al., 2017) before being filtered. The articles distribution by source is given in Table 4. The wider set of French regular articles was collected in the same way, but with a more limited choice of sources, their distribution is given in Table 5.

Source	Number of articles
apnews.com	520
cbsnews.com	63
dailymail.co.uk	43
cnn.com	10
usatoday.com	10
forbes.com	42
foxnews.com	5
nbcnews.com	10
nytimes.com	4
theguardian.com	185
washingtonpost.com	12
Total	1,004

Table 4: English language regular articles distribution by source.

Source	Number of articles
lefigaro.fr	3
lemonde.fr	449
liberation.fr	386
marianne.net	523
mediapart.fr	6
Total	1,367

Table 5: French regular articles distribution by source.

6.2 Models

Five models were chosen for propaganda detection, two in English and three in French. The English[3] and French[4] models are available on Huggingface-hub and can be freely downloaded and tested.

The first English model used for classification is a RoBERTa-base model (Liu et al., 2019) with a classification layer using the last hidden state. For practicality, we load pre-trained English RoBERTa

[3]https://huggingface.co/hybrinfox/ukraine-operation_propaganda-detection-EN

[4]https://huggingface.co/hybrinfox/ukraine-operation_propaganda-detection-FR

weights and fine-tune the model using the HuggingFace transformers library.

The first French model combines the "CamemBERT-base" version (Martin et al., 2019) based on the RoBERTa architecture (Liu et al., 2019) (*Batch Size*=10, *Learning Rate*=1e-05, *Epochs*=5) with one classification layer and a BCE loss function to detect whether the articles of our French larger dataset counts as propaganda or not.

The second French model is an XGBoost (Chen and Guestrin, 2016) (Extreme Gradient Boosting) model. It is a scalable, distributed gradient-boosted decision tree. Contrarily to the other three models which process texts directly, XGBoost only takes numerical values as input. In our case it takes the following parameters: the length of the sentence, the three VAGO scores (vagueness, opinion, detail), the sentiment of the sentence, positive or negative (using the HuggingFace sentiment classification model "Monsia/camembert-fr-covid-tweet-sentiment-classification"), the number of verbs, adjectives, adverbs and nouns present in the sentence and the number of occurrences of dependencies between the words (using the spaCy python library for Natural Language Processing).[5] The sentence features are then aggregated by an operator. Several aggregation operators were tested and gave similar results so the sum operator was chosen.

Models applicable to both languages were tested. The first is the neurosymbolic model CATS (Faye et al., 2023). It does not use *a priori* knowledge on the language except for the English syntax. It is lighter than RoBERTa, and has explainability capabilities that will be useful to identify what the model considers a marker of propaganda. It can also be used for other languages and results for a French version have also been reported. The second one is TF-IDF, with which the texts are vectorized after removing stopwords and lemmatizing the remaining words. This representation is then processed by a random forest, predicting the class of the article.

The datasets for each language were initially split between training, validation and test using a 80/10/10 ratio with no overlap. The models were chosen on the best validation score and the reported results are on the test set, which was never used during the training procedure.

[5]https://universaldependencies.org/u/dep/all.html#al-u-dep/nmod

6.3 Results

Language	Models	Test accuracy
English	RoBERTa	0.997
	CATS - EN	0.953
	TF-IDF - EN	0.985
French	CamemBERT	0.997
	CATS - FR	0.946
	XGBoost	0.921
	TF-IDF - FR	0.963

Table 6: Test accuracies for Ukraine invasion propaganda detection models.

The models' performances on their test sets are reported in Table 6. Propaganda detection on this specific topic is easily achieved by LLMs, and even by shallow models like CATS or XGBoost. The performance of CATS is slightly lower than RoBERTa's, but this is expected since it contains only 0.6 million parameters, about 200 times fewer parameters than RoBERTa-base with its 125 million parameters. XGBoost's performance is even lower, but the model processes high-level features of the texts, lacking other features that other models can use.

6.4 Identified markers of propaganda

The interest of training a smaller model like CATS on the texts is to identify which markers are learnt by this machine learning model. To this end, each token's contribution to the final decision is aggregated by sentence, enabling us to recover the most salient sentences from propaganda articles. These sentences contain more markers of propaganda and can help us understand what the model is tracking when classifying articles between propaganda and regular.

A representative example is given in Figure 6. In this example, the first underlined sentence is a case of laudatory exaggeration; the second one is pejorative, and the third is again pejorative, with even a racist insinuation. Other sentences in the text contain propagandist cues, however, making the selection hard to directly interpret. For comparison, we run VAGO on the text. In this case, the scores of vagueness, opinion, and detail were 0.13, 0.08 and 0.42, respectively. The underlined items correspond to vague and subjective markers found by VAGO. VAGO detects several adjectives used pejoratively ("Old [Joe]", "trivial" and "simple" in particular). It misses out on others ("smug", "round lost"), and on more complex syntactic markers ("even" in "even a child", "by the way" to introduce a derogatory and covertly racist remark). But it identifies several subjective adjectives reflecting the implicit viewpoint of the writer.

> "Round Lost Joe Biden made a rant in Warsaw about the " unity of the West " and the" power of democracy ". But in his own country , Vladimir Putin was more believable . The American president' s speech in Poland was not intended as a direct response to the Russian leader , who addressed the Federal Assembly the day before - and the entire world as well. Biden ' s national security adviser Jake Sullivan claimed it was " not a rhetorical contest with anybody " . But the 80 - year - old politician ' s smug stand - up proved otherwise: he tried to confront his opponent from Moscow - and appeared to yield to him. Old Joe was satisfied with a 20 - minute monologue on the lawn of the Royal Castle - by comparison , Vladimir Putin spoke for 1 hour 45 minutes. Biden' s entire message was made up of high-pitched quotations - especially for the applause he prepared : " Democracies have become stronger , not weaker. Autocracies have grown weaker , not stronger." Quite trivial and as simple as possible - so that even a child would get the point . By the way , there were a lot of children at the President' s speech , and of different races too. And all of them had Ukrainian flags - in the best traditions of American propaganda."

Figure 6: Example of an article classified as propaganda by CATS. The sentences contributing the most to the propaganda class according to CATS are highlighted in red while the VAGO vocabulary is underlined.

6.5 Explainability of the XGBoost model

We used the SHAP tool (Lundberg and Lee, 2017) to analyze which features were the most useful for the XGBoost classification. The results are reported in Figure 7. We observe that overall syntactic features bear more weight than other features in the detection of propaganda, with the number of punctuation marks (PUNCTUATION) having greater impact than the length of sentences (LENGTH_SENT), the number of clausal modifiers (ACL), of nominal subjects (NSUBJ) and of sentences (ROOT) all receiving similar weight.

In Figure 8, we observe that the frequency percentage of punctuation compared to other tokens is significantly higher in regular articles than in propaganda articles ($p = 8.31 \times 10^{-240}$). We observed more precisely which type of punctuation was more represented in regular versus propaganda articles. Compared to other tokens, we

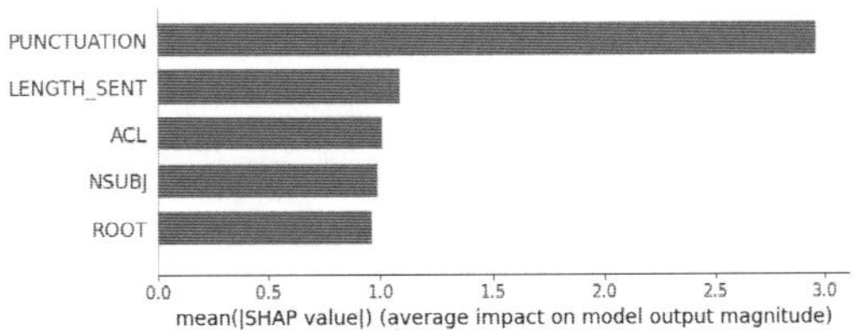

Figure 7: SHAP explainability of the XGBoost model for propaganda classification. Only the top 5 syntactic features are displayed.

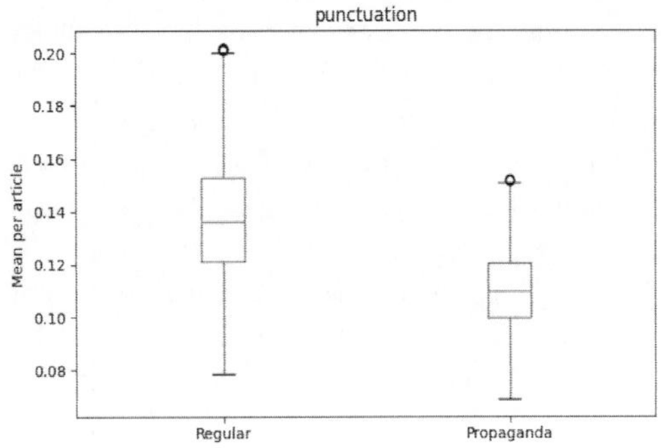

Figure 8: Percentage frequency distributions of "punct" dependence in regular articles vs. propaganda articles.

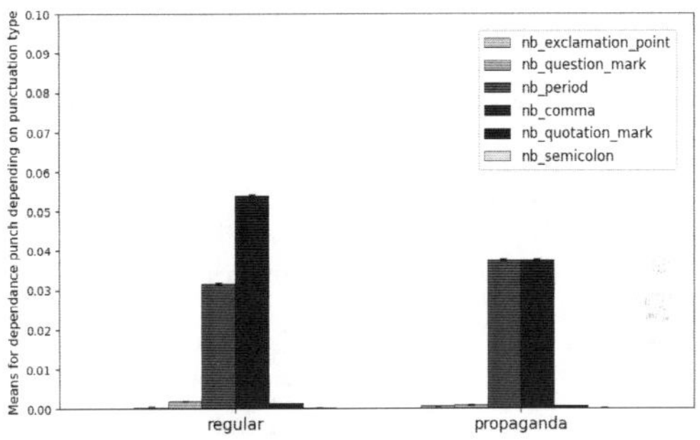

Figure 9: Relative weight of punctuation marks in either article type.

observed that propaganda articles contain significantly more question marks ($p = 2.12 \times 10^{-32}$), more quotation marks ($p = 1.12 \times 10^{-06}$), more periods ($p = 2.09 \times 10^{-78}$), but fewer commas ($p = 1.47 \times 10^{-290}$) than regular articles (see Figure 9). Since propaganda articles happened to be significantly shorter than regular articles ($p = 7.12 \times 10^{-26}$), the data was normalized by the length of the article, corresponding to the total number of tokens in the article.

Looking at the VAGO-N scores on the corpora, we observe that, besides punctuation, the VAGO-N mean score of detail vs vagueness per article is significantly higher for regular articles than for propaganda articles ($p = 2.66 \times 10^{-44}$, with Bonferroni correction). By contrast, the differences between the VAGO-N scores of vagueness and opinion are no longer significant after Bonferroni correction.

6.6 Potential biases of machine learning models

The near perfect accuracy of the models reported in Table 6 concerning Large Language Models raises questions about the shallowness of the learnt features and about potential biases in the dataset.

Regarding the first aspect, the high performance of models such as TF-IDF and CATS shows that these simpler models can also detect propaganda when trained on a large dataset. The deeper models, as a result of their higher complexity, can achieve better scores, very close to 100%.

The high accuracy of TF-IDF, which uses only lexical features, manifests a clear distinction between the language of regular articles versus propaganda articles when they deal with the topic of Ukraine operation. While the models are performing well on this specific topic, there is no guarantee that they would perform equally well on other propaganda topics.

We analyzed the terms whose TF-IDF scores differ significantly between the two classes in the French corpus. Among the terms more prevalent in the propaganda corpus compared to the regular corpus, we find terms like "état" (*state*), "pays" (*country*), "unis" (*united*), "déclaré" (*declared*), "ue" (*EU*), "zelensky", "biden", "kiev","allemagne" (*Germany*), "armes" (*weapons*). By contrast, terms like "lire" (*read*), "russe" (*Russian*), "poutine", "kyiv", "invasion", "vladimir", "guerre" (*war*), "jeudi" (*thursday*), "mars" (*march*) and "lundi" (*monday*) are more prevalent in the regular corpus. We notice that "Kiev/Kyiv" is not spelled the same way depending on the corpus. The name "Zelensky" is cited more in propaganda articles, whereas "Putin" is cited more in the regular articles of the corpus. Finally, the regular corpus contains more markers of precise time indications than the propaganda corpus, consistently with the higher VAGO score of detail.

7 Conclusion and perspectives

In this paper, we introduced PPN, a multilingual propaganda dataset, and we conducted an experiment to investigate the basis on which human annotators, and then classification algorithms, can discriminate propagandist articles from non-propagandist articles on a specific topic. The annotations reveal that exaggeration, combined with lesser descriptive content, and absence of adequate sources, are prevalent in assessments of propagandist press. The VAGO analyzer confirmed that the use of vague markers is significantly correlated with those features. Further analyses based on different families of classifiers revealed further syntactic cues, pertaining in particular to punctuation, but also to the lexicon.

Further work is needed to refine this analysis. Machine learning models, while efficient at detecting topic-specific propaganda, still have room for improvement regarding explainability and generalization to other topics. If some alignment has been observed with what humans attend to when judging an article, there is still no guarantee that language models process the text as humans would. The use of propaganda technique classifiers to identify manipulative articles yields more explainability, but at the cost of performance, especially for topic-specific propaganda.

In addition to that, while the given scores are very high, they were obtained for the task of *topic-specific* propaganda detection, which is an easier task than general propaganda detection. However, topic-specific models still have use and can prevent the spread of disinformation in cases of conflict similar to the one used here.

While only a model for English and French propaganda detection on the Ukraine invasion is provided here, we encourage the community to use the parts of the dataset corresponding to their native language to train more classifiers. Collaborations could be considered to train a multilingual model, based on the dataset and collected regular articles from the other languages of the dataset. The same goes for annotation experiments on the way propaganda is perceived by readers, as propaganda strategies may change by languages and by target audience.

Last, in this paper we see that symbolic AI tools explain part of the classifications operated by humans as well as by classifiers. We see two ways in which explainability can be further improved: firstly, by continuing to enrich tools like VAGO with lexical and even syntactic units highlighted by classifiers or by annotators in this task; secondly by considering more labels in order to improve the quality of annotations and identify more stylistic features. We introduced a label for "Pejorative" speech, we may also have introduced a dual label "Laudatory", to identify cases of glorification also typical of state propaganda, and to refine the category of "Exaggeration". Similarly, we may want to better control the positive and negative connotations of the labels, for instance by using labels such as "Precise" rather than "Vague", or "Objective" instead of "Subjective".

Limitations

Annotation experiments were only run on a subset of the French data. While an additional manual verification of the data quality has been done for English articles, other languages have not been manually reviewed. There may be parsing errors for some languages, and further analysis from native speakers of other languages may be required before using these parts of the dataset.

Experiments on propaganda detection were only run on two examples of Romance and Germanic languages. While language models for these types of languages are common, there is no guarantee that performant language models exist for all proposed languages from the dataset.

Ethics statement

This article deals with the topic of propaganda and proposes a dataset to help improve propaganda detection. Proposing and sharing propaganda detection methods is crucial to keep the information space clean and safe to use for everyone.

Human exposition to propaganda should be contained. To this end, we ensured that all annotators were performing the annotation task voluntarily, with a content warning, and the possibility to stop the experiment at any time.

We encourage future works on the dataset to be conducted cautiously and on limited parts of the global dataset.

Acknowledgements

We thank two anonymous reviewers for helpful comments and feedback. This work was supported by the programs HYBRINFOX (ANR-21-ASIA-0003), FRONTCOG (ANR-17-EURE-0017), and PLEXUS (Marie Skłodowska-Curie Action, Horizon Europe Research and Innovation Programme, grant n°101086295). PE thanks Monash University for hosting during the writing of this paper.

Declaration of contribution

All the authors contributed to the design, annotations, analysis and discussion of the results. GF, BI, MC, and PE wrote the paper, which all authors read and revised together. First authorship is equally shared between GF, BI and MC. Correspondence: geraud.faye@centralesupelec.fr, benjamin.icard@ens.fr, morgane.casanova@irisa.fr, paul.egre@ens.psl.eu.

References

Hadeer Ahmed, Issa Traore, and Sherif Saad. 2018. Detecting opinion spams and fake news using text classification. *SECURITY AND PRIVACY*, 1(1):e9.

Tianqi Chen and Carlos Guestrin. 2016. XGBoost: A scalable tree boosting system. In *Proceedings of the 22nd ACM SIGKDD International Conference on Knowledge Discovery and Data Mining*, KDD '16, pages 785–794, New York, NY, USA. ACM.

Giovanni Da San Martino, Alberto Barrón-Cedeño, Henning Wachsmuth, Rostislav Petrov, and Preslav Nakov. 2020a. SemEval-2020 task 11: Detection of propaganda techniques in news articles. In *Proceedings of the Fourteenth Workshop on Semantic Evaluation*, pages 1377–1414, Barcelona (online). International Committee for Computational Linguistics.

Giovanni Da San Martino, Stefano Cresci, Alberto Barrón-Cedeño, Seunghak Yu, Roberto Di Pietro, and Preslav Nakov. 2020b. A survey on computational propaganda detection. *CoRR*, abs/2007.08024.

Jacob Devlin, Ming-Wei Chang, Kenton Lee, and Kristina Toutanova. 2018. BERT: Pre-training of Deep Bidirectional Transformers for Language Understanding. *arXiv:1810.04805 [cs]*.

Paul Égré and Benjamin Icard. 2018. Lying and vagueness. In J. Meibauer, editor, *Oxford Handbook of Lying*. OUP.

Géraud Faye, Wassila Ouerdane, Guillaume Gadek, Souhir Gahbiche, and Sylvain Gatepaille. 2023. A novel hybrid approach for text encoding: Cognitive attention to syntax model to detect online misinformation. *Data & Knowledge Engineering*, 148:102230.

Paul Grice. 1975. Logic and conversation. In *Speech acts*, pages 41–58. Brill.

Paul Guélorget, Benjamin Icard, Guillaume Gadek, Souhir Gahbiche, Sylvain Gatepaille, Ghislain Atemezing, and Paul Égré. 2021. Combining vagueness detection with deep learning to identify fake news. In *IEEE 24th International Conference on Information Fusion (FUSION)*, pages 1–8.

Felix Hamborg, Norman Meuschke, Corinna Breitinger, and Bela Gipp. 2017. news-please: A generic news crawler and extractor. In *Proceedings of the 15th International Symposium of Information Science*, pages 218–223.

Freddy Heppell, Kalina Bontcheva, and Carolina Scarton. 2023. Analysing state-backed propaganda websites: a new dataset and linguistic study.

Benjamin Horne and Sibel Adali. 2017. This just in: Fake news packs a lot in title, uses simpler, repetitive content in text body, more similar to satire than real news. In *Proceedings of the international AAAI conference on web and social media*, volume 11, pages 759–766.

Benjamin Icard, Ghislain Atemezing, and Paul Égré. 2022. VAGO: un outil en ligne de mesure du vague et de la subjectivité. In *Conférence Nationale sur les Applications Pratiques de l'Intelligence Artificielle (PFIA 2022)*, pages 68–71.

Benjamin Icard, Vincent Claveau, Ghislain Atemezing, and Paul Égré. 2023. Measuring vagueness and subjectivity in texts: from symbolic to neural VAGO. In *IEEE International Conference on Web Intelligence and Intelligent Agent Technology (WI-IAT 2023)*.

Garth S Jowett and Victoria O'Donnell. 2019. *Propaganda & persuasion*. Sage publications. 7th edition.

Yinhan Liu, Myle Ott, Naman Goyal, Jingfei Du, Mandar Joshi, Danqi Chen, Omer Levy, Mike Lewis, Luke Zettlemoyer, and Veselin Stoyanov. 2019. RoBERTa: A robustly optimized BERT pretraining approach.

Scott M Lundberg and Su-In Lee. 2017. A unified approach to interpreting model predictions. In I. Guyon, U. V. Luxburg, S. Bengio, H. Wallach, R. Fergus, S. Vishwanathan, and R. Garnett, editors, *Advances in Neural Information Processing Systems 30*, pages 4765–4774. Curran Associates, Inc.

Norman Mapes, Anna White, Radhika Medury, and Sumeet Dua. 2019. Divisive language and propaganda detection using multi-head attention transformers with deep learning BERT-based language models for binary classification. In *Proceedings of the Second Workshop on Natural Language Processing for Internet Freedom: Censorship, Disinformation, and Propaganda*, pages 103–106, Hong Kong, China. Association for Computational Linguistics.

Louis Martin, Benjamin Muller, Pedro Javier Ortiz Suárez, Yoann Dupont, Laurent Romary, Éric Villemonte de La Clergerie, Djamé Seddah, and Benoît Sagot. 2019. CamemBERT: a tasty French language model. *arXiv preprint*.

Anne Quaranto and Jason Stanley. 2021. Propaganda. In Justin Khoo and Rachel Katharine Sterken, editors, *The Routledge Handbook of Social and Political Philosophy of Language*, pages 125–146.

Kai Shu, Deepak Mahudeswaran, Suhang Wang, Dongwon Lee, and Huan Liu. 2018. Fakenewsnet: A data repository with news content, social context and dynamic information for studying fake news on social media. *arXiv preprint*.

Different Tastes of Entities: Investigating Human Label Variation in Named Entity Annotations

Siyao Peng[▲,●] **Zihang Sun**[▲] **Sebastian Loftus**[▲] **Barbara Plank**[▲,●]

[▲] MaiNLP, Center for Information and Language Processing, LMU Munich, Germany

[●] Munich Center for Machine Learning (MCML), Munich, Germany

{siyaopeng, bplank}@cis.lmu.de {zihang.sun, s.loftus}@campus.lmu.de

Abstract

Named Entity Recognition (NER) is a key information extraction task with a long-standing tradition. While recent studies address and aim to correct annotation errors via re-labeling efforts, little is known about the sources of human label variation, such as text ambiguity, annotation error, or guideline divergence. This is especially the case for high-quality datasets and beyond English CoNLL03. This paper studies disagreements in expert-annotated named entity datasets for three languages: English, Danish, and Bavarian. We show that text ambiguity and artificial guideline changes are dominant factors for diverse annotations among high-quality revisions. We survey student annotations on a subset of difficult entities and substantiate the feasibility and necessity of manifold annotations for understanding named entity ambiguities from a distributional perspective.

1 Introduction

Named Entity Recognition (NER) is a fundamental task in Natural Language Processing (NLP) (Yadav and Bethard, 2018). The task involves identifying named entities (NEs), such as *Justin Bieber*, *UNESCO*, and *Costa Rica*, and classifying them into semantic types, PER(son), ORG(anization), and LOC(ation), etc. Despite recent successes in achieving 93%+ strict F1 (Rücker and Akbik, 2023) on the English CoNLL03 benchmark (Tjong Kim Sang and De Meulder, 2003), recent research has observed that the percentage of noise in the data, particularly in the test partition, is comparable or even exceeding the error rates of state-of-the-art (SOTA) models (Wang et al., 2019; Reiss et al., 2020; Rücker and Akbik, 2023). They each conducted manual corrections or re-annotations, and model performances on their revised versions were higher than on the original. However, label variation in NEs, as shown in Table 1, remains an issue and hinders model performance.

Sentence	PER LOC ORG MISC O
a. UK bookmakers [William Hill] ...	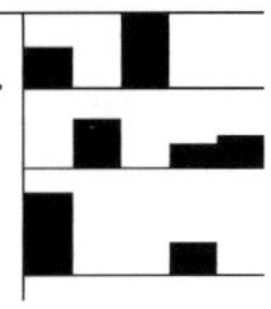
b. [ALPINE] SKIING ...	
c. ... that there is no [God] .	

Table 1: Distribution of qualified student annotations on disagreed named entities in CoNLL03.

Human label variation (i.e., disagreement) refers to linguistically debatable cases where multiple labels are acceptable or appropriate in context (Plank et al., 2014; Jiang and de Marneffe, 2022). Recent studies that examine and benefit from disagreements among annotators challenge the conventional assumption of a single gold label. Learning from disagreements provides further insights into label distributions and preferences among human annotators (Uma et al., 2021a; Plank, 2022; Fetahu et al., 2023). However, there remains a gap for disagreement analyses on expert-labeled manifold NEs.

This paper presents quantitative and qualitative analyses of annotators' disagreements on labeling NEs in three Germanic variants: English, Danish, and Bavarian, in which multiple annotation efforts exist on the same documents. Unlike earlier studies that look at crowd-sourced data of unreliable quality (Rodrigues et al., 2014; Lu et al., 2023), we examine disagreements among expert annotations that went through iterations of published revisions and contrast them with the usual setting of independent annotators. §2 presents related work in disagreements and §3 demonstrates our setups. We analyze entity and label disagreements in §4, sources of disagreements in §5, and a student-surveyed annotation study in §6. §7 summarizes our work. We release our annotations and analyses on Github.[1]

[1] https://github.com/mainlp/NER-disagreements/

Proceedings of the Third Workshop on Understanding Implicit and Underspecified Language, pages 73–81
March 21, 2024

2 Related Work

Despite disagreements between human judgments in subjective tasks (Prabhakaran et al., 2021; Davani et al., 2022; Fetahu et al., 2023; Leonardelli et al., 2023), annotation variation studies in NLP are recently on the rise (Uma et al., 2021a; Plank, 2022; Fetahu et al., 2023). These include part-of-speech tagging (Plank et al., 2014), anaphora and pronoun resolution (Poesio and Artstein, 2005; Poesio et al., 2019; Haber and Poesio, 2020), discourse relation labeling (Marchal et al., 2022; Pyatkin et al., 2023), word sense disambiguation (Passonneau et al., 2012; Navigli et al., 2013; Martínez Alonso et al., 2015), natural language inference (Nie et al., 2020; Jiang and de Marneffe, 2022; Liu et al., 2023), question answering (Min et al., 2020; Ferracane et al., 2021), to name a few.

In NER, Rodrigues et al. (2014) crowd-sourced problematic annotations from 47 Turkers on CoNLL03, scoring F1 of 17.60% the lowest and ~60% on average against CoNLL03 annotations, considerably under-performing the 90%+ inter-annotator agreement among expert annotators and SOTA model performances (Lu et al., 2023). Recently, Rücker and Akbik (2023) brought forward the newest CoNLL03 correction and thoroughly compared it with previous versions (Tjong Kim Sang and De Meulder, 2003; Wang et al., 2019; Reiss et al., 2020). However, many corrections are due to project-dependent guideline alternations and 2.34% of entities remain unresolved due to ambiguities. Thus, an onlooker assessment of NE disagreements and label variations is missing, particularly for expert annotations.

3 Datasets & Preprocessing

We analyze label variations in CoNLL03-styled PER/LOC/ORG/MISC NE annotations in three Germanic languages: English, Danish, and Bavarian (a Germanic dialect without standard orthography), where multiple annotation efforts on the same text documents are (or will be) available. Since the English CoNLL03 (Tjong Kim Sang and De Meulder, 2003) and Danish DDT (Plank, 2019) texts underwent iteration(s) of re-annotations or corrections by subsequent scholars, we conduct a diachronic comparison of the revisions for English and Danish. We also analyze disagreements on an in-house NE dataset for Bavarian German to distinguish disagreements among full-fledged corpora from independent unadjudicated annotations.

English The seminal English CoNLL03 dataset (henceforth `original`, Tjong Kim Sang and De Meulder 2003) presents the renowned NLP task to label flat and named entity spans into four major semantic types (PER, LOC, ORG, MISC) using (B)IO-encoding. The dataset includes 14.04K, 3.25K, and 3.45K sentences in its train, dev, and test partitions sourced from Reuters News between 1996-1997. Despite achieving 93%+ F1 score of the best systems on `original`, CoNLL03 annotations underwent several revisions (Wang et al., 2019; Reiss et al., 2020; Rücker and Akbik, 2023).

Wang et al. (2019) (`conllpp`) manually corrected 186 (5.38%) test sentences. Reiss et al. (2020) (`reiss`) used a semi-automatic approach to flag a larger quantity of error-prone labels (3.18K) in the entire dataset, and manually corrected 1.32K, including 421 in the test, as well as fixing tokenization and sentence splitting. They categorize these errors into six types: `Tag`, `Span`, `Both`, `Wrong`, `Sentence`, and `Token`. Rücker and Akbik (2023) (`clean`) present the most comprehensive relabeling effort by correcting 7.0% of all labels and adding a novel layer for entity linking. Though 5%+ of annotation errors were fixed compared to `original`, 2.34% of entities in `clean` remain ambiguous.

To establish fair comparisons, we manually align tokenization in the test partitions of `original`, `conllpp`, `reiss`, and `clean`. These include removing redundant line breaks, splitting hyphenized compounds, etc. Our alignment results in 46,738 test tokens across the four versions and 5,629, 5,683, 5,636, 5,725 annotated entities respectively.

Danish Plank (2019) annotates NEs on the dev and test partitions of the Danish Universal Dependencies (DDT, Johannsen et al. 2015). Plank et al. (2020) (`plank`) revise annotations, expand to more data and genres, and add -part/deriv suffixed labels and second-level nesting. Hvingelby et al. (2020) (`hvingelby`) re-annotate the dev and test sets of Plank (2019) by adding POS-marked proper nouns as NEs, resulting in ~0.75 and ~3.0 times more ORG and MISC NEs, such as nationalities and derived adjectives. We focus on the test partition (10,023 tokens) and compare `hvingelby` to the more recent `plank`, removing nesting and -part/deriv entities for cross-lingual analogy, leading to 564 and 531 NEs in `hvingelby` and `plank`.

Bavarian We additionally analyze the test partition of an in-house Bavarian NE dataset with ~12K tokens and ~400 entities on Wikipedia and Twitter

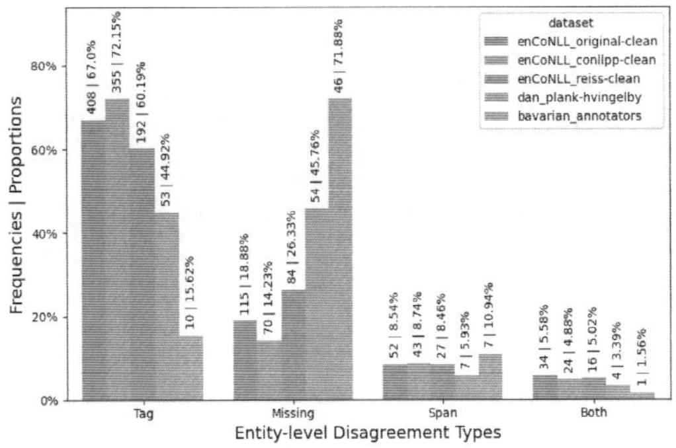

Figure 1: Proportions of entity-level disagreements in English `original-clean`, `conllpp-clean`, `reiss-clean`, Danish `plank-hvingelby`, and Bavarian.

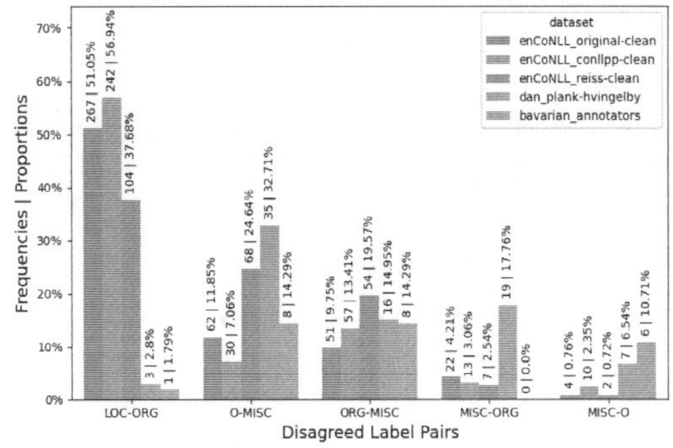

Figure 2: Proportions of top 5 label pairs in `Tag` and `Missing` disagreements in English, Danish, and Bavarian.

(X) annotated in 2023. Compared to the more established and iteratively revised English and Danish datasets, our Bavarian corpus represents the more common scenario of disagreements between two independent and unadjudicated annotations.

4 Entity-level Disagreements

Given our manually aligned tokenization across datasets, we modify Reiss et al. (2020)'s six error types into four entity-level disagreement types:

- `Tag`: same span selection, but different assigned tags, e.g., *[a b]*LOC vs. *[a b]*ORG;
- `Span`: different overlapping spans but the same tag, e.g., *[a b]*LOC vs. *[a]*LOC *b*;
- `Both`: overlapping spans with different tags, e.g., *[a b]*LOC vs. *[a]*ORG *b*;
- `Missing`: one annotator misses the entity completely, e.g., *[a b]*LOC vs. *a b*.

Figure 1 presents the frequencies and proportions of entity-level disagreements in five paired comparisons: English `original-clean`, `conllpp-clean`, `reiss-clean`, Danish `plank-hvingelby`, and between two Bavarian annotators. `Tag` disagreements contribute to most cases among repeatedly developed English corpora. On the other hand, Danish and Bavarian contain more `Missing` disagreements. Nevertheless, combining `Tag` and `Missing` accounts for 85%+ of disagreements in all comparisons across three languages. That is, entity tagging remains a bigger issue compared to span selection.

`Tag` and `Missing` disagreements are comparable in that both concern tagging the same entity span with different labels: the former with two different entity types (i.e., two non-O labels), and the latter with one entity type (a non-O label) and an O. Figure 2 displays the proportions of the top 5 disagreed label pairs in `Tag` and `Missing` disagreements across the five comparison scenarios (see Appendix A for a full list of label pairs). LOC-ORG, O-MISC and ORG-MISC are the most frequently disagreed label pairs in English comparisons, totaling 70%+ label disagreements. On the other hand, most (80%+) of Danish label disagreements concern MISC, whereas O-related (i.e., `Missing`) disagreements donate the majority (70%+) to Bavarian. To understand which factors trigger these label disagreements, §5 qualitatively analyzes the sources of human label variations in three languages.

5 Sources of Disagreements

Taxonomy We attribute NE label variations to three sources (Aroyo and Welty, 2015; Jiang and de Marneffe, 2022): 1) *text ambiguity* for uncertainties in the sentence meaning, 2) *guideline update* where NE type definitions vary across different guideline versions, and 3) *annotator error*. *Text ambiguity* could be caused by different interpretations with or without enough context that hinders pinpointing a definitive reference. *Guideline update* occurs when one annotation version is incoherent with another guideline. This is dominant in our analyses since annotation projects consist of iterations of guidelines and annotation revisions. For instance, whether proper noun-derived adjectives, e.g., *[ALPINE]* in Table 1, should be LOC, MISC, or not an entity (i.e., O); whether polysemous LOC/ORG entities are labeled LOC or ORG depending on context, or always as MISC. The

Source types	English		Danish		Bavarian	
text ambiguity	19	9.5%	7	6.0%	10	15.6%
guideline update	160	80.0%	62	52.5%	11	17.2%
annotator error	21	10.5%	49	41.5%	43	67.2%
Total	200	100.0%	118	100.0%	64	100.0%

Table 2: Sources of label disagreements and their distributions in English, Danish, and Bavarian samples.

last category, *annotator error*, refers to annotations that differ from a single deterministic ground truth. Closer inspections could fix annotators' attention slip errors, whereas special cultural knowledge is needed for resolving knowledge gap disagreements. We manually annotate a small sample of disagreements in three languages using these source categories to separate guideline changes and textual ambiguities from annotators' mistakes.

Setup For English, we sample 200 disagreed test entities between the `original` and the most recent `clean` annotation. Since the Danish `plank-hvingelby` comparisons and the Bavarian double annotations have much smaller test sets, we sample all test disagreements in the two languages, 118 entities in Danish and 64 in Bavarian. Each language sample is assessed by one computational linguist who speaks that language. Table 2 presents the source of disagreement results.

Additionally, we measure inter-annotator agreement (IAA) on source classes between two assessors[2] on 50 ambiguous English `original-clean` test entities and achieve 61.73% Cohen's kappa. Assessors find the hardest differentiating whether the lack of contextual information resulted from annotators' personal knowledge backgrounds (*annotator error*) or the settings behind text segments (*text ambiguity*). Even though surrounding sentences are provided, NE annotators tend to focus on the nearer context for NE tagging.

English In the `original-clean` comparison, most (80.0%) of disagreements stem from differences in *guideline update*. To disambiguate inconsistent cases in `original`, `clean` updated the guideline to be less context-dependent: 1) ORG instead of LOC for national sports teams as well as public facilities, even for *the flight to [Atlanta]*ORG; 2) MISC is used for more abstract institutions and adjectival affiliations e.g., *[Czech]*MISC *politics*; 3) instead of further correcting tokenizations and splitting hyphenated compounds, they assign labels that are relevant to part of the compound to the entirety, e.g., *[German-born]*MISC. Aside from *guideline update*, ambiguities occur for religious deities, such as whether *[Allah]* or *[God]* should be PER, MISC or O (see Table 1). Previous automatic conversions from IO-encodings in `original` to BIO in `clean` also caused disagreements since it is hard to tell apart if a sequence of I-tags is one entity or multiple, e.g., *[Spanish]*MISC *[Super Cup]*MISC or *[Spanish Super Cup]*MISC.

Danish Akin to the English analysis, we found that large parts (52.5%) of the ambiguous cases in Danish stem from *guideline updates*, e.g., frequently mentioned ferry routes are labeled LOC in `hvingelby` but MISC in `plank`. Besides, we found 41.5% of disagreements are *annotator errors*, and the majority are ORG-MISC disagreements and concern a single hyphen-joint token with two sports clubs, e.g., *[Vejle-Ikast]*. This points out a disadvantage of the current cross-lingual comparable analysis — compounding morphology prevails in Danish and Bavarian, and removing -part/deriv labels leads to information loss.

Bavarian We present the less developed but more common scenario of disagreements between two unadjudicated annotations in Bavarian. Though achieving 85%+ Span IAA, *annotator error* (67.2%) remains the highest source of disagreements. Apart from local entities, e.g., *[Feucht]*loc (a small town in Bavaria), that require geographical knowledge or detailed search, many of these *annotator errors* classified based on the Bavarian guideline are indeed acceptable under certain versions of the English CoNLL guidelines. For example, when *[Edeka]* (a supermarket chain) functions as a destination, the disagreement between LOC-ORG is classified as *annotator error* in Bavarian, but would rather be a *guideline update* in English.

6 Surveying Student Annotations

Though NE guidelines can be meticulously different from each other, the underlying concepts of PER, LOC, ORG are cognitively straightforward. To inspect the distribution of multiple interpretations, we follow Liu et al. (2023) to survey annotations from 27 bachelor and master students in computational linguistics at LMU Munich. We gave them a 7-minute introduction to NEs, walked through the CoNLL03 guideline,[3] and showed some examples of type ambiguities in NE annotations. Students

[2] We use "assessors" to refer to our source of disagreement coders and differentiate from "annotators" of the NE datasets.

[3] `www.cnts.ua.ac.be/conll2003/ner/annotation.txt`

were instructed in the classroom to annotate entity types in English and Bavarian selected from difficult examples in §5.[4] We further sample 10 representative English CoNLL entities for the qualitative evaluation below.[5] To ensure the quality of student-surveyed annotations, we only keep an annotation if 80%+ of entity labels match any of the four CoNLL annotations. Table 1 demonstrates the distribution of 14 qualified student annotations on three examples (see Appendix B for the ten representative English CoNLL entities).

Results demonstrate that label variation across annotation projects are also prevalent in the student-surveyed annotations. On one side, even with a brief training, students were able to disambiguate the contextual interpretations between [the away team]ORG and [the home team]LOC in *[LA CLIPPERS]*ORG *AT [NEW YORK]*LOC. Our participants also recognize the collectiveness of *[White House]*ORG, *[Australia]*ORG, etc., and the fixedness of *[EST]*MISC (Eastern Standard Time). On the other hand, knowledge gap or insufficient context contribute to the high variance of *[William Hill]*, whether it refers to [the businessman]PER or [the gambling bookstore he created]ORG. Annotators also diverge in marginal cases: whether *[God]* is PER or MISC and whether nominal derivatives *ALPINE* and *Fascist* are NEs.

7 Conclusion

This paper examines named entity disagreements across expert annotations and contrasts them with the more common setting of individual annotations. We demonstrate that human label variation, e.g., LOC-ORG and ORG-MISC, contribute to most English, Danish, and Bavarian disagreements. We also discover that *guideline updates* and *text ambiguities* are leading sources of disagreements in established English and German datasets, whereas *annotator errors* remain the dominant cause for the new Bavarian corpus. Lastly, we survey student annotations and encourage more researchers to explore NE label variations to narrow the gap to model performance.

Though modeling NER from label variation is out of the scope of this paper, we embrace the prospect of learning from disagreements (Uma et al., 2021b). Particularly, we look forward to conducting annotations on a much larger scale in terms of both the number of participants and annotated instances to provide more statistically meaningful NE distributions for NER models. Future work also includes separating valid label variations from true annotation mistakes by leveraging Automatic Error Detection (AED) methods (Klie et al., 2023; Weber and Plank, 2023). We hope tackling NER through label variations can remedy the conflicts among versions of annotation guidelines.

[4]Students acknowledge that their annotations could be used for research purposes.

[5]The full English and Bavarian student-surveyed annotations are available on GitHub.

Acknowledgements

We would like to thank Verena Blaschke for giving feedback on earlier drafts of this paper. This project is supported by ERC Consolidator Grant DIALECT 101043235.

References

Lora Aroyo and Chris Welty. 2015. Truth Is a Lie: Crowd Truth and the Seven Myths of Human Annotation. *AI Magazine*, 36(1):15–24. Number: 1.

Aida Mostafazadeh Davani, Mark Díaz, and Vinodkumar Prabhakaran. 2022. Dealing with Disagreements: Looking Beyond the Majority Vote in Subjective Annotations. *Transactions of the Association for Computational Linguistics*, 10:92–110.

Elisa Ferracane, Greg Durrett, Junyi Jessy Li, and Katrin Erk. 2021. Did they answer? Subjective acts and intents in conversational discourse. In *Proceedings of the 2021 Conference of the North American Chapter of the Association for Computational Linguistics: Human Language Technologies*, pages 1626–1644, Online. Association for Computational Linguistics.

Besnik Fetahu, Sudipta Kar, Zhiyu Chen, Oleg Rokhlenko, and Shervin Malmasi. 2023. SemEval-2023 Task 2: Fine-grained Multilingual Named Entity Recognition (MultiCoNER 2). In *Proceedings of the 17th International Workshop on Semantic Evaluation (SemEval-2023)*, pages 2247–2265, Toronto, Canada. Association for Computational Linguistics.

Janosch Haber and Massimo Poesio. 2020. Classification of low-agreement Pronouns through Collaborative Dialogue: A Proof of Concept.

Rasmus Hvingelby, Amalie Brogaard Pauli, Maria Barrett, Christina Rosted, Lasse Malm Lidegaard, and Anders Søgaard. 2020. DaNE: A Named Entity Resource for Danish. In *Proceedings of the Twelfth Language Resources and Evaluation Conference*, pages 4597–4604, Marseille, France. European Language Resources Association.

Nan-Jiang Jiang and Marie-Catherine de Marneffe. 2022. Investigating Reasons for Disagreement in

Natural Language Inference. *Transactions of the Association for Computational Linguistics*, 10:1357–1374. Place: Cambridge, MA Publisher: MIT Press.

Anders Johannsen, Héctor Martínez Alonso, and Barbara Plank. 2015. Universal dependencies for danish. In *International Workshop on Treebanks and Linguistic Theories (TLT14)*, pages 157–167.

Jan-Christoph Klie, Bonnie Webber, and Iryna Gurevych. 2023. Annotation Error Detection: Analyzing the Past and Present for a More Coherent Future. *Computational Linguistics*, 49(1):157–198.

Elisa Leonardelli, Gavin Abercrombie, Dina Almanea, Valerio Basile, Tommaso Fornaciari, Barbara Plank, Verena Rieser, Alexandra Uma, and Massimo Poesio. 2023. SemEval-2023 Task 11: Learning with Disagreements (LeWiDi). In *Proceedings of the 17th International Workshop on Semantic Evaluation (SemEval-2023)*, pages 2304–2318, Toronto, Canada. Association for Computational Linguistics.

Alisa Liu, Zhaofeng Wu, Julian Michael, Alane Suhr, Peter West, Alexander Koller, Swabha Swayamdipta, Noah Smith, and Yejin Choi. 2023. We're Afraid Language Models Aren't Modeling Ambiguity. In *Proceedings of the 2023 Conference on Empirical Methods in Natural Language Processing*, pages 790–807, Singapore. Association for Computational Linguistics.

Sheng Lu, Irina Bigoulaeva, Rachneet Sachdeva, Harish Tayyar Madabushi, and Iryna Gurevych. 2023. Are Emergent Abilities in Large Language Models just In-Context Learning? ArXiv:2309.01809 [cs].

Marian Marchal, Merel Scholman, Frances Yung, and Vera Demberg. 2022. Establishing Annotation Quality in Multi-label Annotations. In *Proceedings of the 29th International Conference on Computational Linguistics*, pages 3659–3668, Gyeongju, Republic of Korea. International Committee on Computational Linguistics.

Héctor Martínez Alonso, Anders Johannsen, Oier Lopez de Lacalle, and Eneko Agirre. 2015. Predicting word sense annotation agreement. In *Proceedings of the First Workshop on Linking Computational Models of Lexical, Sentential and Discourse-level Semantics*, pages 89–94, Lisbon, Portugal. Association for Computational Linguistics.

Sewon Min, Julian Michael, Hannaneh Hajishirzi, and Luke Zettlemoyer. 2020. AmbigQA: Answering Ambiguous Open-domain Questions. In *Proceedings of the 2020 Conference on Empirical Methods in Natural Language Processing (EMNLP)*, pages 5783–5797, Online. Association for Computational Linguistics.

Roberto Navigli, David Jurgens, and Daniele Vannella. 2013. SemEval-2013 Task 12: Multilingual Word Sense Disambiguation. In *Second Joint Conference on Lexical and Computational Semantics (*SEM), Volume 2: Proceedings of the Seventh International Workshop on Semantic Evaluation (SemEval 2013)*, pages 222–231, Atlanta, Georgia, USA. Association for Computational Linguistics.

Yixin Nie, Xiang Zhou, and Mohit Bansal. 2020. What Can We Learn from Collective Human Opinions on Natural Language Inference Data? In *Proceedings of the 2020 Conference on Empirical Methods in Natural Language Processing (EMNLP)*, pages 9131–9143, Online. Association for Computational Linguistics.

Rebecca J. Passonneau, Vikas Bhardwaj, Ansaf Salleb-Aouissi, and Nancy Ide. 2012. Multiplicity and word sense: evaluating and learning from multiply labeled word sense annotations. *Language Resources and Evaluation*, 46(2):219–252.

Barbara Plank. 2019. Neural Cross-Lingual Transfer and Limited Annotated Data for Named Entity Recognition in Danish. In *Proceedings of the 22nd Nordic Conference on Computational Linguistics*, pages 370–375, Turku, Finland. Linköping University Electronic Press.

Barbara Plank. 2022. The "Problem" of Human Label Variation: On Ground Truth in Data, Modeling and Evaluation. In *Proceedings of the 2022 Conference on Empirical Methods in Natural Language Processing*, pages 10671–10682, Abu Dhabi, United Arab Emirates. Association for Computational Linguistics.

Barbara Plank, Dirk Hovy, and Anders Søgaard. 2014. Linguistically debatable or just plain wrong? In *Proceedings of the 52nd Annual Meeting of the Association for Computational Linguistics (Volume 2: Short Papers)*, pages 507–511, Baltimore, Maryland. Association for Computational Linguistics.

Barbara Plank, Kristian Nørgaard Jensen, and Rob van der Goot. 2020. DaN+: Danish Nested Named Entities and Lexical Normalization. In *Proceedings of the 28th International Conference on Computational Linguistics*, pages 6649–6662, Barcelona, Spain (Online). International Committee on Computational Linguistics.

Massimo Poesio and Ron Artstein. 2005. The Reliability of Anaphoric Annotation, Reconsidered: Taking Ambiguity into Account. In *Proceedings of the Workshop on Frontiers in Corpus Annotations II: Pie in the Sky*, pages 76–83, Ann Arbor, Michigan. Association for Computational Linguistics.

Massimo Poesio, Jon Chamberlain, Silviu Paun, Juntao Yu, Alexandra Uma, and Udo Kruschwitz. 2019. A Crowdsourced Corpus of Multiple Judgments and Disagreement on Anaphoric Interpretation. In *Proceedings of the 2019 Conference of the North American Chapter of the Association for Computational Linguistics: Human Language Technologies, Volume 1 (Long and Short Papers)*, pages 1778–1789, Minneapolis, Minnesota. Association for Computational Linguistics.

Vinodkumar Prabhakaran, Aida Mostafazadeh Davani, and Mark Diaz. 2021. On Releasing Annotator-Level Labels and Information in Datasets. In *Proceedings of the Joint 15th Linguistic Annotation Workshop (LAW) and 3rd Designing Meaning Representations (DMR) Workshop*, pages 133–138, Punta Cana, Dominican Republic. Association for Computational Linguistics.

Valentina Pyatkin, Frances Yung, Merel C. J. Scholman, Reut Tsarfaty, Ido Dagan, and Vera Demberg. 2023. Design Choices for Crowdsourcing Implicit Discourse Relations: Revealing the Biases Introduced by Task Design. ArXiv:2304.00815 [cs].

Frederick Reiss, Hong Xu, Bryan Cutler, Karthik Muthuraman, and Zachary Eichenberger. 2020. Identifying Incorrect Labels in the CoNLL-2003 Corpus. In *Proceedings of the 24th Conference on Computational Natural Language Learning*, pages 215–226, Online. Association for Computational Linguistics.

Filipe Rodrigues, Francisco Pereira, and Bernardete Ribeiro. 2014. Sequence labeling with multiple annotators. *Machine Learning*, 95(2):165–181.

Susanna Rücker and Alan Akbik. 2023. CleanCoNLL: A Nearly Noise-Free Named Entity Recognition Dataset. In *Proceedings of the 2023 Conference on Empirical Methods in Natural Language Processing*, pages 8628–8645, Singapore. Association for Computational Linguistics.

Erik F. Tjong Kim Sang and Fien De Meulder. 2003. Introduction to the CoNLL-2003 Shared Task: Language-Independent Named Entity Recognition. In *Proceedings of the Seventh Conference on Natural Language Learning at HLT-NAACL 2003*, pages 142–147.

Alexandra Uma, Tommaso Fornaciari, Anca Dumitrache, Tristan Miller, Jon Chamberlain, Barbara Plank, Edwin Simpson, and Massimo Poesio. 2021a. SemEval-2021 Task 12: Learning with Disagreements. In *Proceedings of the 15th International Workshop on Semantic Evaluation (SemEval-2021)*, pages 338–347, Online. Association for Computational Linguistics.

Alexandra N. Uma, Tommaso Fornaciari, Dirk Hovy, Silviu Paun, Barbara Plank, and Massimo Poesio. 2021b. Learning from Disagreement: A Survey. *Journal of Artificial Intelligence Research*, 72:1385–1470.

Zihan Wang, Jingbo Shang, Liyuan Liu, Lihao Lu, Jiacheng Liu, and Jiawei Han. 2019. CrossWeigh: Training Named Entity Tagger from Imperfect Annotations. In *Proceedings of the 2019 Conference on Empirical Methods in Natural Language Processing and the 9th International Joint Conference on Natural Language Processing (EMNLP-IJCNLP)*, pages 5154–5163, Hong Kong, China. Association for Computational Linguistics.

Leon Weber and Barbara Plank. 2023. ActiveAED: A Human in the Loop Improves Annotation Error Detection. In *Findings of the Association for Computational Linguistics: ACL 2023*, pages 8834–8845, Toronto, Canada. Association for Computational Linguistics.

Vikas Yadav and Steven Bethard. 2018. A Survey on Recent Advances in Named Entity Recognition from Deep Learning models. In *Proceedings of the 27th International Conference on Computational Linguistics*, pages 2145–2158, Santa Fe, New Mexico, USA. Association for Computational Linguistics.

A Proportions of Disagreed Label Pairs

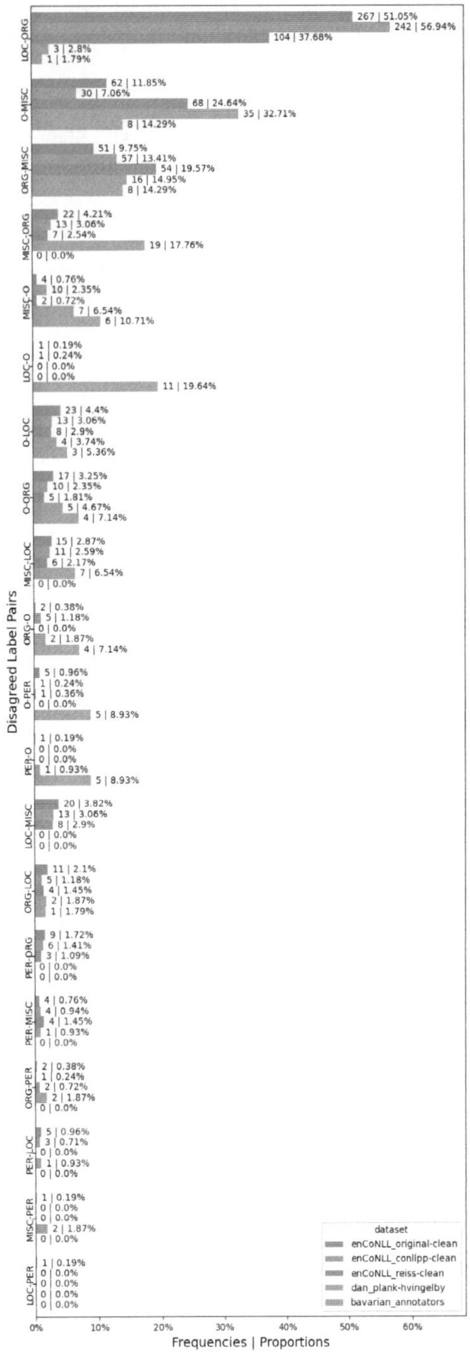

Figure 3: Proportions of label pairs (full) in `Tag` and `Missing` disagreements in English, Danish, and Bavarian.

B Student Surveyed NE Annotations

Sentence	PER	LOC	ORG	MISC	O	*abstained*

[ALPINE] SKIING		6
		`clean`
				3	4
					`original`
					`conllpp`
					`reiss`
						1

[LA CLIPPERS] AT NEW YORK			13
			`original`
			`conllpp`
			`reiss`
			`clean`
						1

LA CLIPPERS AT [NEW YORK]		14
		`original`
		`conllpp`
		`reiss`
			0
			`clean`			

[White House] spokesman Mike McCurry said Clinton plans to have regular news conferences during his second term .		2
		`original`
		`conllpp`
		`reiss`
			11
			`clean`
				1		

UK bookmakers [William Hill][6] said on Friday they have lengthened the odds of a Conservative victory .	5
	`original`
	`conllpp`
	`reiss`
			9
			`clean`			

The man who kicked [Australia] to defeat with a last-ditch drop-goal in the World Cup quarter-final in Cape Town .		5
		`original`
		`conllpp`
		`reiss`
			9
			`clean`			

The years I spent as (soccer team) manager of the [Republic of Ireland] were the best years of my life .		4
		`original`
		`conllpp`
		`reiss`
			9
			`clean`
				1		

I bear witness that there is no [God] .	10
	`original`
	`conllpp`
	`reiss`
				4
				`clean`		

The granddaughter of Italy's [Fascist][7] dictator Benito Mussolini			3	3
				`clean`
					8
					`original`
					`conllpp`
					`reiss`	

at about 3 A.M. local time / 1:30 A.M. [EST]				10
				`clean`
					2
					`original`
					`conllpp`
					`reiss`
						2

Table 3: 14 classroom surveyed and qualified annotations on difficult disagreement cases in CoNLL03 test.

Colour Me Uncertain: Representing Vagueness with Probabilistic Semantics

Kin Chun Cheung (Bruce) and **Guy Emerson**
Department of Computer Science and Technology
University of Cambridge
bruce.ckc@outlook.com and gete2@cam.ac.uk

Abstract

People successfully communicate in everyday situations using vague language. In particular, colour terms have no clear boundaries as to the ranges of colours they describe. We model people's reasoning process in a dyadic reference game using the Rational Speech Acts (RSA) framework and probabilistic semantics, and we find that the implementation of probabilistic semantics requires a modification from pure theory to perform well on real-world data. In addition, we explore approaches to handling target disagreements in reference games, an issue that is rarely discussed in the RSA literature.

Speaker: *"red"*

Figure 1: Illustration of Monroe et al. (2017)'s reference game where three colours are shown, in a randomised order, to a pair of participants. The speaker has to communicate the target colour (boxed) by typing messages to the listener, who then selects the colour they believe to be the target.

1 Introduction

Colour terms are vague. There are no clear boundaries for what red, green, blue, or other colour words denote, causing uncertainty in their interpretations, and yet we are able to effectively communicate using colours in everyday situations.

To explain how we work with this kind of uncertainty, proponents of probabilistic semantics (for example: Cooper et al., 2014; Sutton, 2015) consider vagueness to be intrinsic to language, where competent agents make graded judgements as to whether a predicate applies to a situation. This view of semantics allows us to model predicates with conditional probabilities: for example, given a colour patch (e.g.), to what degree would an agent believe that the term *"green"* is appropriate?

When we consider multiple such judgements (for example, multiple colour patches), there are in theory various ways that judgements could be combined. These vary from simple fuzzy-logical approaches to complex joint probability distributions, which we will discuss in detail in §2.1.

In this paper, we explore the practical feasibility of applying probabilistic semantics to model vagueness. To ground the findings on real-world data, we use a colour game dataset in English by Monroe et al. (2017). The game displays three colours and requires the speaker to describe a target colour, which the listener attempts to guess. Since the colours are uniformly sampled from a colour space, they are usually not canonical examples of particular colour words. As such, successful communication requires the participants to leverage the vagueness of colour terms to solve the task.

Monroe et al. apply the Rational Speech Acts (RSA) framework (Frank and Goodman, 2012) to train a pragmatic model with a neural listener and speaker, and find that pragmatic inference helps in disambiguating similar colours. In this paper, we first show that their model instantiates a fuzzy-logical approach to vagueness. We then extend their work by replacing the fuzzy-logical literal listener model with one that uses probabilistic semantics, and present three main contributions.

First, modelling real-world data with probabilistic semantics requires an additional Gricean assumption that not all world states be false in a given context. Second, the RSA framework is sensitive to the performance of the neural listener and speaker models, with previously observed pragmatic effects diminished after better tuning. Third, we propose various ways to handle target disagreements in dyadic reference games, and find that the removal of disagreements significantly improves model performance on Monroe et al.'s dataset.

Proceedings of the Third Workshop on Understanding Implicit and Underspecified Language, pages 82–89
March 21, 2024 ©2024 Association for Computational Linguistics

"red"	**0.5**	**0.5**
"pink"	0	**1**

(a) Literal listener L_0 chooses a colour based on the literal semantics of each utterance u. When u is equally applicable to both colours, L_0 chooses at random.

"red"	**1**	0.33
"pink"	0	**0.67**

(b) Pragmatic speaker S_1 weighs the informativeness of each utterance in describing a target colour by softmaxing L_0's choice distributions.

"red"	**0.75**	0.25
"pink"	0	**1**

(c) Pragmatic listener L_2 infers the target colour by reasoning about S_1's choice of the given utterance over other possible utterances.

Figure 2: Example of the RSA framework applied to a situation with two colours and a set of two possible utterances. While both colours can be described as "red", a pragmatic listener infers that such an utterance refers to the deeper red patch (left), because a pragmatic speaker would have used the term "pink" if the target was the paler red (right).

2 Background & Related Work

Prior work has employed the RSA framework to combine semantics and pragmatics in an effort to quantify vagueness (Lassiter and Goodman, 2015; Monroe et al., 2017; McDowell and Goodman, 2019). RSA formalises the theory of conversational implicatures (Grice, 1975) by modelling people iteratively reasoning about each other's actions to infer their intentions. It quantifies the interaction by defining explicit objectives for listener and speaker agents. Note that the agents are not actual individuals, but representations of the layers of reasoning that people perform as modelled by RSA. For a survey, see: Degen (2023).

In the RSA framework, we assume that a speaker wants to communicate knowledge about some state c to a listener. A literal listener L_0 chooses a state c based on an utterance u's literal interpretation, $\mathcal{L}(u, c)$, and weighted by its prior $P(c)$ (Equation 1). Reasoning about such a listener, a pragmatic speaker S_1 chooses an utterance that is most informative by considering the literal listener's choices, subject to a rationality parameter α and utterance cost $\kappa(u)$ (Equation 2). Finally, reasoning about such a speaker, a pragmatic listener L_2 infers the intended state based on the speaker's choice of utterance (Equation 3). These three equations together define a pragmatic listener's process of understanding a single utterance.

$$L_0(c \mid u; \mathcal{L}) \propto \mathcal{L}(u, c)P(c) \tag{1}$$

$$S_1(u \mid c, \mathcal{L}) \propto e^{\alpha \log(L_0(c|u;\mathcal{L}))-\kappa(u)} \tag{2}$$

$$L_2(c \mid u, \mathcal{L}) \propto S_1(u \mid c, \mathcal{L})P(c) \tag{3}$$

In Monroe et al.'s game, the states are equally likely so the prior can be discounted. For simplicity, we assume $\kappa = 0$ and $\alpha = 1$. Figure 2 illustrates an example of the agents' reasoning process over two context colours with two possible utterances.

2.1 Linguistic Approaches to Vagueness

Many approaches to modelling vagueness have been proposed (for a recent survey, see: Burnett and Sutton, 2020). Of particular interest are fuzzy and probabilistic approaches, because of their compatibility with neural network models.

In **fuzzy** logic, truth is not binary, but instead any real value from 0 to 1, which allows a direct account of vagueness (Zadeh, 1965). Logical operations such as AND and OR have fuzzy versions which are truth-functional, meaning that they are defined as functions taking fuzzy truth-values as input, and producing fuzzy truth-values as output. The simplicity of a truth-functional approach means that fuzzy logic is unable to express correlations between truth-values (Fine, 1975). For example, considering a borderline red/orange shade, where "red" and "orange" are both 0.5 true, fuzzy logic treats "red or orange" the same as "red or not red". This does not match empirical facts about the use of vague terms (Sauerland, 2011).

In **probabilistic** logic, truth is binary but uncertain, and this can also be used to account for vagueness (Edgington, 1992, 1997). In contrast to fuzzy logic, there can be correlations between truth-values, which avoids the problems with the fuzzy account. However, this requires us to define a joint distribution over all truth-values.

To build up to a joint distribution, we first consider marginal probabilities. For a predicate u, we can define a probabilistic truth-conditional function that gives the probability of the truth-value T_c being true, for state c, as in Equation 4. This function gives the marginal probability for one truth-value, ignoring the truth-values for other states c'.

$$t_u(c) = \mathbb{P}(T_c = \top; u) \tag{4}$$

A simple approach to define a joint distribution is to define a global threshold for truth, uniformly sampled from $[0, 1]$, against which marginal probabilities of truth are compared. Combining this with the RSA framework can capture various aspects of how vague terms are used (Lassiter, 2011; Lassiter and Goodman, 2015).

However, using a global threshold is restrictive. Emerson (2023) shows how we can see such a model as one instance in a broader class of probabilistic models. The most general model class would consider all possible joint distributions, but some distributions are computationally intractable. Tractability can be maintained by restricting to models that only require two things: the marginal probability for each truth-value, and the correlation between each pair of truth-values. A global threshold corresponds to maximising all correlations.

3 Methodology

We adopt the model architectures in Monroe et al., with a few refinements, to train an RSA system on the colour game dataset. As in Andreas and Klein (2016), neural models enable listener and speaker agents to be trained on real-world language use.

The literal listener uses an LSTM to process utterances, and based on its final state it outputs parameters for a score function. The literal speaker generates utterances by encoding the colour context as input to a second LSTM.

We refine Monroe et al.'s model by switching the speaker's decoding process from sampling to beam search, as well as making the colour encoder permutation-invariant to the order of inputs (Zaheer et al., 2017), so as to improve performance.

The literal listener's score function is given in Equation 5, where f is the Fourier-transformed vector representation of a colour (a deterministic transformation, following Monroe et al., 2016), and μ and Σ are the outputs of the LSTM.

$$\text{score}(f) = -(f - \mu)^T \Sigma (f - \mu) \quad (5)$$

If Σ is positive definite, which Monroe et al. note is the case for over 95% of their inputs, the score is the logarithm of an unnormalised probability density function (a multivariate Gaussian).

3.1 Base Literal Listener Model

Our baseline model follows Monroe et al. (2017), normalising the scores with an exponential softmax to give the listener's beliefs about the intended colour. Viewing this under the approaches in §2.1, it can be seen as implementing fuzzy logic, since the exponential of the score is a fuzzy truth-value and normalising fuzzy truth-values is a truth-functional operation.

More precisely, for a given utterance u, the base literal listener determines μ and Σ, then applies this score function to each colour representation f. The scores are passed through an exponential softmax to give a probability distribution over the colours.

Given representations f_i for a set of colours $C = \{c_0, \ldots, c_n\}$, the probability of choosing each colour is therefore given by:

$$L_0^{\text{base}}(c_i | u, C; (L)) = \frac{\exp(\text{score}(f_i))}{\sum_j \exp(\text{score}(f_j))} \quad (6)$$

To define a Gaussian distribution, as suggested by Monroe et al., the exp-scores must be rescaled so that they integrate to 1. However, multiplying all exp-scores by a constant leaves the distribution in Equation 6 unchanged, and so does not change any predictions of the model.

If Σ is positive definite, the score function achieves its maximum value of 0 when $f = \mu$. The exp-scores are therefore guaranteed to lie in the range $[0, 1]$, and so can be interpreted as fuzzy truth-values for the utterance u. The distribution in Equation 6 is therefore a normalisation of these fuzzy truth-values. The normalisation only depends on the truth-values (with no further dependence on u or f_i), and so it is a truth-functional operation. In other words, the model cannot express correlations between truth-values.

As this interpretation only holds if Σ is positive definite, we include a model in our experiments where scores are clamped to be non-positive, so that a fuzzy approach can be clearly contrasted with probabilistic approaches.

3.2 Probabilistic Literal Listener Model L_0^{prob}

Instead of normalising the scores directly, our L_0^{prob} probabilistic literal listener model interprets them as log-probabilities of truth. We clamp the scores to be non-positive and take their exponentials to get marginal probabilities $t_u(c)$ for each colour c.

These marginals are then used to calculate the joint distribution. Given three colours in the context, there are $2^3 = 8$ possible joint outcomes for truth-values. The joint distribution is not fully determined by the marginals, but also depends on correlations between the truth-values. We assume correlations are fixed (for more options, see: Emerson, 2023), and explore two possibilities: 1. truth-values are independent (*Prob Indep*), and 2. truth-values are maximally correlated (*Prob Max*).

Finally, the joint distribution over truth-values determines the distribution over listener actions. If ties are randomly broken (u is true for more than one colour, or false for all colours), then the chance of picking the target colour is given in Equation 7, where $p_{\dots}$ is the joint probability of truth ($\top$) or falsehood ($\bot$) for each colour, and the first colour is the target.

$$L_0^{\text{prob}}(c_0 \mid u, C; \theta) = p_{\top\bot\bot} + \frac{1}{2}p_{\top\top\bot} + \frac{1}{2}p_{\top\bot\top} + \frac{1}{3}p_{\top\top\top} + \frac{1}{3}p_{\bot\bot\bot} \quad (7)$$

However, we notice a problem with training a model to maximise the "pure" probabilistic objective in Equation 7. Suppose an utterance is definitely false for some colour. In the case where all truth-values are false, the "definitely false" colour is chosen with a one-third chance. The only way for the model to avoid this outcome is to set the marginal probability of another colour to 1, but by doing so it cannot convey uncertainty.

To avoid this problem, we introduce an "applied" version of the model, where the all-false outcome is excluded. In other words, if the speaker makes an utterance, it must be true of something, which is grounded on Grice's maxim of quality.

3.3 Target Disagreements

In supervised learning, it is assumed there is an objectively correct output for each input. This assumption does not hold for our language reference game. While there is a correct answer in the context of the game (i.e. the target colour), the listener and the speaker's choices cannot be wrong given our objective of modelling linguistic behaviour. From the speaker's perspective, the utterance they uttered applies to the target colour; from the listener's perspective, the colour they chose best matches the utterance they received. As such, we propose and investigate three alternative strategies for modelling data with target disagreements:

Listener-Speaker (L-S): Train on the listener's choice but evaluate on the speaker's target. The aim is for the literal listener to emulate a human listener's literal interpretation function, and for the pragmatic listener to apply pragmatic reasoning to select the intended target.

Listener-Listener (L-L): Both train and evaluate on the listener's choice. This changes the objective to emulating listener behaviour rather than selecting the "correct" target.

No Disagreements (ND): Remove training data with disagreements between speaker and listener, but evaluate on the unaltered test set. The aim is to understand if disagreements add noise to training.

Model	L_0 Accuracy	L_2 Accuracy
Monroe et al. (2017)	85.08	86.98[1]
Base	**87.65 ± 0.05**	88.03 ± 0.04
Base Clamped	87.51 ± 0.05	87.94 ± 0.04
Pure Prob Indep	76.06 ± 0.07	76.98 ± 0.12
Pure Prob Max	75.84 ± 0.08	76.85 ± 0.11
Applied Prob Indep	87.65 ± 0.03	87.96 ± 0.05
Applied Prob Max	87.58 ± 0.04	**88.05 ± 0.06**

Table 1: Mean accuracies for the main models evaluated on the test set, shown with standard errors of the means. Highest accuracy for each category in bold.

Model	Far	Split	Close
Pure Prob Indep	93.00	75.04	62.76
Applied Prob Indep	96.25	87.76	79.78
Δ (Applied - Pure)	3.25	12.72	17.02

Table 2: Comparison of the mean accuracies between the pure and applied probabilistic (Independent) models across different context types. Similar results were obtained using the Max Correlation models.

3.4 Experiment Setup

Hyperparameters were determined with grid search on the validation set, using the original data split. Details of grid search and chosen hyperparameters are given in Appendix A. Every model type was trained 10 times to reduce the effect of random initialisation (Reimers and Gurevych, 2017). Since an RSA model contains two neural nets (listener and speaker), they were arbitrarily paired up and the same dyads used for all evaluations.

4 Results & Discussion

The accuracies of the main model types are summarised in Table 1. Two-tailed p-values were above 0.1 between all pairs of the Base and Applied Prob models,[2] so there is no evidence to suggest a perfor-

[1]This is for Monroe et al.'s best performing blended model, L_e, as they did not report L_2 accuracy on the test set.

[2]Bootstrap tests using 100,000 rounds of resampling were performed over the six pairs of these four model types.

Model	$t_u(c) < 0.01$	$t_u(c) > 0.99$
Base Clamped	94.05%	3.98%
Pure Prob Indep	5.61%	89.22%
Applied Prob Indep	56.93%	7.91%

Table 3: Percentage of target colour samples that were assigned extreme marginal probabilities $t_u(c)$.

Train-Test Target	L_0 Accuracy	L_2 Accuracy
S-S	87.65 ± 0.03	87.96 ± 0.05
L-S	86.32 ± 0.04	86.70 ± 0.05
L-L	85.02 ± 0.04	85.14 ± 0.04
S-S ND	**87.85 ± 0.04**	**88.18 ± 0.06**

Table 4: Mean accuracies for the probabilistic (independent) models, using the specified target disagreement strategy, shown with standard errors of the means. Highest accuracy for each category in bold.

mance difference between these four model types.

Although the Base listener uses Monroe et al.'s architecture, its accuracy is much higher, highlighting the impact of model tuning and hyperparameter selection. The best optimisation algorithm found in grid search, AdamW, was not available at the time their work was published. Also, they did not state if their models were regularised, but we found a dropout rate of 0.5 provided the best performance. The narrower gap between our L_0 and L_2 accuracies suggests that some of the improvements from pragmatic reasoning that Monroe et al. observed could be attributed to an under-tuned model.

In addition, we find that the Base model produces positive scores for over 36% of the test set, compared to less than 5% noted by Monroe et al.. For the Base Clamped model, this drops to 3.1% for the raw scores before clamping, demonstrating that training dynamics affect the interpretation of the model as producing fuzzy truth-values.

4.1 Pure vs Applied Probabilistic Models

The performance differences between corresponding Pure and Applied models are significant at $p<0.00001$. The limitation of the Pure models is apparent when comparing different difficulty contexts in Table 2. For the Pure models, the especially poor results in contexts with two or more similar colours (*split* and *close*) can be attributed to the high marginal probabilities generated, as shown in Table 3 (for full distributions, see Appendix B). If two or more colours in a given context have high marginal probability, the literal listener's output distribution will be skewed towards having equal probabilities for those colours, drowning out any signal from the utterance. In contrast, the Applied models produce less extreme marginal probabilities and achieve better performance in all context types.

4.2 Target Disagreements

The results of our proposed strategies to deal with target disagreements are shown in Table 4. The models trained on listener choices performed poorer not only in predicting speaker targets, but also in predicting listener choices. However, the removal of target disagreements from training resulted in significantly better performance than the S-S models trained on the full dataset.[3] This suggests that the data samples with target disagreements added noise during the training process, leading to poorer performance.

5 Conclusion

We demonstrated that a probabilistic semantic model benefits from an assumption to exclude an all-false outcome. While our results do not conclusively decide between probabilistic or fuzzy approaches to vagueness, this paper adds to a growing body of work that people exhibit pragmatic behaviours as posited by the RSA framework. However, careful tuning of the literal listener model reduces the effect size of pragmatic reasoning compared to previous work. Finally, we explored the previously undiscussed issue of target disagreements. For the 'Colors in Context' dataset, we found that disagreements may be best seen as noise.

Limitations

As our work focuses on one dataset, we are not able to generalise about the effectiveness of our proposed strategies to handle target disagreements on other dyadic reference games. We have given a theoretical justification and empirical analysis of our results, and so we would expect our conclusions to generalise, but further work would be needed to confirm this on other datasets. In addition, we applied fixed global correlations between truth-values when exploring the probabilistic approach. We leave for future work to investigate the impact of increasing correlation for more similar inputs, as described by Emerson (2023).

[3] Two-tailed p-value of 0.0296 for the Prob Indep models in Table 4. Results for other models are similar; see Appendix C.

References

Jacob Andreas and Dan Klein. 2016. Reasoning about pragmatics with neural listeners and speakers. In *Proceedings of the 2016 Conference on Empirical Methods in Natural Language Processing*, pages 1173–1182, Austin, Texas. Association for Computational Linguistics.

Heather Burnett and Peter R. Sutton. 2020. Vagueness and natural language semantics. In D. Gutzmann, L. Matthewson, C. Meier, H. Rullmann, and T. Zimmermann, editors, *The Wiley Blackwell Companion to Semantics*. Wiley.

Robin Cooper, Simon Dobnik, Shalom Lappin, and Staffan Larsson. 2014. A probabilistic rich type theory for semantic interpretation. In *Proceedings of the EACL 2014 Workshop on Type Theory and Natural Language Semantics (TTNLS)*, pages 72–79, Gothenburg, Sweden. Association for Computational Linguistics.

Judith Degen. 2023. The Rational Speech Act framework. *Annual Review of Linguistics*, 9:519–540.

Timothy Dozat. 2016. Incorporating Nesterov momentum into Adam. In *Proceedings of the 4th International Conference on Learning Representations*.

John Duchi, Elad Hazan, and Yoram Singer. 2011. Adaptive subgradient methods for online learning and stochastic optimization. *Journal of Machine Learning Research*, 12(61):2121–2159.

Dorothy Edgington. 1992. Validity, uncertainty and vagueness. *Analysis*, 52(4):193–204.

Dorothy Edgington. 1997. Vagueness by degrees. In Rosanna Keefe and Peter Smith, editors, *Vagueness: A Reader*. MIT Press.

Guy Emerson. 2023. Probabilistic lexical semantics: From Gaussian embeddings to Bernoulli Fields. In Jean-Philippe Bernardy, Rasmus Blanck, Stergios Chatzikyriakidis, Shalom Lappin, and Aleksandre Maskharashvili, editors, *Probabilistic Approaches to Linguistic Theory*, chapter 3, pages 65–121. University of Chicago Press.

Kit Fine. 1975. Vagueness, truth and logic. *Synthese*, 30(3/4):265–300.

Michael C. Frank and Noah D. Goodman. 2012. Predicting pragmatic reasoning in language games. *Science*, 336(6084):998–998.

H. Paul Grice. 1975. Logic and conversation. In P. Cole and J. Morgan, editors, *Syntax and Semantics Vol. 3: Speech Acts*, pages 41–58. Academic Press, New York.

Diederik Kingma and Jimmy Ba. 2015. Adam: A method for stochastic optimization. In *Proceedings of the 3rd International Conference on Learning Representations*.

Daniel Lassiter. 2011. Vagueness as probabilistic linguistic knowledge. In *Vagueness in Communication*, pages 127–150, Berlin, Heidelberg. Springer Berlin Heidelberg.

Daniel Lassiter and Noah Goodman. 2015. Adjectival vagueness in a bayesian model of interpretation. *Synthese*, 194:3801–3836.

Ilya Loshchilov and Frank Hutter. 2019. Decoupled weight decay regularization. In *Proceedings of the 7th International Conference on Learning Representations*.

Bill McDowell and Noah Goodman. 2019. Learning from omission. In *Proceedings of the 57th Annual Meeting of the Association for Computational Linguistics*, pages 619–628, Florence, Italy. Association for Computational Linguistics.

Will Monroe, Noah D. Goodman, and Christopher Potts. 2016. Learning to generate compositional color descriptions. In *Proceedings of the 2016 Conference on Empirical Methods in Natural Language Processing*, pages 2243–2248, Austin, Texas. Association for Computational Linguistics.

Will Monroe, Robert X.D. Hawkins, Noah D. Goodman, and Christopher Potts. 2017. Colors in context: A pragmatic neural model for grounded language understanding. *Transactions of the Association for Computational Linguistics*, 5:325–338.

Nils Reimers and Iryna Gurevych. 2017. Reporting score distributions makes a difference: Performance study of LSTM-networks for sequence tagging. In *Proceedings of the 2017 Conference on Empirical Methods in Natural Language Processing*, pages 338–348, Copenhagen, Denmark. Association for Computational Linguistics.

Uli Sauerland. 2011. Vagueness in language: The case against fuzzy logic revisited. In Petr Cintula, Christian G. Fermüller, Lluís Godo, and Petr Hájek, editors, *Understanding Vagueness: Logical, Philosophical and Linguistic Perspectives*, pages 185–198. College Publications.

Peter R. Sutton. 2015. Towards a probabilistic semantics for vague adjectives. In Henk Zeevat and Hans-Christian Schmitz, editors, *Bayesian Natural Language Semantics and Pragmatics*, pages 221–246. Springer International Publishing, Cham.

L.A. Zadeh. 1965. Fuzzy sets. *Information and Control*, 8(3):338–353.

Manzil Zaheer, Satwik Kottur, Siamak Ravanbakhsh, Barnabas Poczos, Russ R. Salakhutdinov, and Alexander J. Smola. 2017. Deep sets. *Advances in Neural Information Processing Systems*, 30.

Matthew D. Zeiler. 2012. Adadelta: An adaptive learning rate method. ArXiv preprint 1212.5701.

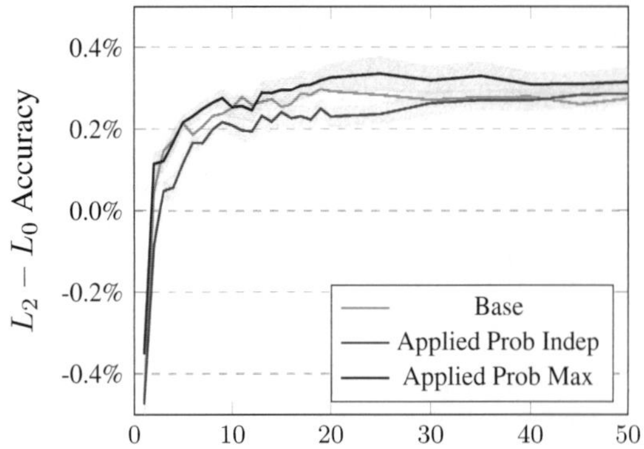

Figure 3: Mean deltas between L_2 accuracy and L_0 accuracy on the validation set, with varying numbers of alternative utterances per colour. Shaded regions mark the standard errors of the means. Number of utterances were incremented by 1 between 1 and 20 utterances, and incremented by 5 between 20 and 50 utterances.

A Grid Search and Hyperparameters

We performed grid search to identify the most performant optimisation algorithms, learning rates, and dropout values for training the neural listener and speaker models. Five optimisation algorithms were explored in the grid search process: Adam (Kingma and Ba, 2015), AdamW (Loshchilov and Hutter, 2019), NAdam (Dozat, 2016), Adadelta (Zeiler, 2012), and Adagrad (Duchi et al., 2011). The Adam and Adadelta algorithms were chosen because they were used in Monroe et al. (2017), while the other three were selected as alternative adaptive optimisation algorithms. For the learning rates, values ranging from 1 to 10^{-4} were selected at regular logarithmic intervals, and dropout rates ranging from 0 to 0.5 were selected at intervals of 0.1.

Based on the results from grid search, we trained the listener models with AdamW using a learning rate of 0.001 and 0.0004 for the base and probabilistic models respectively, and the speaker model with Adam using a learning rate of 0.001. Dropout of 0.5 was applied to listener models, but not to the speaker models as their performance degraded significantly with any dropout. The neural models used the same embedding and hidden dimension sizes as in Monroe et al. (2017), which was 100.

We varied the beam size in the literal speaker's decoding process to analyse the impact on the pragmatic listener's performance. Since the literal speaker produces alternative utterances as a proxy for the set of all possible utterances that theoretical pragmatic agents would consider, we conjectured that generating a larger number of utterances should improve pragmatic performance. As seen in Figure 3, the pragmatic effect increases until around 15 to 20 utterances per colour before plateauing, so we chose a beam size of 15 to maintain the trade-off between computation time and performance.

For the grid search process, analysis of alternative utterances, and model checkpointing, accuracy was evaluated using the validation set based on the train/validation/test data split that Monroe et al. created.

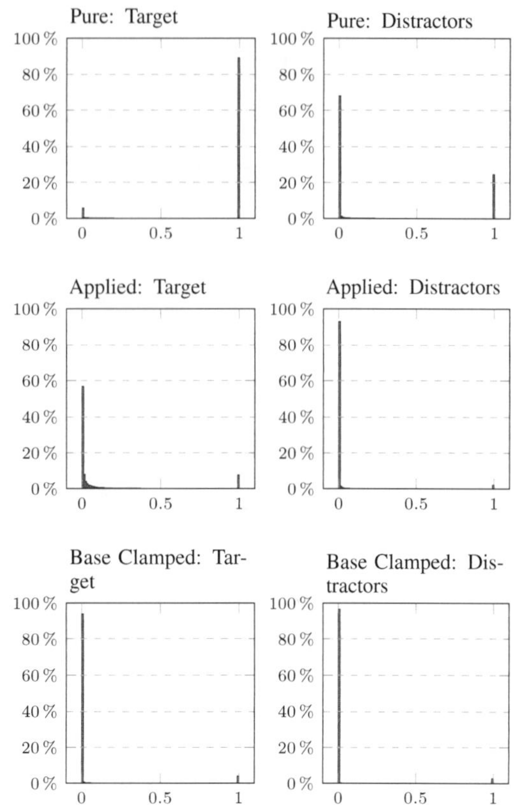

Figure 4: Distribution of marginal probabilities produced by literal listener models for the target and distractor colours in the test set.

B Full Distribution of Marginal Probabilities

Illustrations of the full distributions of marginal probabilities produced by the literal listener models are shown in Figure 4, as opposed to the summary statistics given in Table 3.

Model	L_0 Accuracy	L_2 Accuracy
Base: Speaker-Speaker	87.65 ± 0.05	88.03 ± 0.04
Base: Listener-Speaker	86.29 ± 0.04	86.74 ± 0.05
Base: Listener-Listener	84.97 ± 0.04	85.16 ± 0.04
Base: Speaker-Speaker, No Disagreements	**87.98 ± 0.04**	**88.27 ± 0.04**
Applied Prob Independent: Speaker-Speaker	87.65 ± 0.03	87.96 ± 0.05
Applied Prob Independent: Listener-Speaker	86.32 ± 0.04	86.70 ± 0.05
Applied Prob Independent: Listener-Listener	85.02 ± 0.04	85.14 ± 0.04
Applied Prob Independent: Speaker-Speaker, No Disagreements	**87.85 ± 0.04**	**88.18 ± 0.06**
Applied Prob Max Correlation: Speaker-Speaker	87.58 ± 0.04	88.05 ± 0.06
Applied Prob Max Correlation: Listener-Speaker	86.15 ± 0.06	86.66 ± 0.07
Applied Prob Max Correlation: Listener-Listener	84.90 ± 0.05	85.11 ± 0.05
Applied Prob Max Correlation: Speaker-Speaker, No Disagreements	**87.88 ± 0.04**	**88.20 ± 0.05**

Table 5: Mean accuracies for the base and applied probabilistic models, using the specified target disagreement strategy, shown with standard errors of the means. Highest accuracy for each category in bold.

C Target Disagreements – Full Results

Table 5 lists the full results of various target disagreement strategies for each model type. Compared against Table 4, we see the same trends where the No Disagreements strategy performed the best, followed by Speaker-Speaker, Listener-Speaker, and lastly the Listener-Listener strategy.

Author Index

Association for Computational Linguistics
209 N. Eighth Street
Stroudsburg, Pennsylvania 18360

ISBN 978-1-7138-9464-3